STET

D0073985

SYSTEMATIC TRAINING FOR EFFECTIVE TEACHING

Don Dinkmeyer, Ph.D.
Gary D. McKay, Ph.D.
Don Dinkmeyer, Jr., Ph.D.

AGS ® American Guidance Service Publishers' Building Circle Pines, Minnesota 55014

Dedication

Dedicated to our parents, wives, and teachers who encouraged us. To Rudolf Dreikurs, our teacher and friend.

© 1980.
American Guidance Service, Inc.
All rights reserved.
Printed in the United States of America.

ISBN 0-913476-75-7

Contents

Introduction

Welcome to STET! You are probably wondering, "What will I get out of the course?" and "What is expected of me?"

STET is based on a theory of human behavior which the authors and their colleagues have found effective for thousands of teachers. Its study method is based on reading, discussing, practicing human relationship skills, mutual encouragement, and implementing the principles and techniques with your students.

Be realistic in your expectations of your leader. The leader will not serve as an expert, nor give you answers to all your teaching challenges. The leader's role is to facilitate the implementation of the total program. The leader guides discussion of the materials, leads the training exercises, keeps the group on track, and makes assignments from the leader's manual. The materials themselves are the resources, not the leader. Helpful answers to the challenges of teaching are in the materials and in the group discussions.

To get the most out of this experience, you must be willing to do the reading, participate in the discussions and exercises and, most of all, apply the concepts and methods with your students. The purpose of this program is to study a theory and set of practices which have been demonstrated to be effective in working with students.

The STET program was developed after the wide success of STEP: Systematic Training for Effective Parenting (Dinkmeyer and McKay, 1976) indicated a need for a companion program for educators.

Today's teachers face many challenges. We believe STET, carefully studied and applied, can help teachers meet those challenges.

Don Dinkmeyer, Ph.D.
Diplomate, Counseling Psychology
American Board of Professional Psychology
President, Communication & Motivation
   Training Institute, Inc. (CMTI)
Coral Springs, Florida

Gary D. McKay, Ph.D.
Educational & Psychological Consultant
Western Regional Representative of CMTI, Inc.
Tucson, Arizona

Don Dinkmeyer, Jr., Ph.D.
Educational & Psychological Consultant
Editor, CMTI Press
Coral Springs, Florida

CHAPTER 1
UNDERSTANDING BEHAVIOR AND MISBEHAVIOR

Who is in control in our classrooms?
How do we establish a democratic classroom?
What is a practical theory of behavior?
What are the goals of misbehavior?
How do we recognize and respond to students' misbehavior?
What are the positive counterparts to the goals of misbehavior?

You're a teacher. Maybe a new teacher. You took the required courses, did your student teaching, graduated, and found yourself a job. Now you have your own students — with real needs, expectations, and problems — and you must bring to bear all your training, all your convictions about what education should be. Whether you've taught for thirty years or three months, you enter your classroom each day with the determination to do what you've chosen to do. You want to teach.

Experienced teacher or beginner, you need little time in the schools to see your good resolutions collide with others' demands. You're expected to be a drill sergeant, a secretary, a babysitter, a judge. You're drowning in conflicting advice: Be in charge! Let them be free! Structure every minute! Let them do what they want! Most disturbing of all, many students *won't cooperate, won't listen, won't do what you tell them.*

What's the explanation? Many believe discipline problems are the primary threat to our system of education. Today's teachers face students raised in a generation continually shaken by social upheavals. The traditional authority of men, whites, employers, parents, and teachers can no longer be taken for granted. Gains made by organized groups in their struggle for equality under the law will not be relinquished. Whether we feel encouraged or threatened by society's changes, we must live and teach in the world as we find it. Our students have certain expectations. When they demand their own rights, when they question our authority, we must know how to answer them. The old answer — ''You'll do what I say because I'm your teacher!''— won't work anymore.

Who Is in Control?

Beyond understanding why many of today's students don't respond to traditional methods of discipline, teachers need new ways to ensure the order and direction required for teaching and learning — without denying students the freedom they need and expect. How can we motivate and discipline our students in an era of equality?

Power struggles, especially between teachers and students, have no place in a classroom. Yet someone must take responsibility for maintaining order so teachers can teach and students can learn. The teacher may choose to be an old-fashioned autocrat, controlling through position and power, doling out rewards and punishments. Such a classroom may be orderly, but it won't prepare students to live in a democratic society. Nor do rewards and punishments encourage anyone's intrinsic desire to learn. We will not turn out self-motivated, self-disciplined students if we attempt to control them without their consent or understanding. And many teachers neither enjoy nor do well at controlling.

Should we let students do what they want, then? Is a permissive classroom the only alternative? Should we be passive observers, letting learning happen when and where it will? Few can function, much less teach and learn, in the absence of guidelines and limits. If young people need direction and order as much as freedom, then the most promising learning environment is the *democratic* classroom. The democratic classroom mirrors the most positive features of a democratic society, allowing freedom within responsible limits.

A Democratic Approach

STET promotes a democratic classroom where choices are clear, discipline is logical, and self-discipline is encouraged. Within such an environment, teachers who understand their own and their students' behavior can teach creatively, successfully.

How do you begin to establish a democratic atmosphere in your classroom? Here, briefly stated, are four plans of action that future *STET* sessions will detail.

1. *Establish a climate of equality and mutual respect.* You and your students differ in age, knowledge, and experience, but you share a common humanity. You are all entitled to be treated with dignity. This kind of teacher-student equality is no "demotion" for you; it may, in fact, give *you* certain rights and freedoms you've lacked. Equality carries with it responsibility for one's own behavior. Your students can profit from the opportunity to learn self-direction and self-control. You may feel better as a contributing group member, instead of an overseer.

Respect your students' rights and expect them to respect yours. Involve students in a cooperative learning experience; stimulate their own resourcefulness and desire to succeed; be responsive to them as human beings. And respect yourself enough to refuse the roles of drill sergeant, babysitter, or doormat. Develop and maintain a self-concept you can feel comfortable with. Help your students do the same.

2. *Encourage your students.* Every person wants to feel worthwhile. Everyone wants to belong. Focus on your students' assets and strengths; accent the positive. You don't have to be a Pollyanna. You know that thoughtful encouragement improves your students' motivation to learn and strengthens their relationship with you. Help them build on their successes, not their failures. Bolster their confidence.

3. *Offer your students a role in decision making.* Would you be happy within a system of policies and guidelines you had no part in developing? Your students also dislike dictatorships. They can't decide everything about their educations because they haven't the knowledge or experience. But they can help decide how fast they can learn certain things, what kinds of projects, committees, and bulletin boards their class will have, what their seating arrangements will be, and so forth. Learning to make decisions is an important part of education, a vital preparation for adulthood. Students will be more likely to accept with enthusiasm a classroom policy they helped create.

4. *Develop students' self-discipline by offering them consistent, logical, fully understood guidelines for behavior.* Most of us learn early lessons in natural consequences. If we don't bring our umbrellas to school and it rains, we get wet. If a baby touches a hot burner, she gets burned and she learns.

Similarly, our society has certain rules, the violation of which leads to certain predictable outcomes. If we don't pay our debts, we'll probably be denied further credit. Such consequences, the arranged results of violating the social order, aren't as inevitable as getting wet in the rain. But they have a certain consistency and we are not surprised when they occur. Nor do we question the relationship between our action — reneging on our debts — and the result — being denied further credit. Such consequences are logical.

Classroom discipline can have the same consistency and coherence. If policies are reasonable and if the exceeding of limits leads to logical, predictable consequences, and especially if students have some voice in the formulation of those policies and consequences, then you can foster self-discipline in your students as you maintain order in your classroom.

Democracy — Then What?

Instituting democratic, humane principles in your classroom will not automatically eliminate discipline problems. Human beings are imperfect and their behavior is frequently puzzling. But we can begin to understand behavior if we apply our common sense and the findings of the experts. First, consider five popular but not very helpful theories about why kids act the way they do.

Dad hollered like that. Jamie may have her father's red hair, but it's hardly sensible to blame her short attention span on her heredity.

It's not us. It's everything around us. David's neighborhood, his family's finances, his previous school, his parents' relationship: environmental factors are often blamed for why kids fight or interrupt. But David's brother Alvin is quiet and peace-loving.

It's just a stage. Maybe Harriet's extreme shyness is "just a stage," but other children don't seem to pass through it. If we tolerate all kinds of behavior problems, assuming students will outgrow them, we may see the tantrums of the five-year-old become the rebellion or depression of the teenager. The specific behavior may change, but the underlying patterns remain.

Boys will be boys. Girls will be girls. Attempting to explain behavior through sex role stereotypes gets riskier every year. If boys are like this, and girls are like that, then what about Matthew? What about Marcia?

All students are like that! What we expect often comes true. Expect the worst and you're likely to get it.

A Practical Theory of Behavior

Trained observers of human behavior — most notably psychiatrists Alfred Adler and Rudolf Dreikurs — point to the need to belong, to be accepted, as a basic human characteristic and goal. Our students are social beings; their behavior can be understood as attempts to reach this fundamental goal of belonging. If they misbehave, they reveal certain faulty beliefs about what belonging means. Misbehaving students have adopted certain short-term goals that we can determine by examining the results of their misbehavior, the *consequences* or payoff. When Marvin writes a bad word on the chalkboard, he annoys you and delights his friends. Both reactions point to the goal of his behavior.

If we believe that our students' misbehavior is aimless, without reason or motive, we will likely succumb to frustration, even despair. But if we assume that behavior is understandable, that our students do what they do for a purpose, however little they are aware of that purpose, then we can begin to see the world through their eyes. Sharing their point of view allows us to respond to them rationally, confidently, effectively.

Our students want to belong, to be significant, and their behavior frequently points toward that goal. If they believe they can be significant to you and to their peers only by misbehaving in your class, they will misbehave. But their misbehavior springs from a feeling of discouragement; they don't believe they can belong through constructive, useful behavior. Our efforts to redirect these students, then, must center around our attempts to *encourage* them.

Teachers can provide opportunities for students to succeed and be significant within the boundaries of a democratic classroom. When a student decides, "I just can't do math," "I'm no good at gym," "Nobody likes me," the teacher can work to change those attitudes through encouragement. Without encouragement, the student will probably look for significance outside the limits and guidelines of your classroom.

Classroom misbehavior gains a student immediate recognition, even if that recognition is negative. In a sense, misbehavior is a shout into echo canyon; the echo (our response) is more important than the shout. If we build our students' self-confidence and give them recognition for useful, constructive behavior, they won't need to shout.

What Is Misbehavior?

What you consider misbehavior in your classroom may not be misbehavior in the classroom next door. Students may not agree with either definition. Still, if we are to respond successfully when students misbehave, we need a fairly specific description:

> Misbehavior
> violates the rights of others or jeopardizes their safety
> is self-defeating or self-damaging
> is contrary to the requirements of the situation.

Sonya teases smaller children. Harvey refuses to complete writing assignments, saying, "I can't write." Jennifer shouts out during class discussions.

Having described misbehavior, we can begin to understand and then deal with it.

Four Goals of Misbehavior

In order to respond effectively to a misbehaving student, you need to know the *purpose* of the misbehavior. Sheila had a reason for not doing her assignment. Bert had a reason for drumming on his desk during the class discussion. Determining those reasons, that purpose, will help you choose your method of getting Sheila to work and Bert to stop drumming and pay attention.

Why do students misbehave? After much observation, Rudolf Dreikurs identified four short-term goals of misbehavior. According to Dreikurs, children misbehave because:

1. They want **attention**.
2. They seek **power**.
3. They're looking for **revenge**.
4. They've given up, want you to leave them alone, and so choose to **display their inadequacy**.

Understanding these goals can be useful as you begin to redirect Sheila's and Bert's behavior into useful channels.

How do you find out which of the four goals the student is pursuing? Looking at the *consequences* or results of the misbehavior will help you discover its purpose.

First, consider your own feelings. When Sheila failed to do her assignment, were you annoyed? angry? hurt? Did you despair?

Second, look at how Bert responded when you told him to stop drumming. Did he stop, but only temporarily? Did he scowl at you? Did he ignore you?

Your feelings and ***the student's response to what you do or say*** are the two consequences of misbehavior that will direct you toward the student's goal. You were angry with Sheila. When you said to her, "Everyone else managed to do the assignment. Why couldn't you?" she merely gave you a defiant grin. When Bert did his drum solo, you felt annoyed. You reminded him that music class is in the afternoon and he stopped. In both cases, the students got what they wanted from you; you recognized them in a specific way. What you did met the goal of each student's misbehavior.

Be aware of your feelings. They are important clues to the reasons for misbehavior. Your students may *want* you to feel as you do. Your feelings and behavior give them a significance they were unable to gain any other way.

To summarize: In attempting to deal with misbehaving students, first identify the goal of the misbehavior. To do that, examine your feelings and then analyze the student's reaction to your attempt at correction. That reaction will usually confirm your guess about the purpose of the misbehavior.

Once you identify specific misbehavior as illustrating one of Dreikurs' four goals, you can deal with that misbehavior.

Attention. We all seek attention at one time or another. But young people seem to have a particularly keen desire to be noticed. They need some way to confirm their existence and significance: "Hey! Notice me! I'm here and I'm important!" If students can't get attention through achievement and cooperation, they'll get it any way they can. They may disrupt the class, but they know they'll be remembered.

Jack goes to the pencil sharpener while the class is quietly reading. He begins to grind his #2 pencil to a stub. Mr. Clark looks up, annoyed. "Jack, as I've told you before, we don't go to the pencil sharpener during reading because it disturbs others. Now, please sit down.'' Some of the other students look up and laugh. Jack returns to his seat, smiling sheepishly. This is the third time this week Jack has broken the rule. Can't he remember?

Jack remembers. He remembers, ''Mr. Clark and the other kids notice me when I sharpen my pencil during reading.''

Jack interrupted the class. Mr. Clark was annoyed — not angry, just annoyed — and asked him to return to his seat. Jack stopped sharpening and sat down. Mr. Clark's annoyance and the other students' giggling suggest that Jack wants attention and is actively seeking it through specific misbehavior.

Other attention-seekers use passive ways to make you notice. Randy can never find his notebook, so you help him look. Cynthia must always be reminded to turn in her math problems. Joanna dawdles when the class lines up for assemblies, so you coax her. The services you provide for these students reinforce their beliefs about the only way they can be important to you.

Students who seek attention through active or passive misbehavior aren't getting enough notice for the useful, cooperative things they do, and too much notice for their misbehavior. Our job is to help those students feel significant without giving them attention on demand. Mr. Clark's reaction told Jack, ''You wanted to be noticed and I'm noticing you. Now you're important.''

Similarly, reinforcing ''good'' behavior on demand, when the student's goal is primarily attention, only strengthens the belief that being noticed confers significance. We want students to feel secure and self-confident without needing anyone's approval. Tempting as it is to call on William when he waves his arm wildly and constantly, wait and notice him at other times: when he's reading quietly or leading a small-group discussion. Gradually he may realize that he needn't be center-stage all the time. You'll be redirecting his beliefs and goals, not just modifying his behavior.

The general guideline for responding to attention-seeking students is:

> ***Never give attention on demand, even for useful behavior. Help students become self-motivated. Give attention in ways they don't expect. Catch them being "good."***

In Jack's case, Mr. Clark might have ignored the behavior and later commended Jack when he participated in a class discussion. Jack would then be getting attention he didn't expect, attention for achievement and cooperation. Letting Randy, Cynthia, and Joanna know that you expect them to be self-reliant, and then refusing to notice their attention-seeking behavior, might be the best thing you can do for them.

This method may not work for all attention-seeking students. But the process of identifying the goal of attention and then responding to the misbehavior accordingly will be useful when you attempt to redirect your students toward self-motivation and personal responsibility.

Remember: If you feel annoyed, the student's goal is probably attention. If your blood pressure rises, if your feelings intensify, if you're *angry,* the student likely wants power.

Power. Power-seeking students feel significant only when they challenge authority, resist rules, undermine instructions. Our usual response is to feel provoked and angry and to force the student to obey. Power struggles make a classroom tense and unpleasant; the student who seeks power may be the most difficult to deal with.

"Line up to go to lunch." "Make me!"
"Don't turn in messy papers." "I will if I want to."

These students believe they belong only when they're in control. They'll defy you, trying to see just how far you can be pushed. Or they'll do just enough to appease you, counting on your reluctance to keep fighting. You finally accept Samantha's messy paper after the fourth "rewrite." You're tired of the battle. Samantha's "defiant compliance," then, pays off. Some days you're willing to accept her *first* messy paper: you don't want to fight at all.

If we decide to fight power with power — "How dare you not listen to me? I'm in charge here!" — we merely impress students with the usefulness and desirability of power. They may escalate the struggle. If we give in, we've reinforced their belief that power gets results.

The general guideline for responding to power-seeking students is:

Withdraw from the conflict. Let the consequences of students' behavior occur. Win their cooperation by enlisting their help.

Nobody can fight without an opponent. Lead the other students to the lunchroom. Quietly refuse to accept the messy paper. Later, after the bid for power has subsided, enlist the help of the student in some socially useful task. Help such students use their power constructively: ask them to tutor other students, to lead discussions, to take charge of a project, to be responsible for collecting milk money. Redirect their energies.

Revenge. No matter what you do, some students will consider you a tyrant with all the advantages on your side. They feel defeated, hurt, unhappy. So they (knowingly or unknowingly) adopt another goal: revenge.

They can't defeat you but they can still inflict hurt. "You hate me and wish I weren't here. I'll make you pay for that." Whether their injury is real or imagined, these students feel mistreated; they are motivated by their private sense of injustice to hurt others as they have been hurt.

Students can pursue revenge physically, verbally, or passively, through inactivity. Their revenge can be entirely silent, revealing itself through hateful looks and gestures. Roger notices that his sullenness has "gotten" to Ms. Schwartz. He tells himself, "Now I'm getting even with her for keeping me after school." If Ms. Schwartz decides to punish Roger again, she provides him with a fresh reason to get even.

A student may pursue revenge against a teacher indirectly, by picking on other students or writing on a desk. The effect is the same: The teacher feels insulted and hurt.

When dealing with revengeful behavior, remember:

Avoid feeling hurt. Don't get hooked into seeking your own revenge. Instead, work to build a trusting relationship.

The revenge-seeking student is troubled and deeply discouraged. Understanding Roger's perceptions and goals can take the sting out of his sullen looks; he is more hurt than you are. You may not deserve his attacks, but you're just another "enemy" among many for him. Revenge offers hollow satisfaction, for you or for him. Show Roger he's a full member of your class. Be kind and patient with him. Find his strengths and encourage him to use them constructively.

Display of inadequacy. The deeply hurt and discouraged student may decide to withdraw completely from any challenges. "I just can't do these problems, Ms. Montez." "This book is too hard for me." "I'm no good at geography." These students may have set unrealistically high standards for themselves and failed once too often. Now they've surrendered to their feelings of hopelessness. They don't believe they can ever fit in or contribute anything to the group. They want to be left alone, finding their only significance in your acceptance of their inadequacy. Students rarely choose to display inadequacy in *all* aspects of their lives. Sandra may go home from school and pitch a no-hitter in her backyard. But in your class, her response to all writing assignments is, "I can't."

Once you're sure Sandra's "I can't" doesn't mean, "You can't make me," if your immediate feeling toward her is hopelessness or even despair, realize that Sandra has given up on herself and it's your job to help her. Start where she is; develop realistic expectations for her. Eliminate all criticism of her work. Encourage her slightest effort, her smallest sign of progress. If she manages one paragraph of an essay, even one sentence, note what she's written and encourage her. Sandra needs to be told she can belong, she can succeed, she doesn't have to be perfect. Encouragement can redirect any mistaken goal, but it is especially needed by students who demonstrate feelings of inadequacy.

When dealing with students who display their inadequacy:

Don't give up. Avoid criticism and pity. Encourage any positive effort.

The four goals of misbehavior don't necessarily follow the sequence presented here. Dependent students who bid for attention by always asking for help may surrender to feelings of inadequacy if they become convinced they can't do anything for themselves. Today Roger may pursue revenge; next week he may try a power play. Much depends on a student's changing perception of how to belong.

Similarly, the four goals may expand as students get older. Beyond the ages of 10 or 12, young people may spend most of their time seeking the approval of their peers. They may also seek excitement or thrills. Their pursuit of these added goals may go on outside school, beyond your relationship with them. And they won't necessarily misbehave: some will gain recognition by running for office, excitement by playing basketball. But others may come to believe that significance lies *only* in peer acceptance and excitement. Such students will probably misbehave in your classroom. When they do, you'll likely find them bidding for your attention, challenging you for power, seeking revenge, or displaying inadequacy. The four goals are operative throughout life, and they persist in the teacher-student relationship, regardless of the student's age. Understanding Dreikurs' four goals should give you a firm basis for evaluating the problems and misbehavior of teenagers and young adults.

Helpful Assumptions about Misbehavior

You can make certain assumptions about misbehavior that will help you respond effectively to it.

Misbehavior stems from discouragement. Misbehaving students have decided they can belong only by pestering, fighting, getting even, or giving up. They're discouraged about their ability to find a place in the group through constructive, useful behavior. They're afraid to try, afraid to risk failure, afraid to change their pattern of believing and acting. Their discouragement may be mild (leading them to bid for attention) or extreme (persuading them to display inadequacy). But all misbehaving students are discouraged in some way.

Students are usually aware of the consequences of their behavior, but unaware of their goals. Even if they deliberately set out for revenge, they don't realize the implications of their behavior. They don't recognize their belief that revenge offers them their only significance. Ramon is not likely to tell himself, "I'm going in today to have a power struggle with Mr. MacDonald."

Students may change goals, depending on the situation. At home, Nathan may find that attracting attention helps him feel significant. At school, he may resort to forcing the teacher to notice him. All four goals of misbehavior are immediate and short-range. What remains constant is the major objective: belonging.

Students may use different misbehavior for the same goal, or the same misbehavior for different goals. Helen gets attention by coming in late from recess. Don gets attention by humming under his breath. Gary gets attention by needing all instructions repeated. Same goal — different behavior.

On the other hand, Don may come in late from recess not for attention, as Helen does, but for power. "I'll show him who's boss!" Same behavior — different goal. The student's perception of what it means to belong is all-important.

Attention, power, and revenge can be pursued actively or passively. Coretta can get attention by chattering, Wayne by being shy and getting the teacher to coax him. Sven can seek power by throwing a temper tantrum, Rebecca by being stubbornly silent. Julio can pursue revenge by verbal attack, Linda by hateful stares.

Misbehavior remains a mystery unless we consider not only a student's actions, but our own feelings and the student's response to

14

correction. Misbehaving students make demands on us. We must identify their goals and alter our responses so we no longer satisfy those demands. *Our* goal is to channel students' energy and creativity into constructive, healthy behavior.

Decide how you will respond to misbehavior. You don't want to confirm Anthony's sense of inadequacy by exempting him from all assignments. You don't want to "pay off" Shirley by lashing out at her when she defies you. Teachers don't *cause* misbehavior, but they can *reinforce* it. If we want to help change behavior, we must change our responses to misbehavior.

No guarantees. Students will test you, and they may fail to respond to anything you do or say. But if you refuse to reinforce their mistaken beliefs and actively strive to redirect their goals, you will likely see results. Establishing a democratic classroom of equality and mutual respect will help convince students of your confidence in yourself and in them.

What about Goals of Positive Behavior?

You may be asking, "Don't students ever behave *constructively,* because they *like* school?" Certainly they do. Each goal of misbehavior has a positive counterpart.

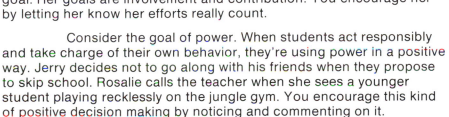

Attention? We all need attention. The question is how much and what kind. Imogene always takes an active part in group projects because she enjoys contributing and takes pride in her work. The attention you give her is a pleasant result of her behavior, but not its goal. Her goals are involvement and contribution. You encourage her by letting her know her efforts really count.

Consider the goal of power. When students act responsibly and take charge of their own behavior, they're using power in a positive way. Jerry decides not to go along with his friends when they propose to skip school. Rosalie calls the teacher when she sees a younger student playing recklessly on the jungle gym. You encourage this kind of positive decision making by noticing and commenting on it.

Can revenge be positive? Probably not. But a student can "get even" in a constructive way by returning kindness for hurt. You got impatient with Aaron and scolded him. He chose to cooperate willingly in class activities, rather than waste his energy on revenge. You respond by appreciating his ability to redirect his own behavior.

Even withdrawal can be positive. Molly withdraws from her shouting match with Malita so she can consider their disagreement and resolve it. Robert decides to be content with *B*s he works hard for, instead of endlessly competing with his brother, who gets *A*s so easily. You recognize their efforts to behave maturely.

How do you feel when students pursue these positive goals? You feel good.

15

Works Cited

Dreikurs, Rudolf; Grunwald, Bronia; and Pepper, Floy. *Maintaining Sanity in the Classroom.* NY: Harper & Row, 1971. 2nd ed., 1980.

Recommended Readings

Combs, Arthur; Richards, Anne; and Richards, Fred. *Perceptual Psychology.* NY: Harper & Row, 1976.

Dewey, Edith. *Basic Applications of Adlerian Psychology.* Coral Springs, FL: CMTI Press, 1978.

Dinkmeyer, Don, and Carlson, Jon. *Consulting: Facilitating Human Potential and Change Processes.* Columbus, OH: Charles E. Merrill, 1973.

Dinkmeyer, Don; Pew, W.L.; and Dinkmeyer, Don, Jr. *Adlerian Counseling and Psychotherapy.* Monterey, CA: Brooks/Cole, 1979.

Dreikurs, Rudolf. *Fundamentals of Adlerian Psychology.* NY: Greenberg, 1950.

Dreikurs, Rudolf; Grunwald, Bronia; and Pepper, Floy C. *Maintaining Sanity in the Classroom.* 2nd Ed. NY: Harper & Row, 1980.

Gould, Shirley. *Teenagers: The Continuing Challenge.* NY: Hawthorn Books, 1977.

Ignas, Edward, and Corsini, Raymond. *Alternative Educational Systems.* Itasca, IL: F. E. Peacock, 1979.

Journal of Individual Psychology 33 (November, 1977). Supplement on Individual Education.

Manaster, Guy J. *Adolescent Development and the Life Tasks.* Boston: Allyn & Bacon, 1977.

Wood, Pat, and Wood, Murray. *Living with Teens and Surviving.* Toronto: Alfred Adler Institute of Ontario, 1979.

Study Questions

1. What changes in society have made teaching more difficult?

2. Why are rewards and punishment no longer effective methods of discipline?

3. What constitutes a democratic classroom?

4. In what sense are teachers and students equal?

5. How does the goal of belonging influence our students' behavior and misbehavior?

6. What are the four goals of misbehavior?

7. What are the positive counterparts to the four goals of misbehavior?

8. Why is it important to understand which goal the student is seeking? How do our own feelings and reactions serve as clues to the goal?

9. How do we feel when students seek attention? Power? Revenge? When they display inadequacy?

10. What are appropriate responses to students who misbehave for attention? For power? For revenge? To display inadequacy?

11. Why do we need to change our behavior first, instead of helping students change theirs first?

12. What role does discouragement play in misbehavior? Encouragement?

Problem Situation

You have just assigned the class 10 arithmetic problems to be done now. Most of the students get busy, but you notice Francis just sitting, staring out the window. When you get to his desk you see that he hasn't started the first problem. You ask him to tell you why he hasn't begun and he says, "The problems are too hard. I can't do them." You sigh in despair, but try to determine what he finds especially difficult. Francis just stares blankly and doesn't even pick up his pencil.

1. What is the purpose of Francis' behavior? How do you know?
2. What do you usually do about students like Francis?
3. Do you have any other ideas of how to motivate Francis?

Activity for the Week

Take a student that is a behavior problem for you and analyze her or his misbehavior in terms of the four goals: attention, power, revenge, and display of inadequacy. By considering your feelings and the student's response to what you say and do, decide the purpose of the misbehavior.

Take notes describing what the student did, your feelings and exactly how you reacted, the student's response to your reaction, and the purpose of the misbehavior.

Since you're also interested in helping students develop positive goals, record examples of any positive behavior.

Recommended Resource Book Material

Chapter 1; Chapters 2-8, stories for group discussion; Chapter 12, "Operating democratically in the classroom."

The Four Goals of Misbehavior

Student's Faulty Belief	Student's Goal	Teacher's Feelings	Teacher's Reactions	Student's Response to Teacher's Reaction	Guidelines for Redirecting Misbehavior
I belong *only* when I'm noticed or served.	Attention	Annoyed.	Remind, coax.	Temporarily stops misbehavior; later resumes same behavior or seeks attention in another way.	Recognize that reminders and warnings only reinforce the goal. Ignore behavior when possible. Give attention in unexpected ways. Notice positive behavior.
I belong *only* when I'm in control or when I'm proving that no one can make me do anything.	Power	Angry, provoked.	Give in or fight power with power.	Intensifies power struggle or submits with defiant compliance.	Withdraw from conflict. Help students use power constructively by enlisting their help.
I belong *only* when I hurt others and get even. I can't be liked.	Revenge	Hurt.	Retaliate, get even.	Seeks further revenge.	Avoid punishment, retaliation, feeling hurt. Build trusting relationship.
I belong *only* when I convince others that I am unable and helpless.	Display of Inadequacy	Despairing, hopeless, discouraged.	Agree with student that nothing can be done. Give up.	Shows no improvement.	Recognize student's deep discouragement. Don't give up, pity, or criticize. Encourage all positive effort.

To identify student's goal:

1. Examine your own feelings and reactions to the misbehavior.
2. Analyze the student's response to what you do and say.

The Goals of Positive Behavior

Student's Belief	Goals	Behavior	How to Encourage Positive Goals
I am responsible for my own behavior.	Attention. Involvement. Contribution.	Helps. Volunteers.	Let student know the contribution counts and that you appreciate it.
I can belong by contributing.	Autonomy. Responsibility for self.	Shows self-discipline. Does own work. Is resourceful.	Encourage decision making. Let students experience both pleasant and unpleasant outcomes. Express confidence in student.
I am more interested in cooperating than in getting even.	Justice. Fairness for all.	Returns kindness for hurt. Ignores belittling comments.	Let student know you appreciate the interest in cooperating.
I can decide to withdraw from conflicts.	Withdrawal from conflict. Refusal to fight. Acceptance of others' opinions.	Ignores provocations. Withdraws from power contest to decide own behavior.	Recognize student's efforts to act maturely.

Recording Worksheet

The Four Goals of Misbehavior

This recording illustrates the four goals of misbehavior. As you listen to each scene, ask yourself:

1. How did the teacher *feel* about the student's misbehavior?
2. What did the teacher *do* about the misbehavior?
3. What was the student's *response* to what the teacher did?
4. Based on the evidence, what was the goal of the misbehavior?

Concentrate on identifying the goals of misbehavior, not on generating alternative behavior for the teacher.

If necessary, refer to Chart 1A. Be prepared to discuss your responses with the group.

NOTES

Chapter 1

Points to Remember

1. To promote a democratic classroom:
- Establish a climate of equality and mutual respect.
- Encourage your students.
- Offer your students a role in decision making.
- Develop students' self-discipline by offering them consistent, logical, fully understood guidelines for behavior.

2. The need to belong is a basic human characteristic.

3. Students who misbehave reveal certain faulty beliefs about what belonging involves.

4. Misbehaving students are discouraged.

5. Dreikurs' four goals of misbehavior are: Attention, Power, Revenge, Display of Inadequacy. Attention, power, and revenge can be pursued actively or passively.

6. Discover a student's goal by examining your feelings and the student's response to what you say and do.

7. The guideline for dealing with attention-seekers: Never give attention on demand, even for useful behavior. Help students become self-motivated. Give attention in ways they don't expect. Catch them being ''good.''

8. The guideline for dealing with power-seekers: Withdraw from the conflict. Let the consequences of students' behavior occur. Win their cooperation by enlisting their help.

9. The guideline for dealing with revenge-seekers: Avoid feeling hurt. Don't get hooked into seeking your own revenge. Instead, work to build a trusting relationship.

10. The guideline for dealing with students who display inadequacy: Don't give up. Avoid criticism and pity. Encourage any positive effort.

11. The four goals don't follow any prescribed sequence. Older students may also pursue goals of peer acceptance and excitement.

12. Teachers don't cause misbehavior. But they may reinforce it by reacting in expected ways.

13. If we want to help change behavior, we must change our responses to misbehavior.

14. Each goal of misbehavior has a positive counterpart to be encouraged.

Personal Record Chapter 1

1. My experience with the weekly assignment

2. My reactions to the reading

3. Topics to discuss with the group

4. Skills I intend to improve

5. My beliefs which impede progress

6. My successes in applying program ideas

7. My difficulties in applying program ideas

8. My progress this week: A specific example

9. This week I learned

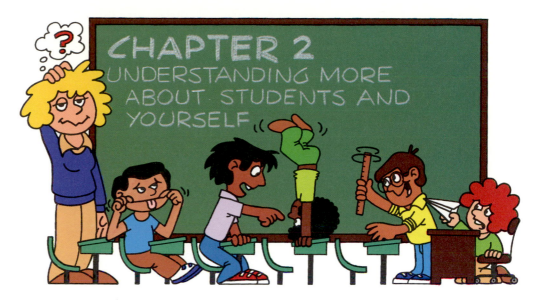

CHAPTER 2
UNDERSTANDING MORE ABOUT STUDENTS AND YOURSELF

What is lifestyle?
What factors most influence students' lifestyles and our own?
How does the family constellation affect beliefs and behavior?
Which of our own beliefs may hamper our relationships with students?
How do emotions influence classroom behavior?
How do students and teachers misuse their negative emotions?
How can we redirect our negative emotions?

The behavior and misbehavior we encounter in our classrooms is energized by emotions. Students misbehave because they're discouraged. They want to belong but believe they can't in any constructive way. Depending on their emotional perception of their place and circumstances, they choose one of the four goals of misbehavior. Our emotional response to misbehavior — our annoyance, anger, hurt, or despair — has much to do with whether that misbehavior continues or stops.

Teacher or student, the way we react to people and situations depends upon our *lifestyle,* the unique, unifying aspect of our personality, the pattern by which we conduct our life (Dreikurs, 1958). Lifestyle reflects our beliefs about ourselves, other people, and the world, and influences the long-range goals we formulate to support those beliefs. We may be unaware of our beliefs and goals, but our behavior will reflect them. A man who believes life is unfair, for example, may strive for justice and fairness in his own life — even though he may be unaware of his belief.

Lifestyle begins to be formed early in life, even before we learn to speak. Even the youngest students, then, come to school with many generalizations about experience, many often-mistaken ideas about life. Lifestyle beliefs, stated or implied, are absolutes: ''I *must* be first''; ''You can't trust *anyone*''; ''*Everyone* is looking out for Number One''; ''Life is *always* dangerous.'' Such all-or-nothing beliefs can have a profound influence on behavior. People will cling to the beliefs they formed as children, even though experience calls those beliefs into question.

Lifestyle is made up of convictions or beliefs. People demonstrate their beliefs by choosing from a wide variety of behavior, both positive and negative. For example, a person who believes in being first and best may become a top athlete, surgeon, or criminal. That person may also decide that life's demands can't be met, that withdrawal from participation is the only answer.

Studying the factors that most influence our students' lifestyle and our own can deepen our understanding of behavior and misbehavior. Those factors are:

Heredity. It's impossible to assess the exact influence of heredity on development and potential. Genetic factors do set certain boundaries or limits. But as teachers we're most interested in what students *do* within those boundaries. We meet many students who have high potential for achievement, but whose faulty or limiting beliefs keep them from becoming all they could.

Family atmosphere and values. The social climate of the home, established by parents, greatly influences children's perceptions of the world. Our students come from homes whose atmospheres may be chaotic or orderly, rigid or flexible, competitive or cooperative, inconsistent or consistent. Relationships within the family may be autocratic or democratic, based on fear or on love. Adults may set reasonable standards, unreasonable ones, or no standards at all. Although children in a family often share certain characteristics, each child responds to the home environment a little differently, according to his or her perceptions (Dewey, 1978).

Values form a significant part of the family atmosphere. Anything important to parents, even if they disagree on the issue, becomes important to children in some way. Each child has to decide her or his position on topics vital to a family.

Family members may be aware of certain values: religion, money, work, education. Other values may be held as firmly but not as consciously: winning, controlling, being right. Each child responds to all family values.

We teachers create the atmosphere of our classrooms. As significant people in our students' lives, we also transmit certain values, intentionally or unintentionally. We too profoundly influence students' behavior.

Role models. Children learn what to believe, even how to think, from watching their parents and other adults. They observe how men and women behave and the ways adults respond to stress. They may choose to model themselves after one or the other parent, or they may combine certain traits of both. Or they may reject both parents.

Unfortunately, children often adopt adults' least desirable traits, since these seem to work best. If Raymond's mother usually sulks to get what she wants, he may try her technique.

Our students use us as role models too. If we control by using power, for example, they will learn how desirable power is.

Methods of discipline. The way parents and teachers discipline can lead students to certain conclusions about life. Adults who stress democratic problem solving based on mutual respect usually do better at influencing a child's sense of responsibility and self-discipline than those who use authoritarian or permissive approaches.

Children look to adults as models for handling human relationships. This profound influence can be seen most tragically in the case of child abusers who were themselves abused as children.

Family constellation. The most significant influence on a person's lifestyle is the family constellation. The family constellation refers to the psychological position of each child in a family in relationship to siblings; this position may or may not correspond to birth order. For example, if a firstborn child feels incapable of staying ahead of a second child, she or he may switch roles with that sibling. Since boys in our culture are often expected to develop more slowly than girls, a discouraged older brother may permit his sister to take the firstborn role.

Each child in a family is born into a different set of circumstances (Dreikurs & Soltz, 1964). The firstborn is an only child for a while, but his or her situation changes if a second child is born. The second child and any born thereafter will always have to contend with a more advanced sibling, unless the sibling is physically or mentally handicapped.

If the family atmosphere accounts for personality similarities in children, the family constellation accounts for the differences. Children often feel they must compete for a place in the family.

Suppose Georgia is an A student; her younger sister Diana must work hard for Bs and Cs. Diana becomes more and more discouraged about ever catching up with Georgia. Since she's more athletic than her sister, Diana decides to stop trying in school but to excel at sports. Georgia begins avoiding any athletic participation, concentrating all her energies on school. In this way, each girl creates a distinct place for herself in the family. Georgia is the student, Diana the athlete. Possibly they could each have done well at both activities if they didn't feel they had to compete.

Georgia's and Diana's parents and teachers may have unintentionally encouraged the competition by praising Georgia for her good grades and ignoring or criticizing Diana. If we want to encourage all students, we must value everyone's uniqueness and focus on strengths. Had the pressure been removed from Diana and her assets appreciated, she might have been more cooperative, more willing to try in school. We particularly need to avoid all comparisons between members of the same family.

The brother or sister most different from us in temperament is usually our major competitor. That sibling is often the one closest to us in age. He or she exerts the most significant influence on us, because it is often with this sibling that we vie for a place in the family. If we feel our major competitor can be overcome, we may choose to compete directly by excelling at the same activities. But if we feel the sibling has certain activities "sewed up," we will compete indirectly by excelling at different activities, ones in which the sibling isn't strong.

We are usually aware of direct competition with a sibling, but often unaware of indirect competition. We do not see that we have developed certain attitudes and characteristics as a result of comparing ourselves with a brother or sister.

Regardless of the size of the family, competition between the first and second child is frequently most pronounced. Those two are for a time the only children who must find a place for themselves and so they may compete intensely.

Twins have an interesting place in a family constellation. They are almost always aware of who was born first, and this influences their personalities. One often takes the role of the older child, the other becoming second. Twins, especially identical twins, may be treated as a separate unit in a family — "the twins." This treatment as one unit can influence each twin to strive for a separate identity. Twins may have many similarities and many distinct differences.

The only child has no sibling to come between or to buffer his or her relationship with parents. Living in an adult world may influence the only child either to become a miniature adult or to stay a baby.

Psychologically, there are five possible positions in the family constellation: only, first, second, middle, and youngest. Other birth-order positions reflect one of these five psychological positions. For example, the third child in a family of four may be, at various times, the elder of two, the middle of three, the youngest of three, or an only child if there's at least five years' difference between this child and siblings. This child may be in a dual position, taking on the complementary characteristics of both positions. If you have such a child in your class, you can determine her or his position only by learning about the other children in the family.

In large families, the children often form groups: the older, middle, and younger children, for example. Within each group may be a psychologically oldest, second or middle, and youngest child. Some children in large families may be in dual positions. For example, consider this family constellation:

Clark	15
Rosalind	13
Lois	10
Craig	8
Barry	3

Lois may be in a dual position as the youngest of three and also the oldest of two, or the youngest of the older three as well as a middle child.

Besides family grouping and the number of years between siblings, the family constellation can be affected by cultural and subcultural expectations. One's sex and the expectations for that sex can affect one's position in the family. The only boy or girl in a family may be unsure of his or her place. Such a child may feel special, choosing the behavior that gains the most status in the family. If one sex is valued over the other, the child may choose either to conform to the valued sex role or to rebel. Fortunately, sex differences are having less and less influence on family constellations. But since past stereotypes persist in some families, we need to keep sex roles in mind when considering our students' family positions.

Age differences can also affect perception. Since lifestyle is usually formed between the ages of four and six, a difference of five years can be used as a rule of thumb to determine if a child competes with an older or younger sibling, or if one is psychologically an only child.

With all these variables affecting our students' psychological place within their families, why should we know the typical characteristics of each position (as shown on Chart 2A)? Because some knowledge of the typical can help us begin to develop a tentative hypothesis about each student's basic outlook and fundamental beliefs. Then we have a starting point for seeing the world from our students' point of view.

Lifestyle and the Immediate Goals of Behavior

In response to heredity, family atmosphere, role models, methods of discipline, and the family constellation, students develop their basic convictions and their *long-range* or *life* goals.

The four goals of misbehavior and their positive counterparts are *short-range* or *immediate* situational goals that help students achieve their long-range goals. The all-important general life goal is belonging; when students become discouraged about ever belonging through constructive behavior, they misbehave and find the place they need. Students may express their life goals through any of the four immediate goals.

For example, suppose Karen believes she must be the best at everything she does. As long as she succeeds most of the time, she probably won't misbehave. But when she discovers certain activities she can't be best at, she may express her long-range goal through misbehavior. She may decide not to participate in gym class because she knows she'll never be the best athlete. Instead, she may choose to be the best at getting attention, showing power, seeking revenge, or displaying inadequacy. Her choice of goal depends on her perception of how to belong most successfully.

Matt is in the same gym class as Karen. He's not much of an athlete either but he doesn't believe he *has* to be better than everyone else. He simply does his best, choosing to pursue his long-range goals constructively. He feels more secure, more encouraged in his life than Karen does.

Some students, however, are "good" for the wrong reasons. Renee always volunteers to help, answers questions on cue, and is one of your best students. She also tattles and seems to enjoy putting others down. She is "good" out of self-interest only. Similarly, Doug gets attention by being cute and charming. He too has no real concern for others. Both Renee and Doug are discouraged in some way, believing that being "good" at the expense of others or getting by on one's charm is the only way they can belong. We do our best for such students by refusing to praise them, ignoring tattling, being unimpressed with put-downs, and giving recognition when the attention is unexpected and only for real contributions.

Students who pursue positive goals feel encouraged in some or all areas of their lives. They are as interested in the welfare of others as they are in their own welfare. They have a well-developed sense of social interest.

How Can We Learn About Our Students' Lifestyles?

With older elementary and secondary students especially, our knowledge of lifestyle, beliefs, and long-range goals is important. Emotionally disturbed students change their immediate goals frequently; insight into their lifestyles is also helpful.

We can begin to understand our students' lifestyle and family constellation by meeting with parents, the class, small groups, and individual students. We can teach the theory of family constellations to our students. The effort we make to understand the environment students come from can help us respond appropriately to all kinds of classroom behavior.

What About Our Own Lifestyles?

Teachers too have many long-held beliefs, formed by the same circumstances that influence students. We act on those beliefs with the best of intentions. But five typical beliefs may actually *hamper* our relationships with students.

I must control. "Stop that or you'll get a detention!" "Listen, I had better not hear any more bad reports about you from other teachers. I won't have a student in my class bothering other teachers!" "Stop your daydreaming and get to work!"

When we believe we must control students, we create restricting environments of either dependency or rebellion. A democratic classroom lets us establish order according to the requirements of a specific situation. We offer logical choices, freedom within limits.

Suppose Fred and Benny are disturbing a class discussion with their private conversation. Instead of yelling at them, you ignore them. They persist. You say, "I'm sorry, but we can't hear each other. Would you like to continue your conversation later, or move away from each other?" You didn't demand they be quiet. You simply responded to the needs of the situation — everyone must hear the class discussion — and offered the misbehaving students a choice within limits. You didn't make a futile attempt at control. Instead, you asked yourself, "What does this situation require?"

Sometimes we try to control by watching our students' every move. We remind them of everything, demand they ask permission to move or speak, appoint monitors to watch them when we must be out of the room, encourage tattling. Such "snoopervision" may include notes to parents detailing misbehavior and demanding that parents help us discipline.

When you ask Ted's parents to force him to study, you're forgetting that his behavior problems probably aren't solved at home either. Even if you have some short-range success using parental pressure, Ted now has both teacher and parents to defeat.

Once we've improved our own relationships with students, we can help parents get along better with their children. We can report *encouraging* news. We can explain to parents in conferences and let our students know that we believe students can make decisions within limits and learn from those decisions. Such a belief promotes confidence. Students begin to feel they can make good decisions.

I am superior. We want students to learn independence, take responsibility, and develop self-discipline. Dominating and over-protecting them out of a sense of superiority can only promote feelings of inadequacy and worthlessness. No matter how young students are, they can be treated as human beings and trusted to learn from experience (dangerous situations excepted, of course).

For example, Charles is dawdling and not finishing his assignment. You give him a choice. "Charles, you may finish the assignment in class or stay after school until it's done. You decide when you'll do the work." If Charles continues to dawdle, you'll know he's decided to do his work after school. You've let Charles know you believe him capable of learning from the consequences of his decisions.

We may have more knowledge, experience, and responsibilities than our students. But teachers and students are equal in human worth and dignity.

I am entitled. In order to create an atmosphere of mutual respect, both students and teacher must behave responsibly. Respect must be earned. Yet sometimes we feel entitled to obedience and respect simply because we're adults and teachers. When we dominate, control, or over-protect students, we foster distrust. We violate respect for students. We need to be firm but kind, offering students logical choices in a respectful manner. When students feel respected, they often return that respect.

I don't count. We violate respect for ourselves by becoming doormats. Teachers also have rights in a democratic classroom. We must believe in our own value and abilities.

For example, Mr. Torres recognized that by repeating instructions to several students who constantly sought his attention by "forgetting," he was showing disrespect for himself and for those students' capabilities. So he began writing all instructions on the chalkboard. Whenever a student asked for a repetition, Mr. Torres simply pointed to the board.

We promote mutual respect not only by respecting our students' rights but by standing up for our own.

I must be perfect. Some of us have grown up believing we must be mistake-proof. Perfectionists will not tolerate errors in themselves; as teachers, they also resent mistakes their students make. This fear of failure often rubs off on students. They begin believing their work is never good enough and become overly concerned about the opinions of others. They believe they must look good at any cost.

Perfectionism in teachers is quite understandable, considering some of society's unrealistic expectations and demands. As we strive to be all things to all people, we get trapped into attempting to satisfy too many people with too many conflicting ideas about what a teacher should be. Our students suffer because our attention is focused elsewhere.

We need to develop "the courage to be imperfect" (Dreikurs, 1971). We need to accept the fact that we are fallible beings so we can set realistic standards for ourselves and our students. Recognizing that mistakes help us learn, we can encourage our students to attempt new things without fear of failure.

The Importance of Emotions

We can't overestimate the importance of emotions in our classrooms. Caroline feels picked on so she responds by sulking and

refusing to speak. Her teacher feels hurt by Caroline's attitude and punishes her. The cycle of revenge continues.

"Emotions are the fuel that take us where we want to go" (Dreikurs, 1967). Yet most of us don't understand our feelings, don't believe we can control them. The following simple experiment may tell you something about your control over your own emotions:

Relax in a comfortable chair. Close your eyes and concentrate on a particularly happy time from your past. Visualize the people you were with, their expressions and what they said. Remember your own expressions and words. Recreate your good feelings and enjoy them.

After a minute or so, think back to a particularly sad or unpleasant experience. Visualize the expressions and words of the people you were with and your own expressions and words. Concentrate on your anger, hurt, depression. After you're keenly aware of those painful feelings, go back to the happy time and stay there until you feel good again (Mosak and Dreikurs, 1973).

What did you discover? Did you have trouble recreating the unpleasant experience or getting back to the happy time? People respond to this exercise in different ways, according to their own perceptions. But most discover they *can* transport themselves from one scene to another and they *can* recreate the feelings.

We can train ourselves to change our feelings because *we feel as we believe.* Our lifestyle, how we view ourselves and others, determines how we act *and* how we feel. If we believe students are trustworthy and deserving of respect, we will form trusting, respectful relationships with them. If we believe students must be watched and controlled at all times, our suspicions will generate hostile feelings and strained relationships.

We need emotions. We couldn't develop close relationships or act with determination without them. Emotions serve the purpose of supplying energy for our actions. But most people tend to overuse their negative emotions. Understanding those emotions in students and in ourselves will help us respond effectively to misbehavior.

Misusing Negative Emotions: Students

Students who pursue one of the four goals of misbehavior act out of strong feelings. They may throw temper tantrums to demonstrate power. Out of hurt, they may coax pity and involvement from teachers. Anger may spur revenge. Self-pity or despair can call forth a display of inadequacy.

Consider Peter, your "sensitive" student. The slightest remark brings out his quivering lips and tearful eyes. Other students pick on him. You feel sorry for him and give him special treatment for a while. Soon, however, you grow annoyed with the constant "waterworks." Your annoyance induces Peter to feel even more sorry for himself. You see he's hurt, feel guilty, and resume the special treatment. The discouraging cycle continues.

We owe it to students like Peter not to give them the attention or power they're seeking. Peter's sensitivity gains him recognition from adults and peers; his peers either give him attention (which Peter likes better than being ignored) or acknowledge his power to get the teacher's sympathy and protection. Yet he doesn't understand the goal of his misbehavior. But you can let him know you believe him to be as capable and resilient as any other student. You can treat him as you do others, refusing to supply the emotional response he wants. You can focus on and encourage his strengths.

Misusing Negative Emotions: Teachers

In order to avoid reinforcing students' mistaken goals, we want to change not only our behavior but also our emotional responses to misbehavior. Since students expect us to feel annoyed, angry, hurt, or despairing, we need to reduce these feelings and change our purpose in those negative interactions with students. More, we need to replace the feelings with positive emotions like empathy and determination. Positive feelings will lead us to constructive responses (McKay & Christensen, 1978).

If emotions give us the energy to act, why do we respond as we typically do to misbehavior? Consider the goal of attention. Our annoyance impels us to stop the interference with our teaching through reminding and coaxing.

We feel angry about power plays because we think they threaten our prestige and authority. The anger spurs us on to control the student through fighting or, if we feel we've lost the battle, getting even.

When we encounter a revengeful student, we usually feel hurt. We may not understand how we created that hurt, since other teachers may respond differently to the student's behavior. But the hurt we created gives us permission to get back at the student. Then we generate anger to carry out our counterattack.

At first we blame ourselves, believing we must be terrible teachers to deserve such an attack. Then we cover up those hurt feelings and generate anger to condemn the student in order to excuse our self-blame. It's usually easier to condemn another than to condemn ourselves (Ellis, 1976).

Our despair over the student who's given up permits us to give up too. We feel unable to help the student; we cover those feelings of inadequacy by viewing the student as inadequate.

How can we get off this emotional merry-go-round? As fallible human beings, we can't completely avoid negative or useless feelings. But with courage and commitment, we can reduce them.

Ways to Redirect Our Negative Emotions

Choose one thing to work on at a time. Perhaps you might decide to cut down on talking when students misbehave. Misbehaving students expect teachers to talk, so we can surprise them by not fulfilling this expectation. If you must respond verbally to misbehavior, choose your words carefully, be brief, and speak in a firm but friendly tone.

34

Once you've chosen a specific response to change, decide on a reasonable time to experiment. Give yourself a week to work on it. You've been behaving and feeling in certain ways for a long time and you'll want to be realistic about your attempts to change.

Plan your experiment scientifically: apply a specific procedure for a certain period of time, delaying evaluation until that time is up. Refrain from unnecessary talk regardless of how students react at first. When you evaluate your results at the end of the week, focus on what you've accomplished. Then decide whether or not to continue.

As you work on changing or modifying your customary responses to misbehavior, consider the following mental and behavioral strategies. These are best used in combination, some for times of quiet thought and some for times of contact with misbehaving students.

1. *Fully acknowledge and accept your own imperfections.* All people are imperfect. Decide what in yourself you want to change and don't be discouraged by slow progress or setbacks. Take the risks required to make you a more effective teacher.

2. *Recognize and change your purpose.* Once you recognize the purpose of your annoyance, anger, hurt, or despair, you can decide to change that purpose.

Instead of "paying off" the attention-seeking student by feeling annoyed and then reminding and coaxing, decide to stimulate the student's self-reliance. You want such students to feel they can belong without constantly seeking your attention. So you will feel *determined* not to reinforce the mistaken goal. You'll avoid giving attention on demand, ignore inappropriate bids for attention, and give attention in unexpected ways and at unexpected times by catching them being "good."

Instead of deciding to show power-seeking students who's boss or giving in and then getting even, choose to win their cooperation. You'll then feel *determination* not to fight or give in and *regret* that such students have decided to make their own lives so difficult. Your determination and regret will motivate you to withdraw from conflicts and let students learn from the consequences of their own behavior. You will teach students to use power constructively by enlisting their help.

Instead of getting even with revengeful students, decide instead to show compassion. Realize such students' deep discouragement; you are probably just one more adult "enemy." Showing compassion will bring feelings of *regret* and *empathy* for the student's plight and *determination* to avoid seeking your own revenge. These feelings will make it easier for you to build a trusting relationship with revenge-seekers.

Instead of giving up on students who display inadequacy, choose to demonstrate confidence in their ability. You'll then feel *faith* in the student, and *determination* not to despair. You'll be able to avoid criticism and pity, arrange success experiences for the student, and encourage any positive efforts.

3. *Think positive.* Consider how much more useful and productive it is to think in positive, constructive terms about students who misbehave.

Harold continually shouts out. You get angry and try to force him to behave but he ignores your efforts. You think about Harold: "That little monster *has* to learn to raise his hand. *I just can't stand it* when he shouts out. *What's the matter with me* that I can't control a nine-year-old?"

Realizing that such a train of thought is useless to you and to Harold, you attempt to view the situation in a different light: "Look, if I keep feeling angry, he'll resist me, disrupt more, and make the whole class suffer. I don't like it when he shouts out but *I can stand it.* It's frustrating when I can't control him but *it's not the end of the world.* It doesn't mean I'm incompetent. He's only misbehaving because *he's discouraged. I can help him* by refusing to fight. I'll simply give him the choice of cooperating or leaving the group until he's ready to behave. He'll probably leave the group but eventually he'll decide to cooperate. *I can redirect* his desire for power by letting him collect the essays. He'll like that job and feel better about himself and me."

Negative thinking only reinforces our negative emotions (Ellis & Harper, 1975). Most misbehavior *can* be understood and *can* be dealt with.

4. *Have a plan.* If certain kinds of misbehavior keep recurring in your classroom, plan what your response will be *before* you come to school. Think about the misbehavior and how students will respond to your new approach. Create the scene in your mind and imagine what will happen. Consider each possible response to your new behavior and plan what you'll do about each one. You'll build up a "response repertoire" that will also help you deal with the unexpected.

5. *Do the unexpected.* Your first impulse is usually to respond to misbehavior as students expect, with the feelings that reinforce their goals. Resist that first impulse (Dreikurs and Soltz, 1964). If they expect you to talk, remain silent. If possible, walk away or busy yourself with something else. Give yourself time to think. Your new response will give your students something to think about.

6. *Speak in a firm, friendly tone.* Your tone of voice is the best indicator of your true attitude and feelings (Dreikurs and Soltz, 1964). As you change your feelings, your tone will become more positive. Similarly, adopting a more positive tone can help you lessen your negative feelings. For example, when Harold chooses to leave the room rather than cooperate, express regret. Let students know you accept them as persons, even if their behavior is unacceptable. (You can practice tones of voice by rehearsing with a tape recorder.)

7. *Watch your nonverbal communication.* Students can tell your real feelings when your words are friendly but your face isn't. Make sure your words and body say the same thing by practicing in front of a mirror, with a friend, or in role-playing exercises with your STET group.

8. *Distract yourself.* When you know it's best not to say anything but your feelings are intense, deliberately concentrate on something else. Think of that tennis match after school, your favorite song, what you have to teach next, what someone said in the teachers' lounge. Move around the room, talk to other students or the class — whatever works for you.

9. *Make yourself reminders and signals.* Use cartoons, a red flag, stop signs. Put them where you'll see them so you'll remember not to respond to misbehavior in the usual way.

10. *Use your sense of humor.* Humor releases tension. If you've been locked in a power struggle with a student during the day, later when you're alone, deliberately exaggerate your negative thoughts. ''You know, for that kind of action you were lucky not to wind up in my student trophy case. Beautiful case — probably has about 50 students mounted in it. I exhibit my collection on holidays . . . .'' Look for the humor in situations.

If you make a mistake in front of the class, laugh about it. Your students deserve to be taught by a human being.

Often you can kid a student out of misbehavior. ''Is that the best you can do to bug me? You can do better than that!'' If your tone is *friendly,* students may see they're being ridiculous. You may all end up laughing.

11. *Avoid the language of discouragement.* Human beings use all sorts of verbal evasions to avoid taking responsibility for their actions. Four phrases are especially common (McKay, 1976):

''I can't.'' Most people use ''I can't'' when they really mean ''I won't.'' ''I can't teach math''; ''I can't stand that kid''; ''I can't help getting mad.'' We say ''I can't'' when we don't want to do something but want others to admire our good intentions, when we choose to proclaim inadequacy and so make others serve us, or when we really feel incapable and want to be left alone. It helps to substitute ''I won't'' for ''I can't'' and then see if you want the refusal to stand. Stop and ask yourself the purpose of your ''I can't.'' Who prevents you? Realize that willingness to change is all that's needed.

''He *made* me blow up!'' Are you sure you had no choice in the matter? He may have *invited* you to explode but didn't you make the decision? It's useful to remind yourself of your own control over your feelings.

''I'll try'' can often be a weak commitment with a built-in insurance policy against an expected failure. When we do fail, we can say, ''Well, at least I tried'' or ''I knew it wouldn't work.'' Make sure you're sincerely committed to change.

''Well, I'd like to do that, *but''* is really a polite way of saying no. We agree with a proposal and then negate our agreement with ''but,'' ''except,'' ''however,'' ''although,'' ''still.'' It's usually better to say no outright than to hedge. No one can force us: we decide.

12. *Set realistic goals.* Sometimes we fail to change our behavior because we demand perfection of ourselves and others. But change needn't be an all-or-nothing proposition. Focus on *decreasing* anger rather than *eliminating* it. Set goals you feel you can achieve.

13. *Recognize your own effort and improvement.* Give yourself credit for any progress toward your goals. If you decided to ignore

Sally's bid for attention and you managed to do so two of the four times she was late to school last week, you accomplished something. You deserve to feel encouraged.

14. *Don't feel guilty.* Guilt feelings sometimes work to impress ourselves and others with our sincerity; we "pay the price" for our mistakes and so feel free to behave the same way again. Guilt wastes energy and accomplishes nothing. If you forgot your good intentions and yelled at Helene today, simply acknowledge your mistake and resolve to respond differently tomorrow.

Students and teachers alike, we all come to school with emotional baggage we've carried for a long time. We can't hope to unload all the beliefs and emotions that interfere with teaching and learning. But we teachers can develop our understanding of the motivations and goals surrounding behavior. Only with understanding can we hope to accomplish change.

Works Cited

Dewey, Edith. *Basic Applications of Adlerian Psychology.* Coral Springs, FL: CMTI Press, 1978.

Dreikurs, Rudolf. *Psychodynamics, Psychotherapy and Counseling.* Chicago: Alfred Adler Institute, 1967.

Dreikurs, Rudolf. *Social Equality: The Challenge of Today.* Chicago: Henry Regnery, 1971.

Dreikurs, Rudolf. *The Challenge of Parenthood.* NY: Meredith Press, 1958.

Dreikurs, Rudolf, and Soltz, Vicki. *Children: The Challenge.* NY: Hawthorn, 1964.

Ellis, Albert. "Techniques of Handling Anger in Marriage." *Journal of Marriage and Family Counseling* 2 (1976): 305-315.

Ellis, Albert, and Harper, Robert A. *A New Guide to Rational Living.* Englewood Cliffs, NJ: Prentice-Hall, 1975.

McKay, Gary. *The Basics of Encouragement.* Coral Springs, FL: CMTI Press, 1976.

McKay, Gary D., and Christensen, Oscar C. "Helping Adults Change Disjunctive Emotional Responses to Children's Misbehavior." *Journal of Individual Psychology* 34 (1978): 70-84.

Mosak, Harold H., and Dreikurs, Rudolf. "Adlerian Psychotherapy." In *Current Psychotherapies,* edited by Raymond Corsini. Itasca, IL: F.E. Peacock, 1973.

Recommended Readings

Ansbacher, Heinz L., and Ansbacher, Rowena R., eds. *The Individual Psychology of Alfred Adler.* NY: Harper & Row, 1956.

Asselin, Cheryl; Nelson, Tom; and Platt, John. *Teacher Study Group Leader's Manual.* Chicago: Alfred Adler Institute, 1975.

Baruth, Leroy, and Eckstein, Daniel. *Life Style: Theory, Practice and Pesearch*. Dubuque, IA: Kendall/Hunt, 1978.

Dinkmeyer, Don. *The Basics of Self-Acceptance*. Coral Springs, FL: CMTI Press, 1977.

Dyer, Wayne. *Pulling Your Own Strings*. NY: Avon Books, 1977.

Dyer, Wayne. *Your Erroneous Zones*. NY: Avon Books, 1976.

Eckstein, D.; Baruth, L.; and Mahrer, D. *Life Style: What It Is and How To Do It*. Chicago: Alfred Adler Institute, 1975.

Ellis, Albert. *How to Live With and Without Anger*. NY: Reader's Digest Press, 1977.

Ellis, Albert, and Harper, Robert. *A New Guide to Rational Living*. Englewood Cliffs, NJ: Prentice-Hall, 1975.

Losoncy, Lewis. *You Can Do It: How to Encourage Yourself*. Englewood Cliffs, NJ: Prentice-Hall, 1980.

Mosak, Harold. *On Purpose*. Chicago: Alfred Adler Institute, 1977.

Shulman, Bernard. *Contributions to Individual Psychology*. Chicago: Alfred Adler Institute, 1973.

Study Questions

1. What is lifestyle? How does it influence behavior and misbehavior?

2. What are the five major influences on a person's lifestyle?

3. What is the family constellation? How can knowing about students' family constellations help us teach more successfully?

4. "Students may express their life goals through any of the four immediate goals." Explain.

5. How can we learn about our students' lifestyles?

6. Discuss the five typical beliefs held by teachers that may hamper relationships with students.

7. How do our beliefs influence our feelings? Why is it possible to change our feelings?

8. How do students misuse their negative emotions? What can we do about it?

9. How do teachers misuse their own negative emotions?

10. Discuss ways teachers can redirect their negative emotions in order to respond more appropriately to students' misbehavior.

Problem Situation

Joe has been teaching for three years. He was an all-A student in his education major and had an A average for his other undergraduate work. He's recently completed an M.A. and regularly enrolls in any self-improvement workshop offered. You know he works well with highly-motivated students, but has difficulty with average or slow-learning students. He has high standards and is impatient with any mistakes made by students or himself. He often feels very tired at the end of the school day but his doctor cannot find any physical cause. One day, Joe comes to you and says, ''Those kids are impossible. I'm just exhausted trying to get them up to grade level!''

1. How would you respond to Joe?
2. What do you think is the source of his frustration?
3. How might you help him change?

Activity for the Week

Study Chart 2B and identify one of your own effective beliefs, skills, or ways of behaving. Also identify one ineffective belief, skill, or way of behaving.

This week, record times when your effective characteristic helped and times when your ineffective characteristic got in the way.

Recommended Resource Book Material

Chapter 2; Chapter 3, ''Top Student''; Chapter 4, ''Building a feeling vocabulary,'' ''Recognizing nonverbal communication of feelings,'' ''Listening for feelings,'' ''Listening,'' ''Feelings''; Chapter 14, ''Moving from negative to positive self-talk,'' ''Developing a system for change.''

Typical Characteristics of Each Position in Family Constellation*

Please note: The following characteristics will not apply to *all* children in *every* family. *Typical* characteristics, however, can be identified.

Only Child[1]	Oldest Child	Second Child	Middle Child of Three[2]	Youngest Child
Pampered and spoiled.	Used to being center of attention.	Never has parents' undivided attention.	Has neither rights of oldest nor privileges of youngest. Feels life is unfair.	Behaves like only child. Feels everyone bigger and more capable. Lets others do things, make decisions, take responsibility.
Feels incompetent compared with adults.	Must gain and hold superiority over other children. Being right and controlling important.	Always has more advanced siblings. Acts as if in race, trying hard to catch up with or overtake first child. If first child is "good," second child is "bad." Develops abilities first child doesn't have. If first child successful, may feel uncertain of self and abilities.	Feels unloved, abused, "squeezed." Feels lack of definite place in family.	Feels smallest and weakest. Not taken seriously.
Is center of attention and enjoys position. Feels special.				
Self-centered.	Responds to birth of second child by feeling unloved and neglected. Strives to keep or regain parents' attention through conformity. If this fails, chooses to misbehave.		Becomes discouraged and a "problem child" or elevates self by pushing other siblings down.	Becomes boss of family in getting service and own way.
Depends on service from others rather than own efforts.				
Feels unfairly treated when doesn't get own way. Feels entitled to own way.	Either develops competent and responsible behavior or becomes discouraged.	A rebel. Often doesn't like position.	Adaptable since must deal with both oldest and youngest siblings.	Develops feelings of inferiority or becomes "speeder" and overtakes older siblings.
Plays "divide and conquer" to get way.		Feels squeezed if third child is born. Pushes down siblings.		Keeps baby role and places others in service.
Has poor peer relations as child but better relations as adult.	Strives to protect and help younger siblings.			In family of three, allies with oldest child against middle child, the "common enemy."
Pleases when wants to.	Wants to please.			
Creative.				
Has striving characteristics of oldest and inadequacy feelings and demands of youngest.				

NOTES: 1. Only children usually want to be adults and so don't get along with peers very well. When they become adults, they often believe they've finally "made it." Only children live primarily in the world of adults during their formative years. Being at a disadvantage, they must learn how to operate in the big people's world as well as how to entertain themselves. As a result, they often become very creative in their endeavors. 2. The middle child of three is usually different from the middle child of a large family. The middle children of large families are often less competitive. Parents don't have as much time to give each child and so the children learn to cooperate to get what they want.

*Adapted from Dinkmeyer, McKay, Dinkmeyer. *Parent Education Resource Manual.* Coral Springs, FL: CMTI Press, 1978.

Ineffective and Effective Characteristics of Teachers

Ineffective Characteristics

Teacher's Belief	Teacher's Behavior	Results for Students
I must control.	Demands obedience. Rewards and punishes. Tries to win. Insists is right and students wrong. Overprotects.	Rebel; must win or be right. Hide true feelings. Feel anxious. Seek revenge. Feel life is unfair. Give up. Evade, lie, steal. Lack self-discipline.
I am superior.	Pities students. Takes responsibility. Overprotects. Acts self-righteous. Shames students.	Learn to pity selves and blame others. Criticize others. Feel life is unfair. Feel inadequate. Become dependent. Feel need to be superior.
I am entitled. You owe me.	Is overconcerned with fairness. Gives with strings attached.	Don't trust others. Feel life is unfair. Feel exploited. Learn to exploit others.
I must be perfect.	Demands perfection from all. Finds fault. Is overconcerned about what others think. Pushes students to make self look good.	Believe they are never good enough. Become perfectionists. Feel discouraged. Worry about others' opinions.
I don't count. Others are more important than I.	Is permissive. Sets no guidelines. Gives in to students' demands. Feels guilty about saying no.	Expect to get own way. Are confused. Do not respect rights of others. Are selfish.

Continued on next page

Chart 2B continued

Effective Characteristics

Teacher's Belief	Teacher's Behavior	Results for Students
I believe students can make decisions.	Permits choices. Encourages.	Feel self-confident. Try. Contribute. Solve problems. Become resourceful.
I am equal, not more or less than others.	Believes in and respects students. Encourages independence. Gives choices and responsibility. Expects students to contribute.	Develop self-reliance, independence, responsibility. Learn to make decisions. Respect selves and others. Believe in equality.
I believe in mutual respect.	Promotes equality. Encourages mutual respect. Avoids promoting guilt feelings.	Respect selves and others. Have increased social interest. Trust others.
I am human; I have the "courage to be imperfect."	Sets realistic standards. Focuses on strengths. Encourages. Is not concerned with own image. Is patient.	Focus on task at hand, not on self-elevation. See mistakes as challenge. Have courage to try new experiences. Are tolerant of others.
I believe all people are important, including myself.	Encourages mutual respect. Invites contributions. Refuses to be "doormat." Knows when to set limits and say no.	Know and accept limits. Respect rights of others.

Recording Worksheet

Typical Beliefs of Teachers

This recording illustrates typical, ineffective beliefs teachers hold and their possible effects on students. As you listen to each scene, note how the teacher interacts with the students. Listen for signs of beliefs such as "I must control," "I am superior," "I am entitled," "I don't count," "I must be perfect."

If necessary, refer to Chart 2B. Be prepared to discuss your responses with the group.

NOTES

Chapter 2

Points to Remember

1. Lifestyle reflects our beliefs about ourselves, other people, and the world.

2. Lifestyle is influenced by heredity, family atmosphere and values, role models, methods of discipline, and the family constellation.

3. The family constellation refers to the psychological position of each child in a family.

4. Students may express their long-range or life goals through any of the four immediate goals.

5. Five typical beliefs may hamper our relationships with students:
- I must control.
- I am superior.
- I am entitled.
- I don't count.
- I must be perfect.

6. We can train ourselves to change our negative feelings because we feel as we believe. We are responsible for our own feelings and behavior.

7. Certain mental and behavioral strategies can help us change or modify our customary responses to misbehavior. These are:
- Fully acknowledge and accept your own imperfections.
- Recognize and change your purpose.
- Think positive.
- Have a plan.
- Do the unexpected.
- Speak in a firm, friendly tone.
- Watch your nonverbal communication.
- Distract yourself.
- Make yourself reminders and signals.
- Use your sense of humor.
- Avoid the language of discouragement.
- Set realistic goals.
- Recognize your own effort and improvement.
- Don't feel guilty.

Personal Record Chapter 2

1. My experience with the weekly assignment

2. My reactions to the reading

3. Topics to discuss with the group

4. Skills I intend to improve

5. My beliefs which impede progress

6. My successes in applying program ideas

7. My difficulties in applying program ideas

8. My progress this week: A specific example

9. This week I learned

CHAPTER 3
ENCOURAGEMENT:
THE PRIME MOTIVATOR

How is encouragement part of a total approach to our relationship with students?

What is the difference between encouragement and praise?

What are some specific ways we can encourage our students?

What is the language of encouragement?

How can an encouraging classroom help bring our ideals closer to reality?

Encouragement is the most valuable gift you can offer your students. It alone won't teach them to read or spell, but without it, teaching may be more difficult than you ever dreamed. Become an encouraging teacher, an encouraging person, and you'll have come a long way toward turning your classroom into a stimulating, creative place.

Encouragement isn't as easy as it sounds. Helping students believe in themselves and in their abilities is part of a total approach to your relationship with them. When you encourage regularly, even systematically, you demonstrate a basic attitude toward yourself and your students. Encouragement is having faith, giving hope, reducing competition, eliminating unreasonably high standards and double standards. Encouragement means accepting students as they are and separating their work from their worth. Encouragement is also a special language, both verbal and nonverbal.

But, you may say, I *do* encourage my students. When they perform well I compliment them, distribute gold stars, give classroom privileges, write to their parents. I say: "What a good job you did!" "I'm so proud of you!" "You're a fine student." "You have the neatest handwriting in the class." But there are important differences between encouragement and praise. Sometimes you may think you're encouraging students when, in fact, you are praising them. And praise can be *discouraging.*

Encouragement and Praise

When we praise, we send a subtly restricting message: "You're worthwhile only when you do things well" or "I like people who can do better than others." When we encourage, we respond to a wider range of behavior, effort, and improvement.

A student may interpret praise as meaning, "To be worthwhile, I must do what you want." Students who become dependent upon praise may grow to believe their self-worth rests solely in pleasing others. Suzanne may be an excellent flutist, Rodney a high-scoring basketball player, Denise a straight-A student. But your praise may discourage them, making them wonder, "What will I do for an encore?" Some students even get hooked on praise, addicted to the evaluations of others. When we encourage, we lead students to take responsibility for their own feelings of worth.

What about the student who is improving, but not excelling? Harry gets five spelling words correct. Last week he got only one. He's improved 500%, even if he still spells poorly. If Harry believes he'll merit praise only if he spells all his words correctly, or only if he does better than anyone else, he'll grow more and more discouraged. He may rebel against you, refuse to cooperate, or give up completely. When you encourage, you let Harry know that you recognize his improvement. You say, "Harry, look at the progress you've made!" You emphasize cooperative effort, rather than competition. You help Harry feel good about himself.

When we praise, however sincerely, we impose value judgments. "What a good job you did" implies that being worthwhile requires excellence, that a job isn't "good" unless we tell the student it is. "I'm so proud of you" teaches the student to please us, to feel guilty when we're not pleased. "You're a fine student" may not be something the student can be all the time. "You have the neatest handwriting in the class" promotes needless competition. Praise is limiting because it focuses upon the extrinsic: our good opinion, the student's standing in class, predetermined criteria. Encouragement promotes self-motivation, personal achievement, independent action.

With thought and practice, you'll begin to see the subtle differences between praise and encouragement:

Praise is a reward given for a completed achievement.
- Encouragement is an acknowledgment of effort.

Praise tells students they've satisfied the demands of others.
- Encouragement helps students evaluate their own performances.

Praise connects students' work with their personal worth, inviting fear of failure.
- Encouragement focuses on the strengths of the work, helping students see and feel confident about their own abilities. It instills faith.

Praise, however warm, places a cold value judgment on the student as a person.
- Encouragement shows acceptance and respect.

Praise is patronizing. It's talking down, as if the praiser enjoys a superior position.
- Encouragement is a message between equals.

Praise can be withheld as punishment or cheapened by overuse.
- Encouragement can be freely given because everyone deserves to receive it.

After you resolve to become more encouraging, you'll need some specific plans of action.

Accept Your Students as They Are

We communicate our expectations to students not only by words but by looks and tone of voice. If we often send verbal or nonverbal messages like "You're always the last one finished," "I suppose that's too hard for you," or "You can't work without supervision," we may find students fulfilling those expectations.

Instead, accept students as they are. Appreciate their differences. Jody may always be the last one finished, but aren't her drawings imaginative? Our best friends have faults but we concentrate on their good points, their unique qualities. We can do the same for our students. Students who are respected regardless of their faults, who feel they belong and know they are equal as class members, can concentrate their energies on growth and learning.

Accept students regardless of past performances; focus on the present and the future. We needn't approve of all their behavior, but we can accept them as people by *separating the deed from the doer*. We can find something to encourage, even in the most deficient work.

Meryl submits a paper describing her grandfather's farm. She's worked hard on the essay, spent all weekend on it, and now it's smudged and wrinkled. Crossed-out words make the poor handwriting almost illegible.

Her teacher blows up. "Do you expect me to spend my time wading through a messy paper like this? I have 35 essays to read! Don't you have any pride in your work? Now you clean this up by the end of the day or take an F!''

In attacking and shaming Meryl, this teacher has not separated the deed from the doer. Instead of focusing on the heart of the assignment — the essay's content — the teacher has told Meryl she's worthless. Even if her next essay is neater, Meryl isn't likely to take pains with her *writing* anymore. In fact, she may well balk at doing another paper.

An accepting teacher would have commented on something admirable in Meryl's paper, no matter how messy it was. We can always find something worth pointing out: a clever thought, a vivid word, a well-organized idea. Encouraged by having her strengths pointed out, Meryl would be more willing to tackle future assignments. Knowing that her efforts were noticed and appreciated, she would likely try harder to make her paper neater next time. The teacher would have accepted not a messy paper, but a student who tried.

Ben interrupts the class to speak. You can accept his intention (''I'm sure what you have to say is important, Ben . . .) without accepting his behavior (. . . and we'll hear from you right after Jan has had a turn to talk''). Feeling understood and accepted, Ben is encouraged to respect the rights of others.

Will acceptance prevent students from learning right from wrong? No. Their lives provide more than enough opportunities to taste frustration and failure. Helping them find their real strengths will give them a valuable resource against discouragement.

How do you show acceptance? With a smile, a touch, an accepting silence, or phrases like:

> I like the way you handled that. It wasn't easy.
> It'll turn out all right. Don't worry about the mistakes.
> I'm glad you're pleased with your work.
> You did your best, and that's all anyone can do.
> You're disappointed, I know. Do you want to talk about it?

When you accept, don't qualify. Make an encouraging statement and then stop. When you say, ''George, it looks like you're really thinking,'' don't add a discouraging ''but,'' ''however,'' ''yet,'' or ''nevertheless.'' Don't say, ''See what you can do when you try?'' or ''It's about time!'' Any added words should back up your encouraging statement by pointing to something specific. (''I like that title!'') Acceptance has no strings attached.

Give Students Confidence. Help Them Be Courageous

Believe that every one of your students can learn and wants to learn, and show them you believe in them. Some students are afraid to try for fear of making mistakes. Maybe they've been shamed once too often. Or they've found one thing you'll praise them for, like neat handwriting, and are afraid to push their luck by trying to excel at something else.

Let them know it's all right to try. Further, show them that mistakes are an important and natural part of learning. Strengthen their

self-confidence so they can easily withstand and profit from errors, false starts, wrong directions. Rid yourself of the red pencil mentality; mark their *correct* answers instead of highlighting their wrong ones. Help them be courageous learners by encouraging persistent effort. Let them know they need not fear ridicule or ostracism if their progress is slow or halting. Encourage any attempt, any improvement. If Jeffrey gets most of a word spelled correctly, let him know you noticed. If Martha is attentive during a class discussion, if she smiles, even if she just looks up, encourage her.

Learn to appreciate small successes and gradual growth. An encourager expects things to get better! Be an optimist who is sometimes wrong, rather than a pessimist who is usually right. Have, show, and express confidence in your students. They will come to live up to your expectations.

You might say:

Knowing you, I'm sure you'll do your best.
I have confidence in your judgment.
That's a rough one, but I'm sure you'll work it out.
You can do it. You've made it part way already.

If you show confidence in their sincerity and ability, they'll gradually come to have confidence in themselves.

Accentuate the Positive

That red pencil mentality is deadly. Marking only mistakes deprives students of hope. Be an asset finder. It's never impossible to find some strength, some effort, some indication of progress. The attentiveness you encouraged in Martha may be the only glimmer you've had from her in weeks, so it's doubly important to show her you noticed. Be alert. You are trying to create an eagerness for learning.

Begin to eliminate the negatives from your vocabulary, your actions, and your attitudes. Just as you can show encouragement by smiling, you reveal disapproval and impatience by frowning, sighing, foot-tapping, avoiding a student's eyes. Students will pick up on these nonverbal signs. That's why encouragement requires a major commitment from you. Used consistently and honestly, your positive attitude will promote their self-confidence.

Being positive may mean some change in your teaching approach. For example, instead of twenty problems, assign ten. Ten will be less discouraging for slower students, and students with more ability will still do well. You will create more interest in arithmetic by settling for slower, more positive growth. As you build students' confidence, along with their interest and ability, you can increase assignments little by little.

Why write to parents only when students are having problems? Send home an encouraging word at unexpected times. Each student is an individual, with unique capabilities. Emily may not read well compared with other students, but if she reads better now than she did last month, she and her parents deserve to hear about it. Tell Jamison's parents how he volunteered for a part in the skit; he may be too shy to tell them. Encouraged parents can only make your job easier.

Recognize effort and improvement with positive phrases:

It looks as if you really worked hard on that.
You spent a lot of time thinking that through and it shows.
I'm glad you volunteered.
Look at the progress you've made. (Be specific.)
You're improving in _____ . (Be specific.)
You may not feel you've reached your goal, but look how far you've come!

Being positive will help you instill a quiet self-confidence in your students. Learning then becomes an exciting challenge.

Respect Yourself and Them

You want your students to risk mistakes and accept imperfections. Give them an example to follow in your own behavior. If you make a mistake, admit it. If you don't know the answer to a question, say you don't and work with students to find it. Your students deserve to be taught by a human being. They'll empathize with a teacher who's open and honest.

Double standards are devastating. You're a human being; you'll have favorite students. But an encouraging classroom demands that everyone be treated equally. Don't overlook your "good" students' talking in class or tardiness with assignments. When all students know you treat everyone equally, they'll be more willing to cooperate and participate. You won't be contributing to hard feelings between students.

Double standards apply to you too. Are the rules for your behavior the same as the ones for your students? Students are quick to notice when you expect them to do what you say, not what you do. Eating in class, chewing gum, and drifting in late from the teachers' lounge isn't respectful. Students get the message: you're the boss and can do what you want. Their self-esteem and willingness to cooperate goes down.

Be as consistent as you can. Don't let bad moods or ill health change your behavior — but if they do sometimes, apologize. Admit you're a human being and fallible; have the courage to be imperfect. Students need to know you're reliable. They need to know what to expect from you. Don't assume every student understands what you say or do. Tell them all plainly what is expected of them. Let them see what you expect of yourself.

When your students do something for you or the class, show appreciation:

Thanks. That helped a lot.
It was thoughtful of you to _____ .
Thanks. I appreciate _____ because it makes my job much easier.
I needed your help, and you came through.
Your efforts improved our discussion.
(To the class) I really enjoyed today. Thank you.

It makes sense. Respect your students and they'll return your respect. Respect yourself and they'll learn to do the same.

Help Students Evaluate Themselves. Reduce Competition

Having students work with you in setting their own goals is a good way to encourage their belief in themselves and their abilities. Help Howard set the goal of completing one science experiment per week, and then encourage his efforts. Seeing progress toward goals they have helped establish motivates students. Perhaps most important, individual goals reduce competition.

Competition can be the most discouraging thing a student faces. We must be careful not to create or feed it unintentionally. Reminding Sarah that her sister is very good in math only adds to her feeling of inadequacy, and fuels what may be a lifelong rivalry. "Everybody else understands the metric system and you can too" tells Eric he isn't trying hard enough, that he's worth nothing until he catches up with the rest of the class. "Which row will get their papers in first?" puts speed ahead of quality and tramples on Paul's concern for completeness, correctness, and legibility.

Pitting students against each other makes winning more important than learning. Those who can't compete either rebel or give up. It can be far more productive, far healthier, to let students progress at their own rates as they work toward goals they took part in setting up. So, periodically through the year, make time for individual, face-to-face conferences with each student to evaluate work and set goals. Easier said than done, you're thinking. But even if they're very brief, confined to just one or two areas or projects, they will encourage students about themselves and your interest in them.

Suppose you've assigned essays about pets. Before collecting them, have each student fill out one side of a project evaluation sheet, as Angela Chesler has in the example shown. Such a sheet asks students to evaluate their own work, the strengths and the weaknesses. After you read each essay, you fill out your side of the form and bring the sheet to the conference. (If you see that the student has been overly self-critical, be sure and detail all the strengths you see. Write a positive overall evaluation.) Ask the student to bring the returned essay.

Start the conference with a general question like, "How do you feel about your essay?" The student will probably answer vaguely: "Oh, okay" or "It's all right, I guess" or "Not very good." Then bring out the evaluation form and ask the student to compare both sides with you.

Begin with the strengths; you want to encourage. Say to Angela, "You've said you like the way you described your dog Charlie's dreams. Which sentences do you think are especially good?" (If you found more strengths than the student did, point them out.) Then you can aim toward some weaker areas that need improvement: "Are there any parts you think could be made more clear? I wonder if a neater paper would help people enjoy your essay more." After Angela has analyzed the weaknesses, continue: "All right, here are some things you've said may need improvement. What kind of plans will you make to improve your spelling? Let me see how I can help."

You and Angela agree on the steps to be taken toward the goals she has set. You make sure the goals and plans to achieve them are realistic for this particular student. Write down the plans or have the student write them. Then file the sheet, retrieving it to add notes about follow-up meetings and records of Angela's progress.

PROJECT EVALUATION SHEET

SUBJECT _Language Arts_

PROJECT _Essay about pets_

STUDENT'S NAME _Angela Chesler_

DUE DATE _October 20, 1981_

Student's Comments

Strengths

The way I told about Charlie's dreams.

Areas Needing Improvement

Spelling

Overall Evaluation

Pretty good. I liked writing it.

Teacher's Comments

Strengths _interesting way of telling about dog's dreams. Use of words like "afraid" and "horrible" helps reader understand how it must be to dream Charlie's dream_

Areas Needing Improvement

Spelling and handwriting. Paragraph organization and transitions.

Overall Evaluation

The vivid details make this essay interesting to read.

Our Improvement Plan

Get a student tutor to help with spelling. Copy over the essay slowly, using the handwriting chart as a model. Revise paragraph 2, paying special attention to organization of ideas. Then begin paragraph 3 with a transitional word.

Progress Made

Got 8 out of 10 words correct on spelling test.

Student's Signature _Angela Chesler_

Teacher's Signature _Mrs. Harzoff_

You can expand the system by giving each student a personal record-keeping card. Students then record their own goals and mark their own progress. (If some students can't mark their own records, you or a peer tutor can do the writing for them.)

This evaluation and record-keeping system is also valuable for teacher-parent conferences. With the student's permission, you can share the evaluation sheet and the personal record card with the parents. They'll see positive progress without seeing their child compared with other students. Students are motivated to improve, and parents are better informed.

We want to reduce competition and promote self-evaluation. But what about grades? Since grades are a fact of life for most students and teachers, we need to experiment with ways to make grading more encouraging.

One way is to involve students in deciding what grades they'll receive. Have them grade themselves and then explain the grades. If you fear students will grade themselves too high, you may be surprised. You will very likely find yourself defending higher grades.

Or you might grade by contract. After you have explained the requirements of a specific grade, each student decides what grade she or he wants and contracts with you to work for it. (Chapter 7 has more about contracts.) You might decide to renegotiate the contract periodically, so you can check progress and encourage realistic goals. Contract grading requires that you neither overestimate nor underestimate your students. Contracts are mutual agreements.

These are some phrases to prompt students to evaluate their own work and performance:

How do you feel about it?
Since you're not satisfied, what do you think you can do so you *will* be pleased with it?
It looks as if you enjoyed that.

Many schools have built-in competitive procedures: grades, honors, demerits. We can dilute the competition and make school a more encouraging place by promoting individual goals and personal evaluation.

Involve Students in Helping Each Other

You can help each student develop feelings of worth and belonging by emphasizing cooperation. Encourage them to help each other.

We all have weaknesses and strengths, and we all prefer to display the strengths. We like competition only when we're sure we have some chance of looking good. If we're not good at dancing, painting, writing, or tennis, we avoid those activities and say we're not interested. This in adults is "good judgment." But when students try to save face this way, we call them "underachievers."

Students can benefit from strengths their peers are willing to share. Have all your students list what they do well and what they need to improve on. Then pair strengths and weaknesses for tutoring. You've probably seen that most students learn very well from their peers. The person being helped is more relaxed, freer to fail or make mistakes. Equally important, the person helping feels more accepted, more a part of a class effort. When roles are reversed — and they should be for every student — both learn something about empathy and cooperation.

Cross-age tutoring also works well. Use older students to teach younger ones. Younger students usually look up to older ones and will be eager to cooperate. But don't ask only "good" students to tutor. They may not even be the best tutors, because they may be impatient with slower learners. Choosing tutors who aren't the best students gives them some encouragement too.

You can teach students to encourage each other. Encouragement Council meetings (Schneidman, 1977) are variations on the class meetings described in Chapter 12. But you needn't wait until then: hold an Encouragement Council meeting soon.

Here are some pleasant topics to discuss:

What is something you do well?
What is something you like about yourself?
What is something you like about a classmate?
What do you like about school or this class?
What is something you've learned or improved on recently?
What has our class improved on lately?
What did somebody do for you this week that helped you feel good?
What did you do for someone else this week?
What is something you'd like to do for someone this week?

Four Encouraged Students

1. Gail is withdrawn, sensitive, usually by herself. Her classmates' feelings always register on her face, but she never speaks. Her teacher, Mr. Applebaum, wants to help Gail use her sensitivity to bring her closer to others, not farther away.

He schedules a conference with Gail. He tells her, "I've noticed how sensitive you are to all our feelings. We could all benefit if you'd share with us what you feel. Would you be willing to join our discussions a little more?" Gail slowly agrees, letting Mr. Applebaum know she appreciates his concern.

The next day, during a discussion of a short story, Mr. Applebaum gently encourages Gail to offer her perceptions. She does make one contribution and her teacher responds with, "That's a good point, Gail. I'm glad you mentioned it. Did anyone else notice that about the main character?"

Mr. Applebaum encouraged Gail by bringing her into the group. He noticed and commented upon Gail's real strength. She committed herself to trying harder and so made real progress.

2. Henry is terrified of tests. He can't eat or sleep the day before, and he panics so completely when he gets the test that he can't answer any of the questions.

His social studies teacher, Mrs. Caruso, notices how well Henry does in discussions. He clearly understands the material. Mrs. Caruso calls Henry in for a conference. She tells him, "Henry, I just wanted you to know how well you express your ideas. You're a real asset to our discussions because you can explain things so clearly. Will you lead our next discussion?" Henry eagerly agrees.

The next discussion goes well. Mrs. Caruso is careful to encourage Henry by pointing out how effective he was in getting everyone involved.

Heartened by her interest, Henry asks to speak with Mrs. Caruso. He talks about his fear of tests, knowing now that Mrs. Caruso accepts and respects him. She listens carefully and then says, "I have an idea about why tests are so horrible for you. May I guess?" Henry says yes. She asks, "Is it possible you believe you have to be the best in everything you do?" Henry smiles shyly, suggesting the guess is accurate.

Mrs. Caruso and Henry discuss tests. She points out that tests only measure a limited amount of knowledge. They say nothing about the total person. She asks Henry if he'd like to do half of the next test orally. Henry happily agrees; he's sure of himself verbally. The first part of the test goes very well, and the second part goes a bit better than Henry's previous tests.

Mrs. Caruso encouraged by being a good listener and focusing on Henry's strengths. She discovered his discouraging beliefs about himself and helped him combat them.

3. Felix is the youngest of four children, all excellent students. But although school records indicate Felix's above-average potential, he is rarely prepared in class and seldom completes an assignment.

His teacher, Mr. Meyer, finds out through conferences with Felix's parents that Felix gets lots of attention at home by not doing his work. His parents spend extra time with him, even doing some of his homework. His brothers and sisters expect little of him and do things for him. Felix has a trained set of servants!

In a conference, Mr. Meyer asks if he can guess why Felix does so poorly in school. Felix agrees. The teacher asks, "Is it possible you do poorly so no one will expect anything of you — so everyone will do things *for* you?" Felix says no, but his obvious discomfort suggests that Mr. Meyer is correct.

In a series of conferences, Mr. Meyer helps Felix see that he can increase his self-respect by doing things for himself. He notices and encourages Felix for any signs of progress.

4. Janet seems to have no friends. She sits sullenly by herself at lunch. Other students occasionally tease her. Now she's stopped turning in assignments.

Mrs. McVay talks to Janet in a conference. She sees that the girl is very hurt by her exclusion from classmates. She's tried to get even by withdrawing more and more, as though she doesn't care. Mrs. McVay lets Janet know she understands and empathizes with her feelings. She suggests Janet begin to cooperate with others, instead of withdrawing from them.

She asks, "Who in our class would you like to spend time with or have as a friend?" "Connie," says Janet. Mrs. McVay promises to pair Connie and Janet for the next science project. She encourages Janet to show her caring feelings to Connie.

Because of Mrs. McVay's interest and concern, Janet begins to change. She learns to use her sensitivity as an asset.

Encouragement helped all these students feel worthwhile and involved.

The Ideal and the Real

Most of us leave college with high ideals but little training in how to achieve them. So there is often a difference between what we first set out to do and the ways we behave once we're in the classroom:

Our Ideal Intentions	*What We May Be Doing*
Prepare responsible, independent students.	Set uniform goals instead of letting students help set their own.
	Give unnecessary assistance.
	Force all to work at the same pace.
	Nag and remind.
Develop resourceful students.	Direct and assign all work instead of considering students' interests and concerns.
Get students involved in and excited about learning.	Stifle curiosity by lecturing instead of promoting self-learning.
Teach students to learn from and cooperate with each other.	Restrict learning to that between teacher and student.
	Interfere with socialization and cooperation among students.
Inspire students to respect other people.	Talk down to students.
	Show no confidence in them.
	Criticize, humiliate, and punish them.
	Yell at them.

Our Ideal Intentions	What We May Be Doing
Develop self-confident, courageous students.	Set impossible goals.
	Penalize for mistakes.
	Advise not to attempt difficult tasks.
	Do for students what they can do for themselves.

This whole course is designed to help teachers attain those ideals. Encouragement is the key, the basis for all plans of action. Create an encouraging classroom and the ideals come a little closer to reality.

Are your actual goals and standards reasonable? Would you consider them realistic if you were one of your students? Have you set standards too high for any but the top students? Extra-high standards more often invite discouragement and rebellion than growth. It makes sense to help students take small, attainable steps toward goals they have had a part in setting.

What about your definition of growth and success? What is success to one student may be an impossible hurdle to another. The poor speller getting five words today over only one word yesterday has shown exceptional growth and success, regardless of how the others did. That student deserves encouragement. We all do.

When you use encouragement to help students believe in themselves and their own abilities, you make your life and their lives easier and more productive. When you show them how to encourage each other, you give them a priceless, life-enhancing skill.

What more can be asked of a teacher?

Works Cited

Schneidman, Bruce. Paper presented at North American Society of Adlerian Psychology, Minneapolis, 1977.

Recommended Readings

Avila, Donald; Combs, Arthur; and Purkey, William. *The Helping Relationship Sourcebook.* 2nd ed. Boston: Allyn & Bacon, 1977.

Combs, Arthur; Avila, Donald; and Purkey, William. *Helping Relationships.* 2nd ed. Boston: Allyn & Bacon, 1978.

Dinkmeyer, Don, and Dreikurs, Rudolf. *Encouraging Children to Learn: The Encouragement Process.* NY: Elsevier-Dutton, 1979.

Dinkmeyer, Don, and Losoncy, Lewis. *The Encouragement Book: Becoming a Positive Person.* Englewood Cliffs, NJ: Prentice-Hall, 1980.

Losoncy, Lewis. *Turning People On.* Englewood Cliffs, NJ: Prentice-Hall, 1977.

McKay, Gary. *The Basics of Encouragement.* Coral Springs, FL: CMTI Press, 1976.

Study Questions

1. What are some of the differences between encouragement and praise?

2. How does the language of praise differ from the language of encouragement?

3. In what ways can praise be discouraging?

4. How can expecting the worst invite students to perform poorly?

5. How can we show acceptance by "separating the deed from the doer"?

6. How can we help students be courageous learners? What can be the value of mistakes? What is the "red pencil mentality" and how can we rid ourselves of it?

7. Why do we need to avoid overambition? Why is it important to recognize effort and improvement as well as accomplishment?

8. Discuss the differences for teachers and students in our being asset finders rather than fault finders.

9. What are some ways to eliminate double standards in the classroom? What effects can unreasonably high standards have on students?

10. How can competition be discouraging? How can we make the grading system more encouraging?

11. How can we involve students in helping each other? Discuss the use of "encouragement councils."

12. In what sense is encouragement the key to a democratic classroom? How is encouragement part of a total approach to our relationship with students?

Problem Situation

Jane is the youngest child in a family of five. All her brothers and sisters have done well in school. Jane's classmates this year are competitive, eager students and Jane seems to be having trouble keeping up. She pays little attention to you and seldom completes assignments. She never gets more than five spelling words correct each week. When you talk with her, she says, "I study but I'm just not smart." You can sense her discouragement.

1. How does Jane's belief about herself influence her work?
2. What is the purpose of her behavior?
3. What are some specific ways you could encourage her?

Activity for the Week

Select a student whom you think is discouraged. Identify and write down why you believe the student is discouraged.

Every day, record how you encouraged the student and how the student responded to your encouragement.

Recommended Resource Book Material

Chapter 3; Chapter 4, "Mutual respect," "Respect"; Chapter 5, "Separating the deed from the doer"; Chapter 8, "Focusing on positive qualities of self and others," "A potpourri of exercises."

Chart 3

Differences between Praise and Encouragement

	PRAISE			**ENCOURAGEMENT**	
Focus	**Message Sent to Student**	**Possible Results**	**Focus**	**Message Sent to Student**	**Possible Results**
1. External control.	You are worthwhile only when you do what I want. You cannot be trusted.	Student learns to measure worth by ability to conform. May rebel, viewing any form of cooperation as giving in.	Student's ability to manage life constructively.	I trust you to become responsible and independent.	Student learns courage to be imperfect and willingness to try. Student gains self-confidence and comes to feel responsible for own behavior.
2. External evaluation.	To be worthwhile, you must please me.	Student learns to measure worth by ability to please others. Learns to fear disapproval.	Internal evaluation.	How you feel about yourself and your own efforts is most important.	Student learns to evaluate own progress and to make own decisions.
3. Reward is only for well-done, completed tasks.	To be worthwhile, you must meet my standards.	Student develops unrealistic standards and learns to measure worth by closeness to perfection. Learns to fear failure.	Effort and improvement.	You don't have to be perfect. Effort and improvement are important.	Student learns to accept efforts of self and others. Student develops desire to stay with tasks (persistence).
4. Self-elevation and personal gain.	You're the best. You must remain superior to others to be worthwhile.	Student learns to be overcompetitive, to get ahead at the expense of others. Feels worthwhile only when on top.	Assets, contributions, and appreciation.	Your contribution counts. We function better with you. We appreciate what you have done.	Student learns to use talents and efforts for good of all, not only for personal gain. Student learns to feel glad for successes of others as well as for own successes.

Recording Worksheet

Encouragement

After each scene, write what you would say or do to encourage the student. Be prepared to discuss your responses with the group.

Scene 1: How would you encourage this student?

Scene 2: How would you encourage this student?

Scene 3: How would you encourage this student?

NOTES

Chapter 3

Points to Remember

1. Encouragement is helping students believe in themselves and in their abilities.

2. Encouragement is a basic attitude toward yourself and other people.

3. Encouragement is different from praise. Praise goes to those who excel or come in first; encouragement can be given for any positive movement. Encouragement does not have to be earned.

4. Praise places a value judgment on the student. Encouragement focuses on the work or effort, treating the student with acceptance and respect.

5. Encouragement accepts students as they are, not as they could be.

6. Encouragement helps the learner develop the courage to be imperfect.

7. Mistakes are not failures. They can promote learning.

8. The first step in encouragement is to stop making negative comments about students.

9. Identify talents, assets, positive attitudes and goals. Every student has strengths.

10. Factors which discourage include:
- Negative expectations.
- Unreasonably high standards.
- Competition.
- Overambition.
- Double standards.

11. Be an asset finder, not a fault finder.

Personal Record Chapter 3

1. My experience with the weekly assignment

2. My reactions to the reading

3. Topics to discuss with the group

4. Skills I intend to improve

5. My beliefs which impede progress

6. My successes in applying program ideas

7. My difficulties in applying program ideas

8. My progress this week: A specific example

9. This week I learned

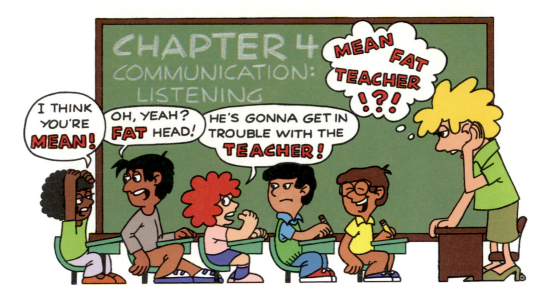

How can sensitive listening help us build better relationships with students?
What traditional roles do we play as we listen to students?
What is reflective listening?
Why are open responses more effective than closed responses?
How can reflective listening help us with students, parents, other teachers, administrators?

Listening is an art. Instead of despairing because "those kids won't *listen* to me," we might profitably examine the ways *we* listen to our *students.* We listen in different ways depending on our moods, our feelings about the person speaking, our opinion of what the speaker is saying and, in the classroom, our beliefs about our role as teacher.

If we agree that it's important to show students we care what they think and feel, then experimenting with better ways of listening makes sense. Many of us are not naturally good listeners. But we can improve once we accept the complexity of this basic communication skill and begin to practice new approaches. We can't understand our students' behavior or provide the right kind of encouragement until we hear precisely what they're saying and feeling. Sensitive listening to their verbal and nonverbal messages is a vital first step.

Who's Listening?

You can tell if someone is really listening to you.

Suppose you've just caught Gregory Loomis fighting for the fourth time this week. One minute he was playing kickball; the next minute he was kicking Peter Simon. You'd only looked away long enough to tie your shoe.

You're furious. You storm into the teachers' lounge and throw yourself into the chair next to Juanita Robb, who's sipping coffee and reading. You begin to pour out your feelings about Gregory Loomis.

Juanita fidgets. She reads. She straightens the papers beside her. She keeps looking toward the door and the clock. She interrupts you with "Mm-hmm," and "Really?" Finally, you've had enough. Your voice tapers off. You can see she's not listening.

How do you feel? Irritated, probably. Perhaps a bit embarrassed, even hurt. You won't be likely to bring your troubles to Juanita again.

Do you ever respond to your students the way Juanita did to you? When they come to you upset or worried, do you fidget or look away? Or maybe you're quick to advise, even before they've finished talking. Do you always stay behind your desk? Does your body language say, "I'm not sympathetic," although your voice says, "I understand?"

Many of us find it difficult to handle other people's strong emotions. We've been taught to conceal our own anger, fear, and hurt, and we're uneasy when we see such emotions expressed. Even outbursts of joy can be unsettling to us when the time isn't "right."

But as teachers we're confronted by our students' strong emotions all the time. Young people quite readily express their feelings. Their days at school are filled with occasions for grief, frustration, excitement, anger, triumph. If we ignore their feelings or try to separate the emotional from the intellectual aspects of learning, we risk losing our students' cooperation and respect. Further, we set up a formidable barrier to a democratic, encouraging classroom. When we fail to recognize feelings, we aren't letting ourselves do our jobs.

Remember your attempt to tell Juanita Robb your feelings about Gregory Loomis? Perhaps you said, "Boy! I've really reached the end of my rope with that kid! Do you know what he *did*?" Juanita fidgeted and interrupted. Consider how you'd feel if someone responded to your outburst in the following, equally frustrating ways.

The Commander-in-Chief. This listener says, "Calm down! You're going to give yourself an ulcer. No student's worth that!" The Commander-in-Chief demands order and control: You are to get rid of those angry feelings immediately and "shape up!" Such a listener, however well-intentioned, *orders* you to stop being angry.

With students, we're not always this polite. We use orders, commands, and threats. We say:

Sit down and be quiet!
Stop that dawdling and get back to your work.
If you bother me with this one more time, I'll _____!

The Moralist. "You shouldn't let Gregory get you so angry," advises this listener. The Moralist is a "shouldist"; the Moralist tells you it's wrong to feel angry. When we play this role with students, we're likely to say:

You know you should study so you'll get a good job someday.
It's wrong to fight. You should know better!
You should apologize!

The Know-It-All. This listener knows just what you should do about Gregory Loomis. The Know-It-All says, "Just call his parents and tell them to punish him." Teachers who play this role try to impress students with their superior knowledge and experience. They lecture, advise, appeal to "reason," and offer the benefits of their own enormous fund of answers:

If you'd studied harder, you'd have passed the test.
The thing to do is talk with Mr. Lopez and find out what he expects from you.
If you keep calling Fred names, he's going to keep hitting you.

The Judge. "Your anger isn't going to help the situation," says the Judge. This listener decides whether or not your feelings are appropriate. Teachers who play Judge are most interested in proving themselves right and the student wrong — guilty without a trial. The Judge says:

All right, what did you do this time?
What did you *expect* to get on the test? You just don't listen in class!
You're not hurt! Go back outside and play.

The Critic. Like the Moralist, the Know-It-All, and the Judge, the Critic likes being right. But this listener relies on ridicule, name calling, sarcasm, and jokes to show you just how ridiculous your feelings are. "Boy, you sure do have a bee in your bonnet!" is the Critic's response to your anger about Gregory. The Critic as teacher says:

You're acting like a baby!
Smart kid! You don't need school. You know everything you need to know already!
Oh, come on now, Kevin. Your sister can't be that bad. Having someone like you around probably drives her batty!

The Amateur Psychologist. This listener questions, analyzes, and diagnoses — in order to set you straight about what your problem really is. "Sounds like you two have a personality conflict," pronounces the Amateur Psychologist. Such teachers say:

I'll tell you what your problem is.
Why did you do *that?*
You feel inferior to your brother, don't you?

The Consoler. The Consoler treats your feelings lightly to avoid getting involved. This listener specializes in verbal pats on the back: "Well, thank goodness the day's over. I'm sure you'll feel better when you get home and unwind." Teachers who are Consolers say:

Don't worry about it. I'm sure everything will be all right.
I've felt that way many times. I got over it and so will you.
I'm sure when you think it over, you'll see it's not so bad.

   Teachers who fall into these common listening roles aren't monsters of insensitivity. They're usually well-intentioned human beings. They don't want to hurt or discourage students; they just don't know what else to say.

How Can I Be a Better Listener?

   Good listening is part of a trusting relationship. We must show students that we accept and respect their feelings. Like most people, our students are happier and do better in an atmosphere of acceptance and mutual respect. We can build that atmosphere by learning to speak "the language of acceptance" (Gordon, 1974).

   This language is only part verbal. Looking and feeling relaxed and comfortable will show students you're listening; you're not begrudging them the time. Lean forward, face the student, maintain eye contact without staring, hold the conversation without a physical barrier, like a desk, between you. Students quickly notice when our words don't match our tone of voice or posture.

   Most important, be willing to hear the student out and suspend judgment. *Empathize:* we needn't feel the same emotions or see the situation as they do, but we can understand their feelings and their point of view. Learn to use silence. We need to restrain ourselves from taking over all conversations with students. Let them talk. Provide some verbal assurance that you're listening and you care, but do avoid interrupting and putting words into their mouths. Students need and deserve the same consideration we would give our good friends.

   After you feel and look receptive, experiment with a special technique of telling students you understand what they're feeling. Use *reflective listening.*

Reflective Listening

Reflective listening calls for a response that reflects back to students their *feeling* and the *circumstances of* or *reasons for* their feeling. You neither interpret nor analyze. You simply show that you've heard and understood.

For example, Martin comes to you with tear-filled eyes. "Those kids won't let me play softball with them." You respond with, "You feel sad because they're leaving you out of the game." You reflected back Martin's feeling:

"You feel sad . . .

You reflected back the circumstances of or reasons for Martin's feeling:

. . . because they left you out of the game."

You became a mirror, reflecting his message by paraphrasing, *not merely by repeating,* what he implied and said. If you'd simply parroted his words, he'd have had no indication that you understood or cared. Martin didn't say he felt sad. You inferred his feeling from his words and from his expression, posture, tone of voice, rate of speech. You didn't really add anything to what Martin said. You simply reflected back in words all that his message communicated to you. In this way, your reflective listening response was interchangeable with what the student said.

When students are upset, they tend to lose perspective. Their problems seem overwhelming, their feelings unbearable. Your use of reflective listening can help them see the situation clearly and rationally. Further, you'll help them articulate their feelings; you'll give their emotions a name.

Sometimes students will use a "feeling word." They'll say, "I'm angry" or "I'm hurt." When they do, you may repeat their word or use another; the important thing is to recognize the feeling behind the content, to translate nonverbal clues into language. Translate, not interpret. As we strive to create a trusting relationship with students, we need first to show them we understand what they're feeling. Giving them words for what may be an inexpressible emotion will also help them put the situation in perspective.

Reflective listening can be useful with students of all ages. Even the youngest will benefit from hearing their teacher accept and reflect back their feelings. But reflective listening, even to the simplest message, takes practice.

Feelings first. Start by concentrating on picking out and reflecting the student's feeling.

Yolanda says, "I'll never learn math. It's too hard."

Delay your response for about 10 seconds while you think about what you heard. Ask yourself what Yolanda is feeling. Then say, "You feel discouraged" or "You feel depressed." Use the word you decide is best for this particular student, the word she'll accept. Sanford may not like being told he feels "afraid," but he may accept "nervous" or "anxious." Speaking in a tentative tone of voice when you reflect will lead students to help clarify their own feelings, and will allow you to avoid sounding like a "know-it-all."

Some messages will contain more than one feeling:

Student: "Every time I raise my hand, you call on someone else!"
Teacher: "You feel both *hurt* and *angry.*"

Similarly, students may have mixed emotions, both pleasant and unpleasant feelings:

Student: "I like this school and the kids here, but I miss my old school too."
Teacher: "You feel both *glad* and *sad.*"

Listen for the whole message.

Choosing the accurate word. "Upset" isn't very specific so don't overuse it. Attempt to use the most accurate word, remembering to be sensitive about the way certain students will respond to certain words. Add your own words to the following two lists:

Words for Unpleasant Feelings

afraid, scared, worried, anxious, nervous, tense

---

angry, mad, turned off, furious, fed up

---

annoyed, bugged, bothered, irritated

---

bad, terrible, awful

---

bored, tired, weary, restless

---

confused, puzzled

---

defeated, beaten

disappointed, let down, dissatisfied

discouraged, inadequate, worthless, hopeless

disgusted, sick, revolted

doubtful, uncertain, undecided, not sure

embarrassed, humiliated

frustrated, stuck, stumped, blocked

guilty, dishonest, rotten, ashamed

hurt, picked on, mistreated

incapable, unable, insufficient

indifferent, uncaring

insecure, not sure of yourself

irritated, grumpy, in a bad mood, gloomy

jealous, envious

put down, humiliated, mocked

rejected, left out, lonely

sad, unhappy, depressed, down, miserable

shocked, surprised

uncomfortable, uptight

---

unfairly treated, cheated

---

unimportant, small, insignificant

---

unloved, unwanted, unappreciated

---

others:

Words for Pleasant Feelings

accepted, respected, valued, important

---

appreciated

---

brave, courageous

---

capable, adequate, confident, sure of yourself

---

comfortable, secure, contented

---

compassionate, caring

---

determined, convinced, certain, sure

---

encouraged

---

excited, thrilled, delighted, elated

---

glad, happy

---

good, great, terrific, wonderful

---

grateful

_____

interested, fascinated, inspired

_____

loved

_____

pleased

_____

proud

_____

relaxed

_____

relieved

_____

satisfied, pleased with yourself

_____

surprised, astonished

_____

sympathetic

_____

trusted

_____

others:

_____

_____

Practice

Reflect the feelings in the following statements. Remember that reflective listening is not a science. The only way you'll know you've been an accurate reflector is by the reaction of the student. If you've hit on the feeling, or at least approximated it, the student will let you know. When you're practicing, use the "You feel _____" or "You're feeling _____" format (Carkhuff, Berenson, and Pierce, 1977):

1. "I'm *never* going to play with her again! She's mean!"

   You feel _____.

2. "I just can't do this problem."

   You're feeling _____.

79

3. "I don't want to eat lunch. I don't want to do anything. Nothing's going right."

You feel _____.

4. "You pick on me!"

You're feeling _____.

Reflect both feelings in the following messages. Use the "You feel both _____ and _____" format (Egan, 1975):

5. "I've tried hard to get along with Ms. Benson, but she doesn't seem to like me and she might give me a bad grade in social studies."

You feel both _____ and _____.

6. "That play we're going to put on sounds really great! But will there be parts for everyone?"

You feel both _____ and _____.

Possible answers: 1. angry or hurt 2. discouraged or frustrated 3. depressed or neglected or bored 4. mistreated or put down 5. both sad and worried, or frustrated and afraid 6. both excited and worried, or happy and concerned.

Along with the feeling, we need to reflect the circumstances or reasons. What led to their feelings?

Yolanda said, "I'll never learn math. It's just too hard!" After you decided she felt *discouraged,* you would ask yourself, What led to her discouragement? When you decided on the answer, you'd say, "You feel *discouraged* because *you find math so tough.*" Notice that you've captured Yolanda's message and made a statement interchangeable with hers.

Work with these again. Remember to keep your responses short and to the point.

1. "I'm *never* going to play with her again! She's mean!"

You feel angry because _____.

2. "I just can't do this problem."

You feel discouraged because _____.

3. "I don't want to eat lunch. I don't want to do anything. Nothing's going right."

You feel depressed because _____.

4. "You pick on me!"

You feel mistreated because _____.

5. "Every time I raise my hand, you call on someone else!"

You feel both hurt and angry because _____.

6. "I like this school and the kids here, but I miss my old school too."

You feel both glad and sad because _____.

7. "I've tried hard to get along with Ms. Benson, but she doesn't seem to like me and she might give me a bad grade in social studies."

You feel both sad and worried because _____ .

8. "That play we're going to put on sounds really great! But will there be parts for everyone?"

You feel both excited and worried because _____ .

Possible answers: 1. she treats you so unfairly 2. the problem seems so hard 3. life seems so difficult 4. you think I treat you unfairly 5. I don't call on you 6. you like it here but also wish you were there 7. you think Ms. Benson doesn't care for you and might give you a low grade 8. you like the idea of a play and want to be in it, but you think you might not get a part.

How Can I Vary the Format?

Using the "You feel _____ because _____" format will help you master reflective listening, but you'll want to vary the approach. You might simply drop "You feel" and substitute "You're": "You're angry because _____ ." Change the preposition: replace "because" with "at," "by," "with," "about," "of." Say, "You're angry about the way she treats you."

As you become more comfortable with this way of responding to students, feel free to vary your "leads." Begin with "It seems" ("It seems you're bored with school"), "You seem" ("You seem disappointed about not being able to go"), or "I'm sensing" ("I'm sensing that you're confused").

You'll probably think of your own ways of beginning reflective listening responses. Here are some other possibilities (Gazda et al., 1977):

> Could it be that . . . ?
> I wonder if . . .
> It's possible that . . .
> Correct me if I'm wrong but . . .
> I get the impression (feeling) that . . .
> Let me see if I understand; you . . .
> As I hear it, you . . .
> _____ . Is that the way it is?
> _____ . Is that what you mean?
> _____ . Is that the way you feel (see it)?

For mixed feelings you could say: "On the one hand you feel _____ because _____ . On the other hand you feel _____ because _____ ."

Any leads you feel comfortable with will work. Do avoid, however, beginning with "You feel that _____ ," since this reflects an opinion, not a feeling. Save this opening for when you want to reflect a student's opinion: "You feel that we should have longer Christmas vacations."

Be as accurate as possible. Be sure you don't underestimate the intensity of a student's feelings. When Ellen stomps in saying, "I'm never going to play with her again. I hate her!" don't respond with, "Sounds like you're annoyed with her." Ellen is more than annoyed; she's furious. Understating feelings may insult students or convince them we don't really care to understand. It's better to overstate than to understate. For example, Jeremiah says, "Aw, gee, it's raining and we can't go out for recess." If you reply, "You seem sad because we have to stay inside," he might correct you with, "No, I'm not sad, but I was looking forward to it" or "I'm a little disappointed, that's all." You want to be an accurate reflector, but if you should overstate the case, students will still know you're trying.

Use adverbs to reflect intensity if they seem right. Being *awfully* boring is much duller than just plain boring. The judicious use of adverbs such as "really," "very," and "terribly" will help you deal with the strongest feelings.

Respond to incomplete messages by giving the student a chance to fill in the blanks. If Carla says, "Iris is a rotten brat!" you understand her feeling but not the reason for it. Simply say, "You sound really angry with Iris." Give Carla the opportunity to tell you why. If necessary, ask, "Do you want to tell me about it?" Avoid saying, "Iris makes you feel angry." When you imply that Iris causes Carla's anger, you take away Carla's control over her own feelings.

Open and Closed Responses

The object of reflective listening is to show students we understand and care about their feelings. Beyond that, we want students to continue to share their feelings so we can help them deal with their strong emotions. We want our responses to be *open,* not *closed.*

Open responses accurately reflect the student's feelings and the circumstances of those feelings; they neither add nor subtract anything. Closed responses add interpretations and judgments that tend to cut off communication; they may also understate or totally miss the student's feelings. For example:

Ralph: I sure wish we didn't have to come to school Monday! The kids in Catholic school get the day off!

Mr. Fieldman: I'd like the day off too, but that's just the way it is.

Ms. Nguyen: You like to stay home from school all the time because you don't think you'll ever do well here.

Ms. Semmelman: You feel mistreated because you don't go to Catholic school.

You: You think it's unfair for them to get the day off when you have to be in school.

Mr. Fieldman told Ralph his feelings don't count. Ms. Nguyen added an uncalled-for interpretation that Ralph will likely see as an accusation. Ms. Semmelman missed the point of Ralph's statement. You recognized and accepted Ralph's feelings, leaving the way *open* for him to explain himself further.

Consider another example. Identify the open response:

Phoebe: (tearfully) Sam's got all the blocks and he won't give me any!

1. "Well, just play with something else."
2. "That Sam is really selfish. I'll tell him to share."
3. "You're upset but you shouldn't be. Yesterday you did the same thing to him."
4. "You're very sad and angry because Sam won't share the blocks."
5. "Seems like you're annoyed with Sam."

The first response is closed because it tries to give advice; the teacher also denies Phoebe's feelings by failing to reflect them. The second is closed because it focuses on Sam and doesn't respond directly to Phoebe's feelings; it also takes away her responsibility for solving the problem. The third is closed because the teacher makes a judgment on Phoebe's feelings. The fourth accurately reflects feelings and circumstances: it is open. The fifth is closed because it understates the case.

Reflective Listening Sounds Good But . . .

"What if I don't understand a student's feelings?" Be tentative. Use leads that tell them you're not sure: "I wonder," "Could it be," or "Is it possible." You might just look interested but remain silent, allowing the student to unravel the thought. Or simply admit your confusion and ask for help. "Sorry, Gina, I don't understand what you're saying and I really want to. Will you tell me how you feel about this?"

"I don't like to have to stop and think before I respond." Maybe you don't have to; you could be doing everything right. With most people, though, responding impulsively leads to misinterpretation. Speaking without considering first may short-circuit communication and reinforce students' mistaken goals.

"I feel silly saying things like that." All new behavior is uncomfortable. The right swing in golf may feel unnatural at first. Habit breeds familiarity. The improvement in your relationships with students will ease any awkwardness.

"I'm a teacher, not a counselor. I don't have time to help students with personal problems. I'm here to teach." No counselor can be everywhere. You are in the best position to influence students. And you know those "personal problems" — the little clashes, the difficulties with attitude and motivation — often make your job impossible. As you reevaluate your role as teacher, you'll want to consider the importance of an improved classroom atmosphere and more trusting relationships. An encouraging, democratic classroom doesn't just happen. We must promote it.

How Will Students React?

You may startle them at first! They may acknowledge your response with "Yeah, that's right" and then shy away from further conversation. But don't worry: both you and your students will become accustomed to reflective listening. You may even decide to discuss with them your attempts to become a better listener.

OH GOLLY GOSH! HONEST TO BETSY! I REALLY AND TRULY UNDERSTAND! CROSS MY HEART AND HOPE TO DIE! GOSH DARN! REALLY?

Never force them to share their feelings. They might be embarrassed or feel you're invading their privacy. Be patient. They will let you know when they're ready.

Some students may be only too ready. Your response may precipitate a dramatic exchange. For example, Steven may charge, "You're the meanest teacher in the world!" You respond with, "You're really mad at me." He comes back with, "Yeah, you always make me do these dumb exercises and I *can't* do 'em!" Now what do you do? *Keep reflecting.* "You feel it's unfair for me to make you do things you believe you can't do." "Yeah, and I try so hard too." "Seems like you're really discouraged." At this point your task is simply to reflect until Steven's tone of voice and behavior indicate he wants to stop. (Later you may want to help him understand his goal; perhaps he seeks revenge because he believes he must be perfect.)

But don't expect students always to work through their problems with you. Just as often, your patient efforts to help them see and understand their feelings will enable them to handle their difficulties on their own.

Don't be concerned if students fall silent instead of responding to you. They may be resisting your efforts, *but* they may also be thinking about what you said. Resist the temptation to fill the silence. We teachers are too prone to talk! Wait — see what happens. If the student remains silent, make a guess about what the silence means and check it out. "You seem disturbed about what I said."

Don't worry about doing reflective listening "just right." If you sincerely want to understand, but get the student's feeling wrong, the student will let you know. Then try again. If you don't have time to talk at the moment, reflect the student's feelings, explain the situation, and arrange to meet another time. For example: "Sounds like you're confused about that, Julie. I have to teach right now. How about if we talk at 2:00?"

Don't give up if reflective listening doesn't produce immediate results. Your students are used to the ways teachers usually behave. Teachers have typically confirmed the goals of students' behavior; students may be reluctant to change the way they behave just because you've changed the way you respond. All of you need time to adjust. It will be time well spent.

Cautions About Reflective Listening

Don't be a mind reader. Be tentative. Your tone of voice and use of various leads should tell them your statements aren't conclusions but hunches.

Don't ask too many questions. You don't want to conduct a quiz. Be judicious with "How did you feel then?" "What happened then?" and "Want to tell me about it?" Sometimes a student will answer "Fine" or "Okay" to a "How do you feel" question. This is the time to respond with another question: "What do you mean by fine?" or "What's okay about it?"

As you develop your relationships with students, you'll find it most helpful to concentrate on reflective listening and play down the use of questions. When you understand a student's feelings, make a statement. Instead of asking, "How do you feel about school?" observe the clues and say, "You seem to be unhappy at school."

Be careful when you interpret nonverbal behavior. One student may show resistance by folding his arms across his chest; another may relax this way. Again, be tentative and sensitive. Say "You seem nervous" rather than "Your twitching tells me you're nervous."

Don't overdo reflective listening. Every question or statement doesn't deserve reflecting. "Where's the glue?" is better answered by "In the cupboard" than by "Sounds like you're anxious to paste." "It looks like rain" usually doesn't need a response like "You feel concerned because of the clouds." Use your sensitivity and common sense. Some questions suggest feelings that need to be reflected and some don't. Learn to recognize the difference.

Be aware of times when your reflective listening is reinforcing a student's mistaken goal. For example, Jerry may complain about his lab partners day after day because your readiness to reflect his feelings and discuss them gives him a good way to get your attention and sympathy. Unless you redirect his behavior, he may continue to use problems instead of solving them. The next time he comes to complain, say, "We've discussed this problem several times before. I guess I can't help you with it but I'm sure you'll be able to handle it." Or "Looks like this is something you'll have to work out for yourself. I'm sure you can take care of it." If he persists, remain silent, busy yourself with something else, or change the subject.

Jerry won't like this, but eventually he'll learn that you're willing to help only if he really wants to solve his problem. Encourage him by paying attention to him at unexpected times; help him find significance in ways that don't require your attention.

Students must learn to solve problems independently, especially problems in getting along with classmates. If they know you'll react to their troubles with each other by asking them to work things out on their own, they'll learn independence. After the teacher reflected Phoebe's feelings about Sam's taking the blocks, she or he might have added, "This is something you and Sam need to talk over. I'm sure you two can solve your problem."

If you feel students are expressing their feelings to gain power over you or for revenge, you may decide to listen or to withdraw from provocation. Once again, use sensitivity and common sense.

Uses of Reflective Listening

Individual conferences are invaluable ways to get to know students. Whether you discuss school, relationships, or anything else, your primary role is to listen, support, and encourage. Your new ways of responding to students, introduced casually as you teach, will help make those conferences enjoyable and productive.

Use your listening skills with parents, administrators, and other teachers. Set Juanita Robb a good example!

Use reflective listening at appropriate moments during the school day. Help students talk out problems: "You seem confused about the assignment." Clarify comments during discussions: "Brady, you seem to disagree with Wanda." "Audrey, you feel the South didn't have the right to secede. How do others feel?" Notice that when no strong emotions are involved, you can reflect beliefs and opinions.

Invite students to talk when you see they have strong feelings about something. Respond to frowns, tears, exclamations: "You look very sad, Jim. Want to talk about it?"

Don't ignore smiles. Be quick to notice, reflect, and encourage happy feelings: "Sounds like you're proud of your work." "You're very excited because you won the game." "You all look very cheerful this morning."

Your students will soon notice and respond to your empathetic concern. Now you're ready for new ways to express your *own* feelings to *students*.

Works Cited

Carkhuff, Robert R.; Berenson, David H.; and Pierce, Richard M. *The Skills of Teaching: Interpersonal Skills.* Amherst, MA: Human Resource Development Press, 1977.

Egan, Gerald. *Exercises in the Helping Skills: A Training Manual to Accompany The Skilled Helper.* Monterey, CA: Brooks/Cole, 1975.

Gazda, George M. et al. *Human Relations Development: A Manual for Educators.* 2nd ed. Boston: Allyn & Bacon, 1977.

Gordon, Thomas. *Teacher Effectiveness Training.* NY: Peter H. Wyden, 1974.

Recommended Readings

Carkhuff, Robert R.; Berenson, David H.; and Pierce, Richard M. *The Skills of Teaching: Interpersonal Skills.* Amherst, MA: Human Resource Development Press, 1977.

Gazda, George M. et al. *Human Relations Development: A Manual for Educators.* 2nd ed. Boston: Allyn & Bacon, 1977.

Gordon, Thomas. *Teacher Effectiveness Training.* NY: Peter H. Wyden, 1974.

Hillman, Bill W. *Teaching With Confidence: Getting Off the Classroom Wall.* Springfield, IL: Charles E. Thomas, 1980.

Wittmer, M., and Myrick, R. *Facilitative Teaching.* Pacific Palisades, CA: Goodyear Publishing Co., 1974.

Study Questions

1. What are some of the traditional roles teachers play when they listen to students? How can these roles discourage students?

2. How can "body language" and silence be just as important as words when we're listening and responding to students?

3. What is the purpose of reflective listening? In what sense is a reflective listening response interchangeable with what the student said? How is reflective listening different from parroting?

4. What is the value of reflective listening? How can reflective listening help us build trusting relationships with students? Why is it important to reflect both the feeling and content of a student's message?

5. Name some "feeling words" which help you accurately reflect your students' feelings.

6. What is the basic format of a reflective listening response? How can the format be varied?

7. What is the difference between an open response and a closed response? Give some examples of both, other than those found in the chapter.

8. What cautions need to be kept in mind about reflective listening?

9. In what school situations can reflective listening be especially useful?

Problem Situation

Your social studies class has just finished a lively discussion about human relations between the races. Now you've returned an essay test. George, a black student, approaches your desk and says, "How can you teach social studies and be so prejudiced? You wouldn't call on me during the discussion, and this exam is graded unfairly."

1. How would you feel?
2. Based on your feelings, what might be the goal of George's behavior?
3. How might you best respond?

Activity for the Week

Practice reflective listening in your class discussions this week. Schedule a conference or two and use reflective listening. Record your experiences and student's reactions.

Recommended Resource Book Material

Chapter 4

Chart 4

Effective Listening

Closed Response: Denies students a right to their feelings by demonstrating the teacher's unwillingness to accept and understand.

Open Response: Acknowledges students' right to their feelings by demonstrating that the teacher accepts what they feel as well as what they say. Indicates that the teacher understands. Is *interchangeable* with students' comments.

Student's Remark	Closed Response	Open Response
(crying) My parents are getting a divorce.	Ah, gee, that's too bad, honey.	You're feeling very sad.
Mrs. Lorenzo, Tom copied from my paper!	Well, I'll take care of him!	Sounds like you're really angry about Tom's cheating.
Going to junior high sounds like a lot of fun. I mean, there's football and stuff like that . . . . I wonder what teachers I'll get. I hear some of them can be pretty tough.	Yes, some of the teachers are tough. But if you do what you're told, you'll be all right.	You feel both excited and worried because there are a lot of neat things in junior high, but you think you might get stuck with some strict teachers.
I'm going to get to go to camp this summer!	That's nice — please sit down so we can get to work.	That sounds exciting!
You're the meanest teacher in the world!	Don't you dare talk to me like that!	You're very angry with me.
I am one of the finalists in the cheerleading tryouts. But the competition is pretty tough.	Don't worry about it. You'll probably make it.	I sense you're worried that you might not make it.

Recording Worksheet

Reflective Listening

After each scene, write an open reflective listening response to the student. Use the "You feel _____ because _____" format. Be prepared to discuss your responses with the group.

Scene 1

You feel _____ because _____ .

Scene 2

You feel _____ because _____ .

Scene 3

You feel _____ because _____ .

Scene 4

You feel _____ because _____ .

Scene 5

You feel _____ because _____ .

NOTES

Chapter 4

Points to Remember

1. Few people are naturally good listeners. Most of us play traditional roles when students come to us upset. We may nag, criticize, threaten, lecture, probe, ridicule, or reassure.

2. "The language of acceptance" requires us to look and feel relaxed, to hear students out and suspend judgment, to use reflective listening.

3. Reflective listening calls for a response that reflects back to students their feelings and the circumstances of or reasons for their feelings.

4. Attempt to use the most accurate word for feelings, remembering to be sensitive about the way certain students will respond to certain words.

5. Be sure you don't underestimate the intensity of a student's feelings. It's better to overstate than to understate.

6. Open responses accurately reflect the student's feelings and the circumstances of those feelings; they open the door to further communication.

7. Closed responses add interpretations and judgments that tend to cut off communication.

8. Be aware of times when your reflective listening may be reinforcing a student's mistaken goal.

Personal Record Chapter 4

1. My experience with the weekly assignment

2. My reactions to the reading

3. Topics to discuss with the group

4. Skills I intend to improve

5. My beliefs which impede progress

6. My successes in applying program ideas

7. My difficulties in applying program ideas

8. My progress this week: A specific example

9. This week I learned

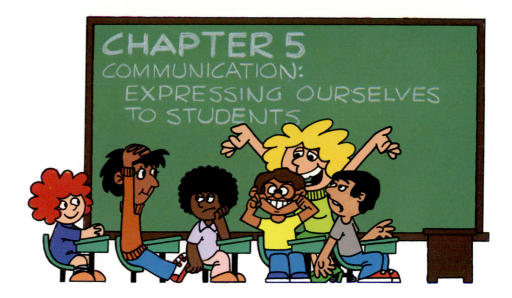

Why is it important to determine who "owns" classroom problems?
What is an I-message?
What is a you-message?
How can I keep from sending angry I-messages?
What are the benefits of expressing my feelings in I-messages?

Reflective listening is a specific way of responding to students. You don't blame, accuse, or diagnose; you reflect their feelings and circumstances. Reflective listening opens the way for constructive discussion and is a first step in helping others solve their problems.

But what about your problems? What if you're the one feeling hurt, annoyed, discouraged, angry, or triumphant? Is there a way of making your feelings known to students without accusing them or turning them off? Teachers are equal members of a democratic classroom: you have the right to express yourself. But you want to do so thoughtfully and productively. You don't want to compound the problem.

The problem. Whose problem is it? We teachers like to talk and we often feel compelled to involve ourselves in everything that happens in our classroom. But some dilemmas belong to our students. We don't help them when we take away their responsibility to solve their own problems.

Problems: Yours, Mine, and Ours

We need first to understand the goal of a student's misbehavior. Then we need to decide who "owns" the problem (Gordon, 1974).

Maureen is upset because Laura doesn't like her anymore. You empathize, you may even try to help, but the problem belongs to Maureen. Her conflict with Laura doesn't directly interfere with your teaching or with other students' learning. Maureen's upset feelings may interfere with *her* performance in school, and for that reason you may decide to help, but she must learn to take responsibility for her own difficulties with relationships.

Now consider this situation: During art class, Roy neglects to cover his desk with newspaper before he uses the paste. You are responsible for the furniture in your room, and so the problem is yours. Roy feels fine, but he's interfering with your responsibilities, which include keeping the furniture clean.

Often, you share in a problem that affects the whole class. You're all participating in a lively discussion about voter registration. Tanya and Pat carry on a private conversation, disturbing the class. How to deal with the disturbance is everyone's problem, but you may have to take the initiative to solve it.

Other problems belong to your students as a group, and they need to experience the consequences of their behavior. If the whole class won't settle down before recess, they'll have to live with a shortened recess. So will you, but by letting students know where their own responsibilities lie, you'll be trading a short-term loss for a long-term gain.

However, if your students are so noisy they disturb another teacher's classroom, then you own the problem. You have an obligation to other teachers and students; when your class violates their rights, you are responsible.

Why is problem ownership so important? Because a democratic classroom requires that all members take responsibility for their own behavior. Problems that interfere with learning must be solved, and students can participate in solving them just as they take part in formulating their own learning goals. You'll very likely be interested in all problems involving your students. But ask yourself, "Who does this problem really belong to? Does it directly interfere with my teaching, my rights, or my safety? Does the problem jeopardize the rights or safety of this student or other students?"

Consider: Even if you're successful in reconciling Maureen with Laura, have they learned to solve their own problems? You may find that permitting students to handle their difficulties themselves frees you to do your own job. Sometimes our interference becomes a problem!

Practice in Problem Ownership

In the following examples, decide who owns the problem and why:

1. Mariana is worried about a test.
2. You're afraid Adam's friends are a bad influence on him.
3. Gerald keeps interrupting when you're trying to give instructions.
4. Homer complains that older students keep pushing him on the playground.

Suggested Responses:

1. You'll want to reflect Mariana's feelings if she confides in you, but the problem is *hers*. Your job is unaffected.
2. *Adam* must choose his own friends. You may decide to advise him but remember: Adam's positive attitude may influence his friends!
3. *You* own this problem. Gerald is preventing you from teaching.
4. *You* are responsible for the safety of your students. However, if you determine that Homer is in no real danger, you may lead him to assume responsibility for his own social difficulties.

When the problem is ours, we often want to let students know how we feel. And we want them to *listen*.

You-Messages and I-Messages

Your class is too noisy. You say, "This class is too noisy! Quiet down!" They do, but only momentarily. Then you say, "Cut it out!" Then, "Okay, let's knock it off." Finally, you get really angry: "That's *it*. I've had it. There will be no more talking!" Now they know you mean business, and they quiet down. But later on, do you find yourself telling them "this is it" once again?

If students respond only to our ultimatums, our *big* messages, then they're not listening to all the *little* ones. We're wasting our breath and expending a lot of useless energy.

If they're not listening, it may be because we're sending "you-messages" instead of "I-messages" (Gordon, 1974). You-messages accuse, blame, and criticize. They contain or imply the word "you," said in a disrespectful or accusing tone. I-messages report the speaker's concerns and feelings, quietly and respectfully.

Teachers aren't always the ones sending you-messages. Suppose your principal, Virgil Turner, follows you into the teachers' lounge, thundering, "David! You still haven't turned in your grades. I'm always being held up by your delaying tactics. Now, I want those grades turned in by noon!"

You'll probably get those grades in by noon. But how will you feel toward Virgil Turner? Angry? Revengeful? Will you be likely to cooperate with him in the future? Or are you likely to be antagonistic?

But what if Turner had followed you into the teachers' lounge and said, "David, when your reports are turned in at the end of the last day, I feel very rushed because I have to get all the grades tabulated and turned in to the Central Office by 4:00."

How would you feel? Perhaps you'd admit to yourself that you *are* often late. Maybe you'd think, "Virgil is just doing his job. I can understand his feelings on this. Maybe in the future I can start getting things in on time."

When we send you-messages to students, they also feel embarrassed, angry, hurt, put down, or worthless. They certainly don't feel like cooperating; some may even internalize these messages as adult judgments on their worth. When we say, "You'd better do that assignment," "You're lazy — now, get to work," "You'll fail if you don't hand this in," we mean to motivate. But instead, we may be inviting hostile, defensive behavior.

You-messages often don't work because:

1. When we expect the worst, we're likely to get it. Students who always hear, "You're wrong," "You're lazy," "You never do anything right," may begin to believe it. They may give us the behavior we seem to expect.
2. When we put the blame for our feelings on students, we risk their refusal to accept that blame.
3. Students expect to be criticized, reminded, and blamed. That's the way teachers usually speak to them. So students' goals of misbehavior can be reinforced by the you-messages they're accustomed to.

When we express our feelings and concerns in I-messages, we appeal to students' good nature and desire to cooperate. We solicit their help. We say, "I'm worried," "I'm discouraged," "I'm concerned," "I'm afraid" — and we tell why. We take responsibility for our own feelings and leave the students' behavior up to them. "When you interrupt, I get worried because we're running out of time and we need to finish."

I-messages don't offer solutions; they trust students to respond appropriately. "When you come in late from the gym, I feel very concerned because it distracts the class." You show students that you expect them to manage their own behavior. You're confident they'll do the appropriate thing or make the needed change.

I-messages are unexpected. They don't reinforce the goals of misbehavior. Students are not prepared to hear teachers divulging their own feelings without blaming anyone.

You may wonder, Why can't I just ask my students for cooperation? You can. But when questions don't work, use I-messages — *before* letting yourself get angry.

Angry I-messages become you-messages. Your language, both verbal and nonverbal, is all-important. Your posture, facial expression, and tone of voice must reflect the nonjudgmental spirit of your I-message. I-messages can help you diffuse your own anger.

Anger is a normal emotion. Sometimes expressing anger can clear the air or dissolve tension. But usually, anger is used to control, win, get even, or to hide other feelings like fear and embarrassment. Attacking students rarely contributes to an encouraging atmosphere. Direct expression of anger may accomplish your immediate goal — Dennis *does* sit down — but it can hinder your future relationship with students. When we're spoken to in anger, we feel threatened. We draw back or mount a counterattack.

How can I keep anger out of my I-messages? Emotions are complex. Anger is usually mixed with other feelings like worry, concern, and anxiety. Learn to express those other feelings, the ones that tell students you care about them. Hostile feelings are usually expressed by blaming the other person. Students will protect themselves against blame, but they'll respect an expression of honest concern.

Suppose Nancy wanders off during a field trip. You're angry. But stop and analyze your feelings. Weren't you frightened also? Tell Nancy, "When you wander away from us, I feel scared because you might get lost and I care about you." Nancy will be surprised! And then she may think, "Hey, I didn't get yelled at. Maybe he really does care."

Remember: I-messages laced with anger (or with similar hostile feelings like annoyance, hurt, disgust) have the same effect as you-messages. Separate your hostile feelings from your feelings of concern and caring. Show those positive feelings in your I-messages. If you're too angry to look for the good feelings, then delay your reaction until you've had time to calm down.

We create emotions to generate energy for accomplishing our goals. If we don't believe we have to control, win, or get even, we won't create hostile feelings.

How Do I Construct I-Messages?

I-messages have a definite structure. They focus on the teacher's feelings and the student's behavior, not on either as a *person*. You are upset with a particular act, not with the total student. You are not irreconcilably angry, just temporarily upset. So I-messages begin with "when"; they separate the deed from the doer. "When I find the library books out of place . . . ." "When I see the paints spilled on the floor . . . ." "When people shout out during class discussions . . . ." "When you run in the hall . . . ." You describe an action; you don't attack a person.

The action you describe is usually not the real reason for your concern. It is the *consequences* the behavior produces, the way it interferes with your job, violates your rights or the rights of other students, that you find upsetting. You see Lucy running in the hall. Are you upset because of the actual running, or because Lucy might fall down, run into something, get hurt, or hurt someone else? You're probably disturbed by the consequences of her running. So I-messages use "because" to connect your feelings with the upsetting consequences of a student's behavior. "When you run in the hall, I worry because you might get hurt or hurt someone else."

You *worry* because you're responsible for your students' safety. The possible consequences of Lucy's running jeopardize that safety.

I-messages, then, have three parts (Gordon, 1974):

1. First describe the *behavior* — don't blame, just describe. "When I find library books out of place . . .

99

2. Then state your *feelings* about the possible consequences of the behavior.
   . . . I feel frustrated . . .
3. Then state what those *consequences* are or might be.
   . . . because it takes so long to find the books when we need them."

A simple format: *When* (describe the behavior), I *feel* (state your feelings), *because* (describe the consequences).

How Can I Vary The Format?

Like reflective listening responses, I-messages can take varied forms. The three parts don't have to be delivered in order, and you may sometimes eliminate the statement of feeling. For example, "I can't hear the intercom when there's so much noise" or "I can't use my worktable when there's paper all over it."

Sometimes, especially when you're speaking to an individual student, your statement will contain the word "you." It's still an I-message if the "you" is merely descriptive and doesn't convey criticism or blame. "Joan, when you speak without raising your hand, I get distracted because I'm trying to listen to someone else."

Choice of words is of course crucial. At times, use adverbs to convey strong feelings: "I get *really* worried," "I'm *very* concerned," "I become *quite* confused." Avoid words that label or judge; such words turn I-messages into you-messages.

You-message	*I-message*
When you make trouble	When you throw erasers . . . .
When you're so noisy	When there's so much noise . . . .

The emotion-laden "make trouble" is vague and hostile; the specific description of throwing erasers is accurate and not threatening. Similarly, calling students "noisy" labels them; speaking of "so much noise" simply reports what's happening.

Remember: I-messages focus on you, not on students. They do not blame anyone. They stress existing and possible consequences of behavior, rather than the behavior itself. When delivered by teachers whose body language reinforces their nonjudgmental, constructive attitude toward students' behavior, I-messages become valuable tools of classroom communication.

Practice

Below are two teacher-owned problems. Write an I-message for each, following the three steps. First, describe the behavior. Then ask yourself, "What am I feeling?" Identify the caring, positive feelings, as distinguished from the anger or annoyance. Review the vocabulary in Chapter 4, but use your own words first. Then go on to the consequences of the behavior. Just describe; don't blame or label. Include adverbs occasionally to convey depth of feeling. Use the format "When _____, I feel _____ because _____."

1. A student promises to help you set up a science experiment before school, and she doesn't show up.

2. A student is using paste with construction paper, and he neglects to cover the desk with newspapers.

Possible I-messages: 1. When you promise to help me and don't show up, I feel disappointed because I was really counting on your help. (Or, I feel very rushed because I have to hurry up and do it myself.) 2. When you paste on the desk without covering it with newspaper, I get very concerned (worried) because we may not be able to get the paste off and the top may be ruined.

How Will Students React?

I-messages will probably be as new to students as reflective listening responses are. Give them and yourself time. Some students will quickly respond to your nonjudgmental approach; they'll do what you ask, without bitterness. Others may fire I-messages right back at you. If this happens, stop and listen. Reflect. Promote cooperation through your words, your tone of voice, your whole attitude.

What if I feel good most of the time? I-messages are particularly important when we must deal with misbehavior. But encouraging teachers are eager to share their happiness, confidence, and pleasure.

Say, "When you participate in a discussion, I feel good because we get so much accomplished." "Thanks for cleaning the chalkboard, Anne Marie. I appreciate it when you help because it makes my job easier."

Let the positive feelings flow. Both you and your students need them.

Communicating Respect

Our students need to feel valued, significant, respected. Reflective listening, I-messages, and other ways of communicating discussed in future sessions will help you convey your feelings. The specific way you respond to students depends upon the situation, the people involved, your own temperament.

Sometimes talking doesn't work. If you feel yourself being drawn into a conflict, withdraw quietly. If Calvin is throwing a tantrum, he's not likely to respond to reflective listening or I-messages. You may have to remove him from the classroom until he calms down. Later, if necessary, talk with him.

Above all, establish a climate in which students feel free to express feelings, and you do too.

To summarize the essentials of classroom communication:

- Use purposeful conversation. Talk with your students in order to understand and to be understood.
- Show you care about students' feelings by using reflective listening responses.
- Send blame-free messages, I-messages, when behavior disturbs you. And be sure to let students know when you feel good.
- Adopt a respectful attitude, free of labels, sarcasm, and ridicule.
- Be sensitive to timing. Respond to specific occasions and situations.
- Fill your conversations with positive, constructive topics; be eager for friendly discussions.
- Show faith and confidence in students. Encourage!

Works Cited

Gordon, Thomas. *Teacher Effectiveness Training.* NY: Peter H. Wyden, 1974.

Recommended Readings

Gazda, George, et al. *Human Relations Development.* 2nd ed. Boston: Allyn & Bacon, 1977.

Gordon, Tom. *Teacher Effectiveness Training.* NY: Peter Wyden, 1974.

Wittmer, M., and Myrick, R. *Facilitative Teaching.* Pacific Palisades, CA: Goodyear Publishing Co., 1974.

Study Questions

1. What is meant by "problem ownership"? Why is it important to determine who "owns" classroom problems?

2. How can we determine who owns a problem?

3. Give an example of a teacher-owned problem, a student-owned problem, and a group-owned problem (other than those given in the chapter).

4. What are the differences between a "you-message" and an "I-message"? Why do you-messages often fail to motivate students?

5. "Angry I-messages become you-messages." Explain. How can we keep anger out of I-messages?

6. What are the three parts of an I-message? How are I-messages constructed? How can the format be varied?

7. What is the value of expressing our feelings in I-messages? Why is it important to stress the consequences of behavior, rather than the behavior itself? Why is it important not to offer solutions or answers when we send I-messages?

8. Why is it important to watch tone of voice, body language, and word choice when sending I-messages?

Problem Situation

You are putting an assignment on the board when you hear giggling and laughing behind you. You turn around and see Lois, a popular student, making faces and mimicking you. You feel angry and hurt.

1. What is the goal of Lois' behavior?
2. How would you use reflective listening in this situation? Would it be appropriate?
3. What would be a typical you-message in this situation? How can you keep yourself from using it?
4. Formulate an I-message.

Activity for the Week

Keep a record of the times when you catch yourself starting to send a you-message. Reword them to I-messages and write them down.

Recommended Resource Book Material

Chapter 5

Chart 5

Communication: Listening and Sending

Situations in which the teacher determines problem ownership and then decides whether to listen reflectively or to send an I-message.

Situation	Problem Owner	Reflective Listening	I-Message
Student crying about low report card.	Student	You feel very sad because you didn't get the grades you wanted.	
Teacher returns to room and finds several students throwing paper wads.	Teacher		When I have to leave the room and return to find things like this happening, I feel very disappointed because I thought we had an agreement on how you would conduct yourselves in my absence.
Student tells teacher she feels sorry because she and a friend had a fight and she called the friend a name.	Student	Sounds like you feel terrible because you think you hurt your friend's feelings.	
Student leaning back on chair as if he might fall over.	Teacher		When you lean back in your seat, I get scared because you might fall and hurt yourself.
Student tells you her mother is in the hospital for surgery.	Student	You're very worried about your mother.	

Recording Worksheet

I-Messages

After each scene, write an I-message for the situation. Use the "When _____ I feel _____ because _____ " format. Be prepared to discuss your responses with the group.

Scene 1

When _____ I feel _____

because _____ .

Scene 2

When _____ I feel _____

because _____ .

Scene 3

When _____ I feel _____

because _____ .

Scene 4

When _____ I feel _____

because _____ .

NOTES

Chapter 5

Points to Remember

1. We need to determine who "owns" classroom problems so all members take responsibility for their own behavior.

2. We can determine problem ownership by asking, "Does this problem directly interfere with my teaching, my rights, or my safety? Does the problem jeopardize the rights or safety of this student or other students?"

3. You-messages accuse, blame, and criticize: "You'll fail if you don't hand this in." They reinforce goals of misbehavior. They may invite hostile, defensive behavior.

4. I-messages report the speaker's concerns and feelings, quietly and respectfully: "When you interrupt, I get worried because we're running out of time and we need to finish."

5. I-messages trust students to respond appropriately.

6. I-messages are often unexpected and so usually don't reinforce goals of misbehavior.

7. I-messages laced with hostile feelings have the same effect as you-messages. We need to reflect our feelings of concern and caring in our I-messages.

8. I-messages focus on the teacher's feelings and the student's behavior, not on either as a person. They connect feelings with the consequences of students' behavior.

9. I-messages can also help convey pleasant feelings. They can be valuable ways to encourage.

10. I-messages can be overused and reinforce mistaken goals.

Personal Record Chapter 5

1. My experience with the weekly assignment

2. My reactions to the reading

3. Topics to discuss with the group

4. Skills I intend to improve

5. My beliefs which impede progress

6. My successes in applying program ideas

7. My difficulties in applying program ideas

8. My progress this week: A specific example

9. This week I learned

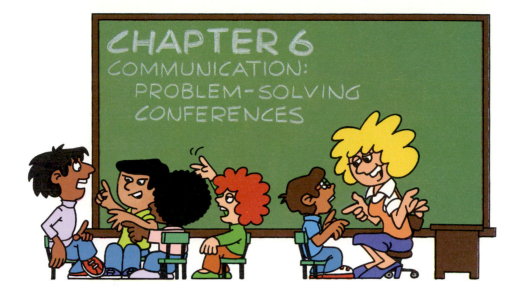

How can I ask effective questions?
How can I help students explore alternative solutions to their own problems?
How can I use conferences to solve classroom problems belonging to me?

You've identified a problem in your classroom, one owned by a student or by you. Using reflective listening and I-messages, you've brought feelings out into the open. Now what do you do?

Problems that interfere with learning must be solved. You'll very likely decide to schedule a conference so you and the student can discuss the situation together, face-to-face. The value of problem-solving conferences is double: you address the specific problem and you teach decision making by encouraging creative thinking. More specifically, you ask *open questions* and together you *explore alternatives.*

How Can I Ask Effective Questions?

Questions are vital to teaching. We use them to stimulate, to clarify, to explore. But in the same way that open reflective listening responses invite further conversation while closed responses tend to cut off communication, open questions improve conferences while closed questions inhibit them. Closed questions often call for a yes or no answer, usually begin with a verb or with *why,* and may stifle further exchanges. They also tend to accuse or blame. Open questions permit many possible responses, often begin with *what, where, when, who, which,* or *how,* and refrain from accusing or blaming.

Consider these *closed* questions:

Are you just going to stare out that window or are you going to get busy?
(No answer required — or wanted.)
Do you really think that's the right way to do it?
(Required answer: no.)
Don't you think that's the right way to do it?
(Required answer: yes.)

111

Have you stopped picking on Rose?
(The old double-bind.)
Why did you do that?
(An accusation.)
Why don't you like Manuel?
(In other words, "You should like Manuel, so why don't you?")
You know that's wrong, don't you?
(A statement masquerading as a question.)

Now see how a simple rephrasing can change closed questions to open:

Closed: Are you still having trouble with your project?
Open: How are things going with your project?
Closed: Aren't you finished with those exercises yet?
Open: How are you doing with the exercises?
Closed: Why can't you get along with Lee?
Open: What can you tell me about your relationship with Lee? or How do you feel about Lee?
Closed: That's what's worrying you, isn't it?
Open: What worries you about this assignment?
Closed: Don't you think you should stop fighting with Morrie?
Open: How do you feel about the fights you've been having with Morrie?
Closed: Why don't you like Thea?
Open: What does Thea do that you don't like?

Be aware that, valuable as open questions are, they may not immediately stimulate conversation. Students may answer some of the ones above with "okay," "nothing," or "fine." (We usually say "fine" automatically when someone asks "How are you?") If conversation lags in this way, attempt to get the real story ("What do you mean by 'fine'?" or "What's okay about it?" or "Tell me more about that!"), even if "fine" or "okay" *is* the real story. You may need to ask further questions (perhaps beginning with "Could it be" or "Is it possible"), and use reflective listening and I-messages. Similarly, while closed questions frequently end discussion, they are completely appropriate when you *want* a yes or no answer ("Do you understand number six?"), or when you need a decision made ("Shall we talk about it next Monday to see how it's going?").

There aren't any hard and fast rules. "Why" questions can be softened and made non-judgmental: "Have you got any ideas about why you're having trouble with him?" Such a question gets students to consider the purpose of their actions; it doesn't *accuse* students. (Phrasing the question "Why do you think you do that?" *may* come across as an accusation.) The *when, where, what, who, which, how* beginnings can launch closed questions if used to belittle or attack: "Where do you think you're going?"

The important thing is to use questions judiciously and sensitively. You don't want conferences to become quiz sessions, and you don't want to alienate students. Remember not to ask questions when you have enough information to make a statement. When James arrives in class beaming after his baseball game, there's no need to ask who won. Instead, say, "You're feeling good about the game!"

Be sure you're asking *necessary* questions in conferences, questions about information you really need to help solve the problem or reach agreement. Use open questions whenever you can, because they don't make judgments and they allow students room to respond. They also encourage students to think about the goals of their behavior. For example, ask "What happened?" "How did the problem start?" "When did it happen?" "What did you do?" "What did they do?" "How did it end up?" Such questions can help you understand the dynamics of a situation.

Exploring Alternatives: Student-Owned Problems

When problems belong to your students, you may decide to let them work things out for themselves. Or you may decide to listen empathetically; sometimes a friendly ear is enough. Reflective listening can help the student feel understood and accepted. But at times you'll want to take a more active role. You'll want to help students consider various plans and choose a solution that makes sense to both of you.

Exploring alternatives isn't the same as giving advice. Most adults are only too eager to advise the young. But giving advice can backfire: students may become dependent upon others to solve their problems; they may resist all advice as a form of control; they may blame us if things don't go well.

Instead of advising students during conferences, consider these six steps:

1. *Understand and clarify the problem.* You need to establish rapport and convince the student you care at *various* times during the conference. Use reflective listening and open questions. Say, "You're discouraged because you and Mr. Reed haven't been getting along. What do you think the problem is?"

2. *Disclose the goal of misbehavior.* Sometimes, especially if the student is in conflict with another person, it helps to look at the purpose of the behavior. Behavior can often be changed after we understand its purpose.

Don't be aggressive; go slowly. First ask *permission* to guess the goal: "Have you considered why you're having trouble getting along with Mr. Reed? Could I give you an idea I have?" If the student agrees, phrase your disclosure in a *tentative* way, as a *question:* "Could it be that you want to keep Mr. Reed busy with you?"

Notice that you've avoided the word *attention,* since you don't want to blame or accuse. Other ways to disclose this goal are: "Is it possible you feel this is the only way Mr. Reed will notice you and you *want* to be noticed? Could it be you want Mr. Reed to do something special just for you?"

Possible ways to disclose *power:* Could it be you want to show her who's boss? Is it possible you want to show her she can't make you work (be quiet, pay attention)? Could it be you want to prove to her that you can do what you want and she can't stop you? Is it possible you're having trouble getting along with Steve because both of you want to be boss?

To disclose *revenge:* Could it be you want to get even with (get back at) him? Is it possible that you want her to feel as hurt as you do?

To disclose *display of inadequacy:* Could it be you believe you just can't write and you want to be left alone? Is it possible that you feel dumb and don't want anyone to know? Could it be you believe math is too hard and you want to be excused?

After making the disclosure, watch very closely for a "recognition reflex" (Dreikurs, 1968), an involuntary sign that your guess is correct. The recognition reflex is often a sheepish, "caught with a hand in the cookie jar" grin. It may be a body twitch or a change in expression or eye contact. Remember that students usually don't realize what their goals are; their goals are below their level of awareness. A recognition reflex indicates that you've successfully brought the goal into the student's conscious awareness.

If the student still denies your guess in words, say, "Your words tell me no but I have a feeling I'm a little bit correct." A recognition reflex tells you you're on target. Students with poker faces or constant smiles often don't give recognition reflexes. With these students, simply proceed on your hunch.

Be sensitive; don't "pounce" on the hesitant student. Be willing to make wrong guesses and then try again. Let the student know you're searching for the goal in order to clarify the upsetting situation. We needn't be psychotherapists to use goal disclosure. Goal disclosure helps students understand themselves, leaving them free to make an informed choice among alternatives.

3. *Explore alternatives through brainstorming.* Now you want students to do some problem solving. You want them to see how what they're doing is interfering with their learning. Depending on the student's goal, use these questions and phrases:

Attention

Why do you suppose it's so important for you to get Mr. Reed's attention? (You can use 'attention' now if the student acknowledged your guess.)
Could it be you believe that getting attention is the only way you can be important (count, belong)?

Is it possible for you to feel important without always having Mr. Reed's attention?

What do you think will happen if you keep disturbing the class to get Mr. Reed's attention?

Power

Who do you think is winning this fight?

Seems like you've proved your point — she can't tell you what to do.

What do you think will happen if you and Steve continue to fight?

Revenge

Could it be that you're trying to get even with him because you think he's out to get you?

Is it possible you feel that all adults want to hurt you, and all you can do is hurt back?

If you keep trying to get even with her, how do you think things will end up?

Display of inadequacy

How did you come to the conclusion that you just can't learn to spell?

Is it possible you believe you can't do math because you want to do it better than anyone else or not at all?

Why would it be so terrible if you couldn't do math better than everyone else?

(Help the student see the humor in the situation by asking, "Why would it be so terrible?" after each rationalization.)

If you continue to convince yourself you can't spell, what do you think will happen?

What do you tell yourself when you have a math assignment? (The answer to this will tell you how the student prepares for defeat.)

To any of these questions, students may respond with, "I don't know." This familiar answer may mean they *do* know but don't want to *tell* you, they are deeply discouraged and see no sense in trying, or they truly *do not know.* Find out what "I don't know" means by lightly saying: "When I hear someone say, 'I don't know,' it sometimes means, 'I know, but I'm not telling.' Could this be what you mean?" (Watch for the recognition reflex. Follow it by saying, "That's okay. You don't have to tell me. I trust your judgment.") Or ask, "Could it be that you say, 'I don't know,' because you feel discouraged and don't think anything will help?" (Follow this by saying, "If we can figure out what to do together, would you be willing to make an effort?") Or ask, "I realize you don't know, but what do you think might happen?" Or, "If you were the teacher, what would you do with a student who behaved this way?" If the student still doesn't know, help by offering an opinion: "Could it be . . ." Remember that students are often telling the truth when they answer, "I don't know." They aren't aware of their purposes.

At this point, have students start looking for new ways to deal with the problem. Ask them if they're satisfied with the way things are now; ask if they'd be willing to consider some other solutions. If they resist, use reflective listening or end the conference — with an invitation to come back some other time. If they seem willing to brainstorm ways of handling the problem, ask:

> How can you get Ms. Robbin's attention in ways she'll enjoy?
> What are some things you could do to get along better with Daryl?
> You're a very powerful person. How could you use all that power to help Mr. Reed?
> How could you go about learning to spell?

Encourage students to offer as many ideas as they can, no matter how silly or strange. Don't evaluate any ideas; just let them come.

If students can't seem to get started, try these techniques to unblock the creative flow:

   a. Take the problem away by asking them to pretend a friend has it. Students then become advisers, offering solutions. You can ask if any of those solutions might work for them. This procedure is especially valuable because it accustoms students to examine alternatives.

   b. Use role reversal. Students play the people they're having trouble with, and you play your students. Then check and evaluate the differences in responses: "What happened here that was different from what usually happens? Do you think this might work for you?" With young children, use puppets.

   c. Offer tentative suggestions. Phrase them as questions so you aren't giving advice: "Have you considered _____?" "What do you think will happen if you _____?" "I've found it helpful to _____ . Do you think this might work for you?"

Use role reversal and give suggestions only as a last resort. Work hard at getting students to come up with their own ideas, to be creative problem solvers.

4. *Evaluate all proposed alternatives.* If brainstorming resulted in more than one suggestion, summarize the proposals and then examine the options together.

5. *Choose a solution.* Now ask which idea the student thinks will work best. Help students consider the logic of their decisions: we are teaching a process, not simply solving a problem. It's important that students understand the *dynamics* of the situation, so they can apply what they learn to other problems.

For example, if Renee complains that students tease her, she needs to understand both their purpose and her goal. They may be asserting their power; she may seek attention, even if she's treated unkindly. If Renee understands the dynamics of her problem at school, she may see how similar her troubles with friends are to her troubles with a brother.

What if Renee chooses a solution you don't think will work? Ask her, "What do you think will happen if you do this?" If necessary, give your opinion ("It seems to me that if you yell at them instead of crying you'll still be letting them upset you. What do you think?"), ask if she'd like to consider other options, but be sure to leave the final decision *to her.* As long as Renee's choice isn't dangerous, let her experiment and learn. Do avoid all "I told you so's."

6. *Make a commitment and set a time for evaluation.* It's easy to say, "I'll try." Explain to Renee that "I'll try" often means "I know it won't work." Get her to make a firm commitment. Explain the way scientists repeat a certain procedure over and over without evaluating their results until the end of the experiment. Ask her if she's willing to give her plan a fair test. If she's not sure, attempt to get a commitment from her to think about it and see you again in a few days. If she agrees, repeat the specific plan of action she has decided on: "Okay, you've decided that every time the other kids tease you, you'll walk away. Right?"

Now help Renee set a realistic time limit. She may want to walk away "from now on," but forever is a long time. Ask her to test her plan for three days, a week, two weeks, depending on the student's age and the nature of the problem. Say, "Shall we discuss it again a week from today at noon?"

If Renee complains the next day that the plan isn't working, simply comment, "I thought you agreed to give it a fair test and not judge the results for a week." During the next conference, evaluate the results. Then decide whether to continue, modify the plan, or look at other alternatives. If Renee didn't do what she said she would, don't ask why. Instead, ask if she's willing to keep the agreement and if so when (Glasser, 1969). If Renee forgets her follow-up appointment, don't remind her. At a later time, ask her how the plan is working, saying you missed her at the scheduled conference. Then the two of you can decide whether another conference is needed.

Cautions and Variations

Go slowly. Limit your responses to reflective listening until you and your students feel comfortable. If you rush into exploring alternatives, students may think you're trying to manipulate them. Return to reflective listening if they become defensive.

Don't let students exploit you by using conferences as a way to get attention. Let them know you're willing to discuss the issue only if they are sincerely interested in solving the problem. You might want to disclose their goal for staying in this holding pattern ("Could it be you have one problem after another in order to keep me busy talking with you?"), and then discuss constructive ways of getting attention.

Don't use problem-solving conferences only for misbehavior and distress. Use the method of exploring alternatives to help students make other kinds of decisions, about school projects, for example.

Better yet, teach students to use the procedure themselves. Explain steps 1, 3, 4, 5, and 6 to them; then you can help them clarify and understand a problem's dynamics. Encourage them to discuss problems with friends before coming to you. Set up class discussion periods when students can get help from the entire group. Use these times also for making group decisions on issues important to everyone.

All these variations will save you time. They'll also allow students to practice and use this valuable procedure.

What if You Own the Problem?

If the problem is yours, there is conflict in your classroom. Keep these four points in mind as you work to resolve that conflict (Dreikurs and Grey, 1970):

• *Maintain mutual respect.* Don't fight or give in. Instead, work for agreement by understanding the other's point of view and discussing your differences openly. Rather than dominating students or becoming a jellyfish, use your listening, responding, and questioning skills. Really *listen* to the student's point of view and be willing to negotiate.

• *Identify the real issue.* On the surface it may look as though the conflict stems from the student's not completing work, not cooperating, creating a disturbance, and so forth. But remember that conflicts arise from the purposes or goals of those involved: these are the real issues. Felice is always late to class and you're having a conference with her on the subject. You have a hunch the real problem is Felice's desire for power. When she arrives late, you get angry. The respectful atmosphere of the conference enables you to ask, ''Could it be you come in late to show me you can do what you want and I can't stop you?''

• *Change the agreement.* Those in conflict have agreed on one thing: they've agreed to fight. Resolve to change *your* behavior, to make concessions. Tell Felice you won't disrupt the class by repeating instructions when she arrives, but you're willing to give her the information after school.

• *Invite participation in decision making.* The democratic classroom requires that everyone have a part in making decisions. To resolve a conflict, you and the student must reach some agreement; you must negotiate calmly and rationally. Unless the situation demands instant action, wait until your emotions have cooled. Then you can have a productive discussion.

The six steps in exploring alternatives can be just as useful for teacher-owned problems.

1. *Understand and clarify the problem.* You own the problem and you need to make the first move to solve it. Jerry plays too roughly on the playground. Open your conference with him by sending an I-message: ''Jerry, I'm concerned about the rough play because I'm afraid someone will get hurt.'' If Jerry replies, ''I'm not playing rough!'' use your listening skills: ''You're angry and feel I'm falsely accusing you?'' Be truly willing to stop and listen. Allow Jerry to feel respected by being sensitive to his feelings. He'll be more willing to negotiate.

2. *Disclose the goal of misbehavior.* Help Jerry see his goal. ''Jerry, I'm wondering if you have any idea why you and I are having trouble about this. May I tell you what I think? Could it be you want to show me who's boss?''

Be sure Jerry is ready to hear this. If he's hostile, wait. Keep trying to reach an agreement. Be quick to admit your part in the conflict: ''I know that sometimes I've tried to pressure you into cooperating.'' Assure him you don't want to fight anymore.

118

3. *Explore alternatives through brainstorming.* You participate in the brainstorming, letting him know you're interested in reaching a decision he'll accept. For example, you might ask, "How can we solve this problem? Maybe you'd like to teach the younger students a game." If Jerry won't cooperate, you may have to insist upon a tentative solution. "If you decide to play rough, I'll have to ask you to take some time out from playing. You can return to the playground when you're ready to play safely." Keep the door open for future discussion. If Jerry *does* want to participate, brainstorm with him, encouraging him to offer all his ideas. Make your own suggestions only if necessary.

4. *Evaluate all proposed alternatives.* Don't rush him; make sure you both understand the other's feelings. Say, "I like that one because _____" or "I'm uncomfortable with that one because _____."

5. *Choose a solution.* If you don't agree, brainstorm some more, end the conference and schedule another, or make a temporary decision yourself if the behavior must stop — again, leaving the door open for future negotiation.

6. *Make a commitment and set a time for evaluation.* Say, "Let's see, Jerry, you've agreed to play basketball instead of wrestle and I've agreed to accept that plan." Build a consequence into the agreement if you need to, letting Jerry help: "Jerry, if for some reason you forget our agreement and begin playing roughly again, what do you think would be a fair thing for me to do?" Then brainstorm again, avoiding loopholes in your agreement. Be sure to set a definite time period for a fair test, allowing for a follow-up conference to discuss how the plan is working. It helps either to write down or tape-record the agreement to avoid misunderstandings. If you write it down, both sign. Students will usually keep agreements if we expect them to, and if we fulfill our part of the bargain.

Scheduling Conferences

We have busy days and many students, but a ten-minute conference is usually long enough. For those who require more time, longer conferences can be arranged. You may only be able to spare time once every few weeks, but do set aside whatever time you can.

Schedule conferences by checking students' study periods and free periods. Use "conference corners," private places that still allow you to see the rest of your class. Have peer tutors answer any questions while you're holding conferences.

Make a concerted effort to add regular conferences to your school year. Simply set them up if you already have a good relationship with your students. Or use your responding skills as you teach so students will begin to see you as accepting and understanding. When you feel the relationship has improved, introduce the idea of conferences. The time you invest can have great value.

Exploring alternatives with students is a constructive way to solve problems. Conferences conducted in an atmosphere of mutual respect and trust can help build the student-teacher relationships you need for a democratic classroom.

Works Cited

Dreikurs, Rudolf. *Psychology in the Classroom: A Manual for Teachers.* 2nd ed. NY: Harper & Row, 1968.

Dreikurs, Rudolf, and Grey, Loren. *A Parent's Guide to Child Discipline.* NY: Hawthorn Books, 1970.

Glasser, William. *Schools Without Failure.* NY: Harper & Row, 1969.

Recommended Readings

Carkhuff, Robert. *The Art of Helping.* Amherst, MA: Human Research Development Press, 1973.

Carkhuff, Robert. *How to Help Yourself.* Amherst, MA: Human Research Development Press, 1974.

Egan, G. *The Skilled Helper.* Monterey, CA: Brooks/Cole, 1975.

Gazda, George, et al. *Human Relations Development.* 2nd ed. Boston: Allyn & Bacon, 1977.

Gordon, Tom. *Teacher Effectiveness Training.* NY: Peter Wyden, 1974.

Hackney, Harold, and Nye, Sherilyn. *Counseling Strategies and Objectives.* Englewood Cliffs, NJ: Prentice-Hall, 1973.

Study Questions

1. What are the differences between open questions and closed questions? Give some examples other than those given in the chapter.

2. What is the value of using open questions in conferences? When are closed questions appropriate?

3. What are the six steps in exploring alternatives?

4. How can we clarify a student-owned problem? A teacher-owned problem?

5. Why is it helpful to disclose the goal of misbehavior? What is a "recognition reflex"?

6. How is exploring alternatives through brainstorming different from giving advice? Why is it important to delay evaluation until after the brainstorming? How does brainstorming differ for student-owned and teacher-owned problems?

7. Why do we evaluate all proposed alternatives before choosing a solution? For a student-owned problem, what can you do if the student chooses a solution you disagree with?

8. Why is it important to make a commitment and set a time for evaluation? How does the evaluation process differ for student-owned and teacher-owned problems?

9. For teacher-owned problems, how can we maintain mutual respect? Identify the real issue? Change the agreement? Invite the student's participation in decision making?

10. "Exploring alternatives with students is a constructive way to solve problems." Do you agree? Disagree? Why?

Problem Situation

Fred has frequent, disruptive arguments with other students when they don't want to do projects his way. You set up a conference with him to negotiate a mutually agreeable solution.

1. What might be the purpose for Fred's behavior? How could you get Fred to understand his goal?
2. How have Fred's beliefs about himself influenced his behavior?
3. How could you help him develop other ways of behaving?
4. What problems might arise in negotiation with a student like Fred? How will you deal with these problems?

Activity for the Week

Set up at least one problem-solving conference, during which you and the student explore alternatives. Record your impressions of the more and less successful parts of the conference. If possible, record a conference and bring the tape to our next session.

Recommended Resource Book Material

Chapter 6

Chart 6

Steps in Exploring Alternatives

Step	When Student Owns the Problem	When Teacher Owns the Problem
1. Understanding and clarifying the problem.	You are very hurt when Sharon calls you names. What do you do when Sharon calls you names?	When you continue to make jokes during class discussion I get very discouraged because I can't get the students to discuss the topic for the day. You get bored during the discussions and want to liven them up.
2. Disclosing the goal of misbehavior.	Have you considered _____? Could it be you want Sharon to notice you? Is it possible Sharon wants to get even with you for teasing her? (Watch for the recognition reflex.)	Have you considered _____? May I tell you what I think? Could it be you want to be in charge of the class? It seems we both want to be the boss.
3. Exploring alternatives through brainstorming.	Why do you suppose it's so important for you to have Sharon's attention? Would you like to look at some other ways you can get Sharon to notice you? What are some things you could do to get Sharon's attention that she would like?	Since we both want to be in charge, let's see if we can work it out so that we both get what we want. Let's brainstorm — give any idea we can think of and not evaluate them until we're through. What ideas do you have to solve our problem?
4. Evaluating all proposed alternatives.	How do you feel about the idea of giving Sharon some compliments?	Okay, which one do we want? How do you feel about a ten-minute period each day for you to entertain the students?
5. Choosing a solution.	Which idea do you think will work best for you? What is your reason for choosing that solution? What do you think will happen if you do this?	Have we decided? Is this the one we want?
6. Making a commitment and planning a time for evaluation.	Are you willing to say one positive thing each day to Sharon? (narrowing to specifics) Okay, you have decided that once a day you will tell Sharon something you like about her. If she calls you a name, you'll walk away. Is that right? Shall we talk about this again on Thursday to see how it's going? You will do this for one week no matter what happens, is that right?	Okay, you've agreed to stop interrupting discussions in return for a ten-minute, one-man show each day and I've agreed to accept that. Is that right? What do you think would be a fair consequence if you decide to make jokes at other times? If I break the agreement, what do you think should happen? Shall we do this for a week and then talk about it next Thursday at this time?

Recording Worksheet

Exploring Alternatives

As you listen to a teacher exploring alternatives with a student, consider the steps in the process. Decide what you would do at each step. Be prepared to discuss your responses with the group.

NOTES

Chapter 6

Points to Remember

1. Problem-solving conferences let us address specific problems as we teach decision making.

2. Closed questions often call for a yes or no answer, usually begin with a verb or with Why, and may stifle further exchanges. They also tend to accuse or blame: "Do you really think that's the right way to do it?"

3. Open questions permit many possible responses, often begin with What, Where, When, Who, Which, or How, and refrain from accusing or blaming: "What worries you about this assignment?"

4. Use six steps during problem-solving conferences:
- Understand and clarify the problem.
- Disclose the goal of misbehavior.
- Explore alternatives through brainstorming.
- Evaluate all proposed alternatives.
- Choose a solution.
- Make a commitment and set a time for evaluation.

5. As you work to resolve classroom conflicts:
- Maintain mutual respect.
- Identify the real issue.
- Resolve to change your own behavior as needed.
- Invite students' participation in decision making.

6. Explore alternatives for both teacher-owned and student-owned problems. Use the technique in class discussions, small-group meetings, and individual conferences.

Personal Record Chapter 6

1.   My experience with the weekly assignment

2.   My reactions to the reading

3.   Topics to discuss with the group

4.   Skills I intend to improve

5.   My beliefs which impede progress

6.   My successes in applying program ideas

7.   My difficulties in applying program ideas

8.   My progress this week: A specific example

9.   This week I learned

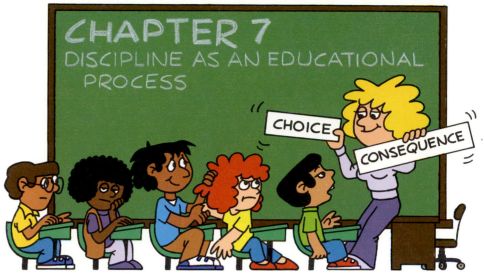

CHAPTER 7
DISCIPLINE AS AN EDUCATIONAL PROCESS

How can I prevent discipline problems by offering students choices and letting them make decisions about their educations?

What can I do myself to prevent discipline problems?

What is a workable substitute for corrective discipline based on rewards and punishment?

What are natural consequences?

What are logical consequences? How do they differ from punishment?

How can I involve students in formulating logical consequences?

When we commit ourselves to the principles of a democratic classroom, we show our belief in the importance of offering choices. Offering choices can in itself be encouraging. Students begin to feel trusted when we allow them a voice in classroom policies, even in learning procedures. Similarly, students are more likely to benefit from disciplinary measures they helped tailor for themselves. If discipline is handled with the same mutual respect that characterizes other classroom activities, it can be a valuable, constructive part of our students' educations.

The most effective discipline, like the best health care, is preventive. Offering choices, getting students involved in their educations, helps reduce the occasions for misbehavior. As mentioned earlier, students can help decide matters such as the way they'll study certain subjects, the way their classroom will be arranged, the distribution of classroom responsibilities, the composition of committees and study groups, and so on. It is essential to increase interest and cooperation by letting students know we respect their opinions and will act upon reasonable suggestions and decisions.

An Ounce of Prevention

We can help invigorate our classrooms by breaking routines, using media, alternating class discussions with small-group and individual work, allowing students to participate in grading, and individualizing students' education as much as we can. Treating our students as unique individuals, worthy of trust and respect, creates an encouraging climate.

Time spent on certain topics. Let students help decide which topics they'd like to spend more time on, which ideas they'd like to pursue. If you've only allotted a week for your discussion of photosynthesis, but your students want to experiment with the process, be flexible enough to revise your schedule.

Since students don't all learn at the same rate, let them participate in establishing their own rates of learning. While Fred may take three lessons to learn how to multiply two-place digits, Carlos may learn how in one lesson. Students can be helped to discover how long certain assignments will take them.

Ways certain topics are studied. Involve students in devising creative ways to study. The class may want to work in small groups, see films, invite guest speakers, go on field trips, produce plays or projects, and so on.

The order of study. Unless some subjects demand a particular sequence, let students help decide what to tackle first, second, and so forth. If it doesn't matter to you whether they study the newspaper first or write poetry first, involve them in the decision. In self-contained classrooms, students can help decide the order of subjects they'll study during the school day.

Methods of evaluation. Tests, book reports, seat work, and compositions are all valid ways to evaluate learning. But consider discussing with students other, more unusual methods. For instance, see if they'd like to hold panel discussions or debates, construct murals or posters, build models, dramatize events or ideas. All these projects can tell us whether or not students have grasped specific material.

Involve them in devising different kinds of tests. Consider group tests during which the group discusses each test item but every student responds individually. Introduce take-home and open-book tests. Have students submit test questions; then use one question from everyone.

Students may fear tests less when they've helped devise them. You'll evaluate other skills besides memorization when you and your students become more creative about methods of evaluation. It's much more important to teach students how to learn than how to memorize.

Activities and projects. Students may want to set up a display table, do a series of drawings, create a book, take an in-depth look at a particular topic: allow them to be creative about how they spend their time.

Committees and small groups. Students can help decide who they'll work with on particular projects. Most of us work better with people we like than with people we only tolerate. Let them form their own groups sometimes, with your systematic guidance. For students who misbehave when they're together, offer the choice of *working* together or joining groups that *you've* chosen. Invite withdrawn students to join groups with lively, talkative students.

Bulletin boards. Instead of making the first bulletin board display yourself, devote one of your first class discussions to the subject. You might say, "I thought you might like to help decide what will be on our bulletin board. What shall we display?" Open the way for students' imagination, cooperation, and involvement. Consider forming committees to take charge of each bulletin board.

Classroom jobs. You and your students share a classroom. You can also share the responsibilities for creating a pleasant, efficient place to learn. Discuss with students what jobs must be done: There are chalkboards to be cleaned, materials to be passed out and collected, shelves to be straightened, milk money to be collected, attendance to be taken, lab animals to be cared for, plants to be watered, and so on. Make the list together and then decide a fair way to share the jobs. Maybe jobs can rotate among class members from week to week.

Seating arrangements. Students can sit at tables and chairs, at desks in a circle, or double circle, or semi-circle, in small groups or large. Let students help decide the arrangement and who they will sit with. Change the arrangements occasionally.

You will have other ideas about ways to involve students in their education. Since students exercise their decision-making powers all the time — as they decide whether or not to do as you say — it makes sense to give them as many choices as possible. Developing their ability to choose will be valuable to them. You'll also be encouraging them to feel like real, contributing members of their class.

Some students, especially young students, will need more guidance than others. You may have to give them some ideas or perhaps limit the alternatives to two or three. Students may need help learning to work together. For them, you might begin with groups of two, then three, and so on; beginning with larger groups may invite chaos. But regardless of your students' experience, getting them involved can be the best possible way to ward off discipline problems promoted by alienation and boredom. For unmotivated students, offering choices can be especially stimulating. Students may take a new interest in learning when they are given a voice in their education.

What Can I Do Myself To Prevent Discipline Problems?

Vary the pace. Everyone likes a change in routine. Varying the pace of the school day and the kinds of activities you call for can help keep students energetic and interested. Alternating discussions, use of media, exercises, small-group discussions, and independent work will avoid monotony and staleness.

Put instructions on the board. To avoid the payoff for attention-seeking students who continually ask for instructions to be repeated, simply refer them to the chalkboard. Use a tape recorder for students who can't read. You'll then show students that not listening will no longer capture your attention.

Individualize instruction. Most teacher-education courses stress individualization, but how do we do it? Several procedures have been found helpful.

1. Have a folder for each student containing individual assignments. Depending on students' ages and the subject, the folder can contain work enough for a period, a day, a week, or a whole unit. Students can get their assignments from their folders as soon as they come to class. Assignments you've graded can be returned to the folders. In this way, work becomes more individualized and students more self-sufficient.

2. Let students help decide their grades. Before report-card time, meet with all students, discuss individual progress, and ask them to grade themselves. They should understand that the final decision is yours but have them explain the grade they chose. You'll very likely find that students will grade themselves too low, rather than too high. If your district insists on competitive grades for achievement, give students grades for effort as well. That way, the student with a C in science may have an A in the effort column.

Establish daily free-time periods. Since students are kept busy much of the schoolday, you can increase their cooperation by giving them a daily free period. During free time students can read, play quiet games, engage in art projects, do homework, and so on. Some may want to work on school projects or contracts. Others will need to use the time to complete work they didn't finish during the day. The consequence of misbehaving during work periods can be finishing work during free time.

Such periods are best established near the end of the day to give you and your students a chance to wind down.

Create learning contracts. Setting up a learning contract is an excellent way to involve students in formulating their own goals. If your district requires grades, contracts can establish grading criteria. Students and teacher decide what work will be required for the grade the student chooses to earn. Contracts can apply to a whole unit or to part of a unit. (See the following sample contract.) In ungraded systems, contracts can detail what is required for a ''pass,'' based on each student's individual level.

<u>Grade Contract</u>

Subject: <u>Social Studies</u>   Student_____

Unit: <u>Indians of the American Southwest</u>   Teacher_____
      <u>during the Nineteenth Century</u>

Instructions:
    You may decide what grade you wish to earn for this unit. Here are some ideas from our class discussion on how you can earn a certain grade. You may have other ideas that you want to discuss with me.
      Grade of <u>A</u>: <u>Four</u> of the projects listed below.
      Grade of <u>B</u>: <u>Three</u> of the projects listed below.
      Grade of <u>C</u>: <u>Two</u> of the projects listed below.
      Grade of <u>D</u>: <u>One</u> of the projects listed below.

NOTE: If you decide to work for a C or above, you may choose only <u>one</u> small-group project. The other project or projects must be individual.

1. Write a composition comparing the daily life of three Southwestern Indian tribes.

2. Form a small group and present a play about the life of one of the tribes. (NOTE: If more than one group decides to do this, each group will have to choose a different tribe.)

3. Form a small group and design a mural or a model village showing the way of life of one of the tribes. (Each group chooses a different tribe.)

4. Give an oral report on a novel about Southwestern Indians and compare the story to the facts about the way the Indians lived.

5. Make a presentation using the overhead projector on the life of a Southwestern tribe. (Each presenter will need to choose a different tribe. Tribes chosen should be different from those presented in plays or art projects.)

6. Either individually or in a small group, make a map showing the location of each tribe.

7. Answer five study questions from the text. (We will decide together which questions you will answer.)

8. Other ideas?_____

_____

_____

REMEMBER: Your grade also depends upon quality. For example, if you decide to work for an A but your work is really B quality, you will have the opportunity to improve the work or accept a B. You and I will decide together the quality of your work.

I have read and understood all of the above. I wish to contract for a grade of _____. I will earn the grade by doing the following projects. (If you're doing a small-group project, name the other members of your group.)

_____

_____

_____

_____

Date_____

Last day to renegotiate_____

Signature of
Student_____

Signature of
Teacher_____

Perhaps you've objected to contracts in the past. You worry that less capable students may set their sights too high, and that more capable students may try to slide through. But you can monitor contracts to prevent unrealistic or unchallenging terms. Students who work only when pressured need to take responsibility for their own learning. Your pressuring them will continue to remove that responsibility. Since contracts are renegotiable, students can revise the terms without losing face. Unmotivated students may try harder when they realize they can't get your attention or defeat you by not working, only by changing their behavior.

Contracts take time, especially at first when you must structure them precisely. But, in the long run, contracts save time and energy. You free yourself from the necessity of reminding and nagging. And you've allowed students to take responsibility for their own achievements.

Contracts are not substitutes for other activities involving the whole class, such as discussions, audiovisual programs, speakers, and so on. But you can adapt them to individual needs. They can include participation in class discussions and classroom jobs. They can lead students toward experiences you think they need, like small-group work or peer tutoring.

To simplify your evaluation of larger projects, stagger the due dates so you won't get everything at once. Collect projects in segments so you can guide students in new directions. With older students, you might assign learning partners to check each other's work.

Contracts can also be used remedially, for reluctant learners. You start where the student is willing to start and gradually increase the work. (See the following example of a remedial learning contract.)

Setting Up a Remedial Contract

Mr. Muellar hasn't been able to get Patty to do any work. He's reminded her, nagged and punished her, but to no avail. She demonstrates her power by refusing to care about grades or about her parents' opinion of her apathy. Finally, Mr. Muellar decides to win Patty's cooperation by involving her in decisions that affect her. He negotiates a contract with her:

Muellar: Patty, we've been having problems ever since school started with you getting your work done. I've stopped nagging and reminding you because I know that doesn't work.

(He has admitted defeat, the first step in working with a power-bent student. He'll now attempt to enlist her cooperation.)

Patty, what I'm wondering is, are you willing to do any work at all?

Patty: Well, yeah, I guess so.

Muellar: Okay, let's look at the afternoon schedule. First, there's reading.

Patty: I hate reading. I don't read very fast and I can't keep up. And the stories are boring.

Muellar: Would you be willing to look through the book, pick out any story that looks interesting, and read the first three pages of it? Then would you answer a few questions I give you about those pages?

Patty: Any story?

Muellar: Yes. The first three pages of any story you choose. All right?

Patty: Well, okay, but what happens if I don't do it?

Muellar: What do you think would be fair?

Patty: I'd have to do it during free time?

Muellar: I'll agree to that. You'll read the first three pages of any story in the book and answer questions about those pages. If you don't do this during reading period, you'll do it during free time. Can we make that agreement?

Patty: Okay.

Muellar: Then let's write it out and both sign so we know what we've agreed to. Tomorrow we'll talk again to see what you want to do during that reading period.

REMEDIAL LEARNING CONTRACT

DATE ___10/9/81___

STUDENT ___Patty_____

TEACHER ___Mr. Muellar_____

SUBJECT ___Reading_____

___Patty___ agrees to complete the following work during regular class time: Read the first three pages of any story and then answer questions about those pages.

If ___Patty___ chooses not to do this work during regular class time, she will finish the work during ___Free time___

_____Patty_____
STUDENT

_____Mr. Muellar_____
TEACHER

If Patty didn't do the work during reading period, Mr. Muellar would say nothing. When free time came, he'd politely remind her of the contract and ask her to fulfill its terms. If she refused to work and didn't fulfill the terms of a renegotiated, smaller contract, Mr. Mueller might have to devise a special contract for Patty — a contract employing the logical consequences of Patty's decision not to be a student.

A Plan for "Non-Students"

Let's say that Patty refuses to honor any contract. Mr. Muellar can show her that she has made a decision; she's decided not to be a student. So he has decided to treat her as a "non-student." (The following plan was developed by Sally Laufketter, a counselor in Ritenour School District, St. Louis County, Missouri.)

He explains that Patty will not participate in any student activity. She'll receive no assignments, remain silent during all class discussions, and stay in one classroom or in her homeroom all day. She may watch the activities but may not participate. Mr. Muellar will speak to Patty only when necessary, since his job is to teach students and Patty has decided not to be a student. He isn't interested in punishing her; he's simply honoring her decision to be a "non-student." Patty will go to the restroom and to lunch by herself. If she forgets and begins to join in some class activity, Mr. Muellar will take her aside and remind her of their agreement: "Patty, remember that you've decided not to be part of this class."

Mr. Muellar presents this plan to Patty during a conference, offering her the choice of setting up another learning contract instead. If she refuses another contract or fails to honor its terms, and if she offers no help to her teacher's "What shall we do?" Mr. Mueller explains his plan regretfully but firmly:

"Patty, you've shown that you're not willing to make any contracts for doing schoolwork. I know that I can't make you keep a contract. You don't seem to want to do the things required of students, and yet the law says you have to come to school.

"I can't control the law but I can arrange it so that you won't have to participate in anything the other students do. You won't have to turn in any papers or assignments or take part in discussions or projects. In other words, you won't have to take any of the responsibilities that go along with being a student. You'll just stop participating in school.

"The only thing I'll require is that you don't disturb others. If you decide to do that, I'll have to ask you to sit by yourself or leave the room until you're ready to stop."

They establish a time limit, perhaps three days, after which the two will have another conference. If Patty is hostile and resistant, he probably decides not to ask her any more questions. He doesn't increase her resistance by reminding her she'll be missing gym, recess, assemblies, and so on. He simply institutes the plan immediately.

After three days, Mr. Muellar meets with Patty again. He offers her another learning contract or a continuation of her "non-student" status. If her behavior indicates she's still not ready to join the class, her teacher continues to treat her as a "non-student," this time for a day or two longer than before.

This plan may require the cooperation of other teachers, the principal, and the parents. If anyone resists, explain that since nothing else has worked, you'd like to experiment with this.

Most students don't choose to be "non-students" for very long. When Patty rejoins the class, her teacher reinforces her decision by encouraging her, getting her involved as a room helper or tutor, and generally welcoming her back. The teacher also plans for peer encouragement so Patty will feel accepted. Patty will come to understand that the social order of school must be maintained for the benefit of everyone. She is a responsible member of that social order.

All the prevention in the world will not eliminate misbehavior. But no matter how disruptive the misbehavior, we need to stop thinking of *punishment* as our final resource. Punishment is based on power, the autocratic control of teachers, administrators, and parents. A democratic classroom requires a system of cooperative discipline. Mr. Muellar's treatment of Patty used this kind of system.

Natural and Logical Consequences Instead of Reward and Punishment

"Boy, am I glad it's my free period! I can't wait until this day is over!"

"What's the matter, Marge? You look all done in."

"I'm *so* tired."

"What happened?"

"Well, yesterday was Bill's birthday and we had a party. Some people didn't leave until one o'clock and then we cleaned up until two. To top it off, I overslept half an hour and just missed my bus! I mean, there I was running for the bus when the driver took off! So I was twenty minutes late to school, the kids were already in the room . . . . Boy! What a day!"

Poor Marge experienced both the *natural* and the *logical* consequences of her birthday party. She stayed up late and so felt tired; that's a natural consequence, the result of a violation of the natural order of events. She overslept and missed her bus; that's a *logical* consequence, the result of a violation of the social order, the rules people have set up for cooperative living. Natural and logical consequences happen all the time in "real life," yet we seldom use them in our classrooms to correct misbehavior. Instead, we often rely on punishment.

Since punishment is based on power, it frequently produces power struggles or induces revenge. Punishment increases conflict, removes responsibility from students, impedes the development of self-discipline, and guarantees negative interaction between teacher and student. With the exception of the "good" youngster who occasionally goes astray, most students respond to punishment only when the teacher is present and the punishment is constantly repeated.

Rewards, the other side of punishment, do similar damage. Rewards invite dependence, discouragement, and rebellion, because they too are based on power and control. Rewards also demand considerable ingenuity from us, since what appeals today may not appeal tomorrow. If students ask themselves, "Is a bowl of jello worth eating the spinach?" their answer will depend on how fond they are of spinach or jello! Rewards have to escalate; the ante must always be upped. If punishment teaches the desirability of power, rewards teach the inevitability of extrinsic motivation, the "never give something for nothing" philosophy. And rewards teach that learning itself is only a means to an end, without real value.

We want to stimulate self-discipline, responsibility, decision making, and independence. Yet misbehavior, both mild and severe, exists and must be dealt with. How can we discipline within the spirit of a democratic classroom?

Dr. Rudolf Dreikurs (1968) suggested a system for cooperative discipline using *natural* and *logical consequences.* This system has distinct advantages over reward and punishment: Students are responsible for their own behavior; students make decisions within limits and are held accountable for the consequences; teachers allow students to experience the reality of the natural and social order and to learn from that experience.

Punishment is often far removed from the misbehavior it tries to correct; this lack of relationship to the event makes such discipline ineffective as a means of changing students' behavior beyond the moment. In contrast, when we allow students to experience natural consequences, we permit them to learn what happens when the natural order of events is violated. For example, if Colleen refuses to eat, she'll be hungry. If Dale doesn't leave himself enough time to finish his science test, he'll do poorly. When we decide not to remind or coax Colleen and Dale, they learn from the natural consequences of their behavior.

Our opportunities to use natural consequences as a way of letting students learn by experience are limited, mainly by our responsibility for students' safety. We can't permit students to hit each other with baseball bats or to play on the highway. Many classroom situations have few natural consequences. But we can use *logical* consequences, the results of violating the *social order.*

We establish guidelines in our classrooms so our students can live and work cooperatively. When students exceed those guidelines, they are offered a logical choice: "Would you like to settle down so we can play the game, or shall we play it another time when you're ready to listen?" We watch their *behavior* to see what choice they've made. Then we follow through with the consequence, if necessary: "I see by the way you're acting that you're not ready to play the game today. We'll try again tomorrow." Logical consequences must be *seen* as logical by the misbehaving student.

Some examples of logical consequences: Students who lose library books pay for them. Students who throw food clean the floor and may temporarily lose the privilege of eating with others. Students who fight during recess temporarily play by themselves or stay inside.

Notice the absence of hostility in applying natural and logical consequences. (The alarm clock that failed to wake Marge up wasn't angry with her. Neither was the driver of the bus she missed.) Natural consequences require only that we stand aside and let events take their course, provided the outcome isn't dangerous. Logical consequences are arranged. But logical consequences are only effective when used by teachers who are both *firm* and *friendly*. Firmness shows we respect ourselves; friendliness shows we respect our students. Tone of voice, gestures, and facial expressions are all-important.

Six major differences between punishment and logical consequences emerge (Dreikurs & Grey, 1970; Dinkmeyer & McKay, 1976):

1. *Punishment expresses the power of personal authority.*

"I *told* you people to quiet down! Now I'll separate you!"

Logical consequences express the reality of the social order. They acknowledge mutual rights.

"I realize you're excited about your project but the noise is bothering the rest of us. Please work quietly or you will need to separate until you're ready to work without disturbing others."

2. *Punishment is arbitrary or barely related to the situation.*

"All right, you will stay after school and write, 'I will not write on my desk' one hundred times!"

Logical consequences are directly related to the misbehavior.

"Since you've decided to write on your desk, when will you clean the desk?"

3. *Punishment is personalized and implies moral judgment. It equates the deed and the doer.*

"You took that book from the library without checking it out! Don't you know that's stealing? Now you march right back there and check that book out!"

Logical consequences imply no element of moral judgment. They separate the deed from the doer.

"Since you're not ready to respect the rules for checking out books, it looks like you're not ready to borrow library books."

4. *Punishment is concerned with past misbehavior.*

"No! You can't help set up the science experiment. The last time you did, you refused to wear safety glasses and we couldn't get started!"

Logical consequences are concerned with present and future behavior.

"You may help with the science experiment as long as you're willing to wear safety glasses."

5. *Punishment threatens; it treats the offender with disrespect. It is a put-down.*

"You embarrassed me in front of our guest speaker! I'm really ashamed of you. We won't be having guest speakers again for quite a while!"

Logical consequences are invoked in a friendly manner, after feelings have calmed. They imply good will.

The teacher says nothing after the speaker leaves because she knows the students are expecting her to yell at them. At a later, more relaxed time she says, "It appears you're not ready for a guest speaker. We'll need to postpone the time for our next guest speaker until you feel you're ready."

6. *Punishment demands obedience.*

"You go sit by yourself right now and finish that assignment!"

Logical consequences permit choice.

"You can either do your assignment now or during your free time. You decide."

The most logical of consequences can become punishment if we inject anger, warning, threats, reminders — *too much talk of any kind.* Hostile body language, gestures, and facial expressions that belie our friendly words can also defeat our efforts. So can hidden motives of power or revenge, the "this will teach them a thing or two" attitude.

Logical consequences require that we're verbally brief and to the point, that we follow through, and that we maintain a friendly, encouraging attitude. They require our willingness to let students experience and learn from the consequences of their behavior. Misbehavior alerts us to the need for a learning experience.

Guidelines in Applying Consequences

1. *Determine the student's goal of misbehavior.* Natural consequences apply to any goal, since they require no application by the teacher. But we must arrange logical consequences without reinforcing a student's mistaken goal. Consequences are usually most effective for attention-seeking students. The approach gives attention in unexpected ways and so doesn't reinforce the goal. Students displaying inadequacy need extra doses of encouragement from a teacher who won't give up on them; logical consequences are less appropriate for such students. However, once these students begin to respond to our encouragement, we can set up learning contracts, based on logical consequences, with them. Students seeking power and revenge may interpret logical consequences as punishment; they're frequently unable to see anything "logical" about us or our actions toward them. We can devise logical consequences for such students, but we must be especially careful and observant so we don't reinforce their goals.

The important thing to remember is that part of the logic of this method of discipline is its ability to fit the goal of misbehavior. Logical consequences are tailored to individual students and specific situations. For example, the student who clowns for attention can be asked for a "command performance," since this will be an unexpected kind of attention. However, the student who clowns for power may get just that when asked to perform; such a student *wants* to take over the class.

The basic guidelines for each goal of misbehavior bear repeating here. They suggest the appropriate kinds of logical consequences.

For attention-seekers who shout out during discussions, we can ignore the outburst and only call on students who raise their hands. The logical consequence of shouting out is being ignored. As soon as these students do raise their hands, we call on them, giving them recognition for positive behavior. We also catch them being "good," remarking quietly, "I see you're really working hard on that assignment." Kindness with firmness is the key.

The guideline: ***Never give attention on demand, even for useful behavior. Help students become self-motivated. Give attention in ways they don't expect. Catch them being "good."***

Power-seeking students can experience the logical consequence of having no one to fight with them. We withdraw from the conflict without giving in, allowing students to be their own boss (unless they are disruptive). If they decide not to work, they don't receive a grade. Meanwhile, we improve our relationship with them by remaining friendly and helping them use their power constructively by enlisting their help. As relationships improve, we can negotiate learning contracts with these students.

The guideline: ***Withdraw from the conflict. Let the consequences of students' behavior occur. Win their cooperation by enlisting their help.***

As with students seeking power, those seeking revenge need to be their own bosses, as long as their behavior isn't disruptive or dangerous. Trying to force revenge-seekers to work will only reinforce their desire for revenge. Instead, we need to improve our relationship with them by remaining friendly, refusing to be hurt, and focusing on any positive behavior. Sometimes you can involve the class in helping the student, perhaps by appointing one or more "buddies" to bring the revenge-seeker back into the group. Once relationships improve, negotiate a learning contract with the student.

The guideline: ***Avoid feeling hurt. Don't get hooked into seeking your own revenge. Instead, work to build a trusting relationship.***

Students who display inadequacy want us to leave them alone. We treat them most logically when we show our concern, give plenty of encouragement, and refuse to give up.

The guideline: ***Don't give up. Avoid criticism and pity. Encourage any positive effort.***

2. Having determined a student's goal, *recognize who owns the problem.* Student-owned problems are often best handled with natural consequences. When Colleen skips lunch and feels hungry for

141

the rest of the day, she learns what happens when she misses a meal. Her teacher needn't get involved. However, problems belonging to the teacher or to the group often call for logical consequences. When our classroom is disrupted, we must take the lead in solving the problem. Certain student-owned problems can be solved with logical consequences. For example, if Marshall won't do his work, his teacher can negotiate a contract with him specifying what work he's willing to do and what the consequences will be if he doesn't do that work.

3. After instituting logical consequences for students whose goal and problem ownership you've determined, *remember to focus on positive behavior.* If you had to remove Duane from the cafeteria, and then after lunch you see him working diligently on his math, make an encouraging comment, pat his shoulder, or simply smile at him. Students need to feel personally accepted, even though some of their behavior may be unacceptable. And *we need to identify for ourselves those positive attitudes and characteristics we'll encourage* — like respect, tolerance, and cooperation. Specifically (the following adapted from Carlson, 1978):

Characteristics to encourage	Behavior to encourage
Respects the rights of others.	Takes turns. Lets others talk. Helps clean up. Shares. Is quiet while others are working.
Is tolerant.	Listens to others. Lets others use their strengths. Is patient with less able students.
Is interested in others.	Includes others in play. Shows concern for absent classmates. Volunteers to help others. Socializes.
Cooperates.	Works well in groups. Completes individual assignments.
Encourages others.	Notices and acknowledges the efforts of others. Gives others a chance to participate.
Is courageous.	Takes appropriate risks. Enjoys novel experiences. Is calm under pressure. Accepts challenges.

4. When we discipline, we want to *choose our words carefully.* Students expect us to talk and we usually oblige. Doing what they expect may reinforce the misbehavior. We can be more successful with misbehavior if we're economical with our words. We want also to be encouraging.

Consider how students hear the following:

"Just *when* is that report going to be turned in?"
"*What's* the matter here? *Trouble* again?"

"If I have to tell you *one more time . . .*"
"*Don't* let me catch you doing that again or there's going to be *trouble!*"
"I can *never* leave this class alone."

Certain words almost always sound negative. Each has an alternative:

Negative	Positive alternatives
never	this time
always	if . . . then
must	could
should	it would be better if . . .
have to	You decide.

We want to encourage all the time, not just when students are behaving. We want them to know we expect the best from them.

5. Discipline becomes more logical when we *respond as consistently as possible.* When students know what to expect, they begin to trust us. Consistency counteracts misbehavior when our responses don't reinforce mistaken goals.

6. We help stimulate self-discipline when we *let all students share the responsibility* for misbehavior when the "culprit" is unknown. Trying to smoke out the guilty party only leads to tattling, hard feelings between "good" and "bad" class members, and embarrassment. If, when you return from the office and find spitwads all over the floor, you ask the whole class to pick them up, individual students will be less likely to cause the group inconvenience in the future. You'll be using peer pressure constructively; students will discipline each other. The "good" students will no longer maintain their halos at the expense of the "bad" students.

7. Finally, *set aside time for training.* We'll be more successful in teaching self-discipline if we do so at relaxed times. Show young students how to button coats and tie shoes before they must scramble to catch the bus. Before the field trip, allow plenty of time to discuss appropriate behavior. Make self-discipline a regular part of every student's education.

Involve Students in Formulating Consequences

Discipline in a democratic classroom is a cooperative effort between teacher and students. We offer choices by taking the time to discuss appropriate behavior with our students. We involve them in deciding what consequences would be fair for specific misbehavior. Classroom rules and your expectations need not be mysteries to students.

Discuss behavior and misbehavior in class meetings (explained in Chapter 12), small-group conferences, and individual meetings. Most classroom problems can be dealt with cooperatively.

At certain times, of course, you'll need to take independent action without involving students. When something must be done immediately, do it. When the problem is rather minor, there's no need to magnify it. Simply give Grant and Ed the choice of ending their private conversation or being separated for the rest of the period. Then go on with the class.

Sometimes students won't know how to formulate a reasonable consequence, so you'll have to take the lead. Other times, the misbehavior is so serious that choices are limited. The student may simply have to leave the classroom or even the building.

Generally, though, we can enlist our students' aid in our disciplinary efforts. Doing so can be tremendously encouraging for all concerned.

Steps in Applying Consequences

• *Provide choices.* Pose alternatives that fit the situation and let students decide either verbally or through their behavior. Offer choices firmly but respectfully:

"Terry, I'm sorry but throwing the blocks is not permitted. You can play with them correctly or stop playing with them for a while. You decide."

"Either help us out on this project or leave the group."

When the alternative is obvious, you need not state it:

"When the books are put away, we can go to lunch."

"If you go to the library, you go to work on your report."

Sometimes you'll want to state your intentions:

"I'm willing to help you with the project, but only after you've given it your best effort."

• *As you follow through with a consequence, assure students they'll have an opportunity to change the decision later.*

"Your behavior tells me you've decided not to help us with the project. Please leave the group and come back when you're ready to cooperate."

• *If students continue to misbehave, extend the time that must elapse before they try again.*

"I see you're still not ready to play with the blocks correctly. You may try again tomorrow."

From this point on, confine your remarks to repeated assurances that the student will get another chance at a specific time. Increase that time if the misbehavior is repeated:

"You may try again in two days."

To make sure your action expresses logical consequences rather than punishment, ask yourself: Am I showing an open attitude? Am I giving students a choice and then accepting their decisions? Am I speaking in a firm but friendly tone of voice? Does my nonverbal behavior match my tone of voice? Are the consequences I devise logically related to the misbehavior? Am I involving students whenever possible?

Typical Misbehavior and Logical Consequences

Note: Sometimes the consequences of misbehavior are the same, regardless of the student's goal. Your relationship with a particular student is crucial, especially with those seeking power or revenge. Logical consequences for such students must be matter-of-fact, related to the needs of the situation, and instituted only for disruptive or harmful behavior in teacher-owned problems. There may be other ways of dealing with the problems discussed below; this section describes only logical consequences and refers to the most *typical* goals of particular misbehavior.

Problem: Wandering out of seat.
Probable goal: Attention or power.
Problem owner: You if the student is bothering others. The student if no one is bothered.

Some alternatives

If for attention:

1. Ignore.
2. Give choice of completing work during class time, free period, or student's own time. Then ignore continued wandering.
3. Remove chair or desk, telling student he or she doesn't seem to need one. Return later to see if student is ready to sit down.

If for power:

Do not challenge student by removing chair or offering choice of working during free time. Instead, give student choice of remaining in seat or leaving the room until ready to behave appropriately.

Problem: Noisy classroom.
Probable goal: Attention or power.
Problem owner: You if the noise prevents you from teaching.

Some alternatives

If for attention, involving one or a few students:

1. Ignore.
2. Give choice of behaving appropriately or leaving group.

If for power, involving one or a few students:

Give choice of behaving appropriately or leaving group.

Regardless of the goal, if most of the class is involved:

1. Busy yourself with other work, ignoring students until they settle down.
2. Give a choice of settling down or making up the time during a free period.
3. As a last resort, take students outside to work off their excess energy; remind them that they'll have to make up the work during a free period since they've had recess during class time.

Problem: Late to class.
Probable goal: Attention or power.
Problem owner: You if lateness disrupts class or inconveniences you.
  Student's problem to decide how work will be made up.

Some alternatives

If for attention:

1. Ask student to wait in hall until ready to enter without disturbing class.
2. Enlist cooperation of class in ignoring latecomer.
3. Plan an interesting class activity that must begin promptly.
4. Have student make up time missed.

If for power:

If disruptive, ask student to wait in hall or ask class to ignore late-comer. If not disruptive, plan an interesting class activity that must begin promptly.

Problem: Running in hall.
Probable goal: Attention or power.
Problem owner: You: safety is involved.

Some alternatives

If for attention:

1. Ask student to be your partner for a few days until ready to walk.
2. Ask student to remain in room until ready to walk.

If for power:

Ask student to remain in room until ready to walk.

Developing Your Skill in Using Logical Consequences

Every classroom is unique. The solutions proposed here for common discipline problems may not work in all circumstances. But understanding the principles behind logical consequences will help you and your students design consequences for specific classroom misbehavior. With patience and creativity, you'll find appropriate consequences for most situations that require them.

We *can* discipline within the spirit of a democratic classroom. We can teach students that they are responsible for their own behavior, that they can make decisions based on choices we offer. Natural and logical consequences make discipline educational.

Works Cited

Carlson, Jon. *The Basics of Discipline.* Coral Springs, FL: CMTI Press, 1978.

Dinkmeyer, Don, and McKay, Gary D. *Systematic Training for Effective Parenting: Parent's Handbook.* Circle Pines, MN: American Guidance Service, 1976.

Dreikurs, Rudolf. *Psychology in the Classroom: A Manual for Teachers.* 2nd ed. NY: Harper & Row, 1968.

Dreikurs, Rudolf, and Grey, Loren. *A Parent's Guide to Child Discipline.* NY: Hawthorn Books, 1970.

Recommended Readings

Baruth, L., and Eckstein, D. *The ABC's of Classroom Discipline.* Dubuque, IA: Kendal/Hunt, 1976.

Dinkmeyer, Don, and Carlson, Jon. *Consulting: Facilitating Human Potential and Change Processes.* Columbus, OH: Charles E. Merrill, 1973.

Dreikurs, Rudolf. *Psychology in the Classroom.* NY: Harper & Row, 1968.

Dreikurs, Rudolf, and Cassel, Pearl. *Discipline Without Tears.* 2nd ed. NY: Hawthorn Books, 1972.

Dreikurs, Rudolf, and Grey, L. *Logical Consequences: A New Approach.* NY. Hawthorn Books, 1968.

Dreikurs, Rudolf; Grunwald, Bronia; and Pepper, Floy. *Maintaining Sanity in the Classroom.* 2nd ed. NY: Harper & Row, 1980.

Study Questions

1. What is "preventive" discipline? What are some ways we can prevent misbehavior by offering students choices? In what areas can students help make decisions?

2. What are some specific ways we can individualize instruction? How can individualization help prevent misbehavior?

3. What is the value of setting up learning contracts? How can learning contracts help prevent misbehavior?

4. How can contracts be used remedially for reluctant learners?

5. What are natural consequences? Give some examples other than those in the chapter.

6. What are logical consequences? Give some examples other than those in the chapter.

7. Why aren't rewards and punishment effective today as discipline?

8. What are the advantages of using natural and logical consequences rather than rewards and punishment? Contrast the two systems of discipline. Specifically, what are the differences between logical consequences and punishment?

9. Why do we need to determine the student's goal of misbehavior and the ownership of the problem before we apply logical consequences?

10. Why is it important to focus on positive behavior soon after correcting misbehavior? Why is consistency of response to misbehavior important? Why is it important to let all students involved in a problem share the responsibility?

11. What determines whether or not to involve students in formulating consequences? If we decide to involve students, how specifically can we do it?

12. What are the steps in applying consequences?

13. How can we make sure our actions express logical consequences rather than punishment?

Problem Situation

Casey is frequently late from recess. Since she wanders in after assignments have been given out, she expects instructions to be repeated. When you ask her to see you privately, she complains that she won't have time to finish. You've lectured her on tardiness, but your efforts have failed to bring any change.

1. What is the probable purpose of Casey's misbehavior?
2. What faulty belief does she have?
3. What is an I-message you might send?
4. What would be a logical consequence of Casey's tardiness? How would you present it to her?

Activity for the Week

Practice applying natural or logical consequences with students when you own a classroom problem. Bring examples of successful logical consequences and of situations for which you couldn't find a logical consequence.

Recommended Resource Book Material

Chapter 1, "Cooperation and responsibility," "Classroom jobs"; Chapter 7, "Logical consequences"; Chapter 9, Sociometrics." Chapter 13, "Behavior awareness and change," "Attention-getting behavior."

Chart 7

Major Differences Between Punishment and Logical Consequences

	PUNISHMENT			LOGICAL CONSEQUENCES	
Characteristics	**Underlying Message**	**Likely Results**	**Characteristics**	**Underlying Message**	**Likely Result**
1. Emphasis on power of personal authority.	Do what I say because I say so! I'm in charge here!	Rebellion. Revenge. Lack of self-discipline. Sneakiness. Irresponsibility.	1. Emphasis on reality of social order.	I trust you to learn to respect yourself and the rights of others.	Self-discipline. Cooperation. Respect for self and others. Reliability.
2. Rarely related to the act; arbitrary.	I'll show you! You deserve what you're getting!	Resentment. Revenge. Fear. Confusion. Rebellion.	2. Logically related to misbehavior; makes sense.	I trust you to make responsible choices.	Learns from experience.
3. Implies moral judgments.	This should teach you! You're bad!	Feelings of hurt, resentment, guilt, revenge.	3. No moral judgment. Treats student with dignity.	You are a worthwhile person!	Learns behavior may be objectionable but not self.
4. Emphasizes past behavior.	This is for what you did — I'm not forgetting! You'll never learn!	Feels unable to make good decisions. Unacceptable in eyes of teacher.	4. Concerned with present and future behavior.	You can make your own choices and take care of yourself.	Becomes self-directed and self-evaluating.
5. Threatens disrespect, either open or implied.	You'd better shape up! No one in *my* class acts like that!	Desire to get even. Fear. Rebellion. Guilt feelings.	5. Voice communicates respect and good will.	It's your behavior I don't like, but I still like you!	Feels secure in teacher's respect and support.
6. Demands compliance.	Your preferences don't matter! You can't be trusted to make wise decisions!	Defiant compliance. Plans to get even another time. Destruction of trust and equality.	6. Presents a choice.	You can decide.	Responsible decisions. Increased resourcefulness.

Recording Worksheet

Logical Consequences

This recording presents typical school situations calling for logical consequences. After each scene, consider the student's goal and the appropriate logical consequence. Be prepared to discuss your responses with the group.

NOTES

Chapter 7

Points to Remember

1. Discipline is an educational process which teaches responsibility.

2. The most effective discipline is preventive. Offering choices, getting students involved in their educations, helps reduce the occasions for misbehavior.

3. Students can help decide such issues as:
- Time spent on certain topics.
- Ways to study certain topics.
- The order of study.
- Methods of evaluation.
- Activities and projects.
- Committees and small groups.
- Bulletin boards.
- Classroom jobs.
- Seating arrangements.

4. Teachers can prevent discipline problems by varying the pace and individualizing instruction.

5. Learning contracts involve students in formulating their own goals. They can also be used remedially, for reluctant learners.

6. Discipline using rewards and punishment depends on power and control.

7. Rewards invite dependence, discouragement, and rebellion. Punishment increases conflict, removes responsibility from students, impedes the development of self-discipline, and guarantees negative interaction between teacher and student.

8. Natural consequences are the result of a violation of the natural order of events. Logical consequences are the result of a violation of the social order.

9. Discipline using natural and logical consequences:
- Holds students responsible for their own behavior.
- Allows students to make decisions within limits and to experience the consequences of those decisions.
- Lets students learn from experience.

10. Logical consequences are only effective when used by teachers who are both firm and friendly.

11. Use the following guidelines when applying consequences:
- Determine the goal of misbehavior.
- Recognize who owns the problem.
- Remember to focus on positive behavior.
- Choose words carefully.
- Let all students share the responsibility for misbehavior when the "culprit" is unknown or when most of the students are involved.
- Set aside time for training.

12. We need to involve students in deciding what consequences would be fair for specific misbehavior.

13. To apply consequences:
- Pose suitable alternatives.
- Follow through with consequences but give an opportunity to change the decision later.
- If misbehavior continues, extend the time that must elapse before students try again.

Personal Record Chapter 7

1. My experience with the weekly assignment

2. My reactions to the reading

3. Topics to discuss with the group

4. Skills I intend to improve

5. My beliefs which impede progress

6. My successes in applying program ideas

7. My difficulties in applying program ideas

8. My progress this week: A specific example

9. This week I learned

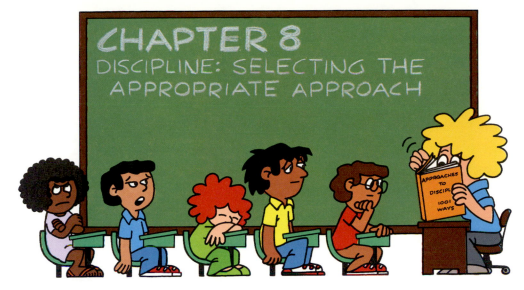

CHAPTER 8
DISCIPLINE: SELECTING THE APPROPRIATE APPROACH

How can I choose the most effective approach to specific discipline problems?

What are some other approaches to discipline besides reflective listening, I-messages, exploring alternatives, and natural and logical consequences?

If I must remove a student from the group, what is the most effective way to do it?

What are some effective approaches to typical misbehavior?

Understanding the goals of behavior, learning to encourage, listening and responding sensitively, involving students in decisions, and applying logical consequences are all ways to approach discipline as part of a total learning environment. They are all ways to initiate constructive behavior, as well as to respond effectively to misbehavior. They all help us emphasize the positive and expect the best.

Which Approach Shall I Use?

The communication skills of reflective listening, I-messages, and exploring alternatives have great value as approaches to misbehavior. Reflective listening helps students feel understood and often paves the way for exploring alternatives. I-messages describe our feelings without blaming or placing demands on students. Exploring alternatives helps students examine all possible ways of solving a problem. Used along with a system of natural and logical consequences, these procedures allow us to promote self-discipline and personal responsibility.

Encouragement is the key to any approach. Communicating faith, recognizing any improvement, stressing assets, separating the deed from the doer, emphasizing the courage to be imperfect, being both firm and friendly — encouragement is the most important ingredient in preventing and dealing with misbehavior.

Your most effective approach to discipline requires you to:

1. *Determine the goal of misbehavior.* The approach you choose must fit the student's goal or you may reinforce the misbehavior. Repeated use of reflective listening with an attention-seeker, for example, gives that student undue attention. If you explore alternatives and find students returning with the same problem, they may have learned that problems get your attention. Express faith in students' ability to solve problems on their own. Be sure they don't feel you will only talk with them if they have a problem.

In a power or revenge struggle, it helps to withdraw from the conflict and wait until you and the student are calm. At a later time you may want to use reflective listening, if you're sure you aren't reinforcing mistaken goals. Exploring alternatives, especially with students whose relationship with you has improved, offers students an active role in formulating new goals and redirecting energy.

Reflective listening can be especially useful with students who display inadequacy. It helps them understand their feelings about themselves. In some cases, the understanding encourages them to explore alternatives with you.

I-messages can be effective with attention-seekers at the time of misbehavior and during non-conflict times with students seeking power and revenge. However, like reflective listening, I-messages can be overdone. Be sensitive to students' responses when you use any approach.

When I-messages don't work, logical consequences are in order. For example, if Lee is leaning back in his chair, you might say: "When you lean back in your chair, I get nervous because you might fall and hurt yourself." If Lee continues to lean back, you could give him a choice: "I'm sorry but leaning back in your chair is dangerous. Please sit properly or I'll have to remove the chair until you're ready to use it correctly."

Allowing natural consequences to happen is appropriate for any goal, provided the situation isn't dangerous. We needn't get involved at all — we just let the consequences occur. Logical consequences, however, work best with students seeking attention; the approach gives attention in unexpected ways. Students displaying inadequacy need extra doses of encouragement from a teacher who won't give up on them, so logical consequences are less appropriate. However, once these students begin to respond to our encouragement, we can set up learning contracts with them.

Students seeking power and revenge may interpret logical consequences as punishment. They're frequently unable to see anything "logical" about you or your actions toward them. We can devise logical consequences for such students, but we must be especially careful and observant.

Discipline is most effective when it fits the goal of misbehavior. We can individualize our teaching by tailoring our discipline to individual students and specific situations.

2. *Decide who owns the problem.* Student-owned problems may be handled differently than teacher-owned problems. Reflective listening focuses on students' feelings and so is useful for students' problems. I-messages focus on our feelings, our problems. We can explore alternatives to help students solve their own problems of misbehavior or motivation, or to negotiate an agreement with a student whose misbehavior is interfering with our or others' rights or safety.

Natural consequences can solve student-owned problems; logical consequences may apply to either student-owned or teacher-owned problems.

3. *Recognize that more than one approach can apply.* A combination may be necessary. When Millie tells you how upset she is about the group she associates with, your reflective listening response can lead to exploring alternatives with her. Sometimes you'll use all four approaches. For example, suppose you've negotiated an agreement with Kevin about his behavior in the library. You used reflective listening and I-messages as you explored alternatives with him. Together, you decided on the appropriate consequences in case Kevin broke your agreement. You used all four approaches, as you do during class problem-solving discussions.

4. *Choose an approach based on your experience with it.* It's always best to use methods you feel comfortable with and find effective. Some students will respond best to reflective listening, others to I-messages. Use the approach that makes sense for particular students and situations.

Some situations will call for logical consequences, rather than I-messages. However, as your relationships with students improve, you may find that you rarely have to use consequences, that students respond well to I-messages.

Other Approaches

Experiment with other techniques of discipline, either in place of the four main approaches mentioned or in combination with them.

Give permission to misbehave. No matter what the goal of misbehavior, humor can be an effective antidote. Humor, free of sarcasm or ridicule, is unexpected. Since misbehaving students expect us to punish them, we can surprise them and so fail to reinforce their goals. When we actually "permit" misbehavior, we often reduce its attractiveness.

Let's say that Arnold is your attention-getter. He continually calls out answers. You have a conference with him and ask, "Could it be you want to keep me busy with you?" Arnold's recognition reflex tells you you're correct. You ask him how many times he thinks he needs your attention each day. He replies, "Five." You agree to pay attention to him five times each day. Then, after each answer he shouts out, you say, "Arnold, 1, " "Arnold, 2," and so on to five. After the fifth time, you ignore Arnold's bids for attention. See how quickly Arnold stops his shouting out when he realizes you're not responding as he wants you to (Dreikurs, Grunwald, and Pepper, 1971).

Suppose Melba throws paper airplanes. During her free time, you have her make 20 airplanes and throw them. Then she must pick them up. She'll soon tire of this way of getting attention.

However, if Melba throws airplanes for power, rather than attention, you could be inviting a power contest. Instead, command her in a *respectful* and *humorous* way to do what she's already doing. Order her to continue her misbehavior: "Melba, please don't throw airplanes while I'm in the room. Whenever I leave the room, make sure you throw at least 25." Melba's bid for power will probably end with that unexpected remark; had you ordered her to stop, she would probably have defied you.

To the power-seeking student who refuses to work, say, "Vernon, I'm going to pass out the worksheets now, but I don't want you to do the work." Or respond to Vernon in another unexpected way:

Vernon: I'm not going to do that worksheet and you can't make me!

Teacher: (walking away) Okay.

Since you refuse to fight with him, he may decide to do the work! Remember to keep sarcasm out of your voice and manner.

Acknowledge the student's power. Power-seekers are out to prove we can't make them do anything. They'd like to make us look bad. To thwart this goal, admit defeat ("You're too strong for me. I can't make you do anything.") or say to the class, "Carlotta's very powerful and it looks like we can't make her join our discussion" (Dreikurs, Grunwald, and Pepper, 1971).

If Oscar likes to correct you, thereby embarrassing you as a form of revenge, admit he succeeded. "You really got me that time." "I guess you're right. Sometimes I can be pretty dumb." These words are easier to say without sarcasm when we realize that students like Oscar want us to feel hurt enough to retaliate. Our feelings aren't hurt when we simply "agree." After their revenge falls flat, revenge-seekers may in time become more receptive to a trusting relationship.

Acknowledge the power of students who try to disrupt discussions by arguing unnecessarily. Simply reflect their opinions and feelings ("You feel strongly about that"); then state your own opinion or call for responses from the class. Acknowledge that everyone has a right to an opinion and move on. Or quietly tell the student, "You could be right but I feel differently." Then move on.

Create alternatives by turning a minus into a plus. Direct negative or destructive behavior into positive, constructive channels. Ask the student who draws on the wall to join the bulletin board committee. Combine this approach with logical consequences where you can. The student who draws on the walls to attract your attention can be required to clean the walls. However, if the student seeks power or revenge, he or she would balk at your requirement. So just asking such a student to join the bulletin board committee may work best. (If the misbehavior continues, you may have to remove the student from the group, your classroom, or the school, or assign a staff escort.)

Other ways to create positive alternatives:

Robert gets attention by not working. Notice him when he *is* working.

Lorraine is so disorganized she can never find anything. You put her in charge of keeping the classroom's magazines organized.

Stewart is the ringleader for most classroom disturbances. You appoint him chairman of the UNICEF committee.

Raymond is a bully. You have him use his strength to help move the risers on and off the stage.

Shanda is mean and revengeful. You cast her as the gentle heroine in your class play.

Gretchen is discouraged about her poor reading ability. She loves animals. You ask her to research the history of zoos, providing her with books she can read easily.

Be alert for ways to encourage misbehaving or disgruntled students. Give them specific ways to succeed.

Removing a Student from the Group

Some behavior is so disruptive it requires us to remove the student from the group, the classroom, even the building. But this radical form of discipline needn't be resorted to out of despair. We can still present the student with a choice. The logical consequence of seriously disrupting the group is leaving the group. "I'm sorry, Dinah, but your behavior is disturbing us. You may settle down and stay with us or leave the group."

Students aren't learning what we're teaching while they're out of the room, but what are they learning while they're disturbing the class? What are the other students learning? Removing a student is a last resort, but teachers need to have this option. We don't always have to remove students from the *room;* sometimes it helps simply to have them sit by themselves. We can, in fact, work with five different kinds of removal (Thompson and Poppen,1972). The level we use depends on the student's goal and reactions. The levels are not necessarily sequential.

Level 1. The student moves to another part of the room, away from the people being disturbed.

For example, Terry disturbs his reading circle by tapping his feet. You offer him a choice: "Terry, either stop tapping your feet or leave the reading circle." If he continues tapping, you accept his decision: "I see you've decided to leave the reading circle. You may return to your group when you're ready to cooperate." You designate an area of the room where Terry can sit.

If Terry returns to the group but continues tapping, it's time for you to decide how long he must stay away. If you again say, "Come back when you're ready," Terry may return too early. Terry's time alone needs to be long enough to make an impact on his behavior. Each time he misbehaves, you extend the time out.

Level 2. The student goes to a part of the room where he or she can't see the group, perhaps behind a partition like a portable chalkboard. Eye contact may continue to reinforce the misbehavior.

If you've already used level 1 with a misbehaving student, then don't say, "Come back when you're ready." Terry has already had the opportunity to control his removal time. Simply tell him you will come for him in a while to see if he's ready.

Level 3. The student goes to a place outside the classroom, either to another classroom or to some other supervised place in the building.

Obviously, this level requires the cooperation of other staff members, unless placing Terry outside your door is sufficient. Another

teacher may permit Terry to sit in the back of her or his classroom; sometimes removal to another social group works, since Terry's misbehavior may not be reinforced there. Your principal may permit you to send misbehaving students to the office, not for punishment but simply as a place to go.

When misbehavior fails to stop with levels 1 and 2, we need to be able to remove a student from the classroom. Level 3 is for students who only require occasional removal, whose behavior changes after a few separations.

Level 4. The student is systematically removed to a designated "time-out" place in the building every time he or she misbehaves.

This level is for students who engage the teacher in numerous conflicts throughout the day, the severely disruptive class members. Such students often start with minor infractions we attempt to correct or ignore, and gradually snowball their misbehavior until we become too angry to respond appropriately. Such students must not be fought with or given in to. Instead, we eliminate all conflict. We make no attempt to force the student to work. After the behavior improves, we negotiate a learning contract, if necessary, but first we concentrate on the disruptive behavior. We remove the student at the *first* sign of disturbing behavior.

We explain our plan to the student in a conference, held during a non-conflict time. We prepare for the conference by listing all the actions the student does that concern us.

At the conference, we say: "Terry, you and I haven't been getting along too well lately. We've been fighting about your behavior, but I've decided to stop fighting with you. I can't make you work or behave unless you want to. So I'm going to let you be your own boss. Maybe that way you can help yourself.

"From now on, you can do whatever you want as long as you don't disturb the rest of us. When you do things like . . . (here, read your list) . . . you disturb us. You're telling us that you've decided to leave the room.

"I've arranged with Mrs. Brubaker for a place by the office where you can go. If your behavior shows you've decided to leave our class, I'll hand you a 'time-out pass' and you'll go to that place. You can take paper, a book, or your work with you if you want, but you don't have to. You'll stay in that place until I come and check whether you're ready to return to us. If you don't have any questions, I'll show you where you're to go."

Let Terry decide how to respond. If he starts to argue, just go on without responding to the argument. Pretend he is listening. Prepare several time-out passes so you won't have to talk when Terry misbehaves; talking may only aggravate the conflict.

The *first* time Terry does any of the things on the list, silently hand him a time-out pass. Have written on the slip "15 minutes" or "30 minutes," depending on the student's age. Increase the time by 15 minutes every time Terry misbehaves. (Establish a maximum of 1½ - 2 hours for older students, 45 minutes for younger ones.)

If he misbehaves just before gym, music, art, or recess, and complains because he must miss the period, say, "I hope you'll get to go tomorrow." If he misbehaves in ways that aren't on your list, add to the list and show him the additions during a brief conference.

It will help to have a conference with Terry's parents so they understand why you've found it necessary to remove Terry from the classroom in this manner. Explain that you allow Terry to take work or other materials with him so his removal won't seem like punishment. If they resist your method, explain the procedures you've tried without success. If they continue to resist, you and your principal may decide to give them the option of this plan or Terry's suspension.

When we systematically remove students from the classroom, we stop any conflict before it starts. We neither argue nor fight. Students gradually learn to manage their own behavior. They know exactly what will show their decision to leave the classroom and what will allow them to stay.

When they're behaving appropriately, remember to notice and encourage them. Be friendly and accepting. Let Terry know it is his *behavior,* not him as a person, that you and the class find unacceptable.

Level 5. Some students are too disruptive to stay in school. They are often suspended or even expelled, revengeful procedures frequently resorted to in desperation. Suspended or expelled students are rarely motivated to return to school; if they do return, they often adopt the goal of revenge. Instead of suspension or expulsion, experiment with a "homebound systematic removal plan" (Keirsey, 1969). This plan has the same rationale and procedures as level 4, except the student goes home when he or she misbehaves.

This plan must involve the principal and the parents (and you'll want to check your school district's policy on due process). You and your principal first hold individual conferences with the parents, other staff members involved, and the student, explaining the reasons for the plan.

Follow these guidelines for the conference with the student:

1. Let Terry know you understand his feelings about school: "I imagine it's pretty miserable being nagged and bossed around."
2. Tell him he won't be nagged or bossed around anymore. From now on, he'll be his own boss, as long as he doesn't bother anyone.
3. Explain that if Terry does bother others, he'll be showing everyone that he's decided to take the rest of the day off. He'll go home and relax, returning the next day for another chance at school. He has a choice. He can stop bothering others and stay in school, or he can go home.
4. Advise Terry of his upcoming conference with his parents, teachers, counselor, and principal. Assure him that only the principal and Terry will talk. The others will be there to learn what they're to do in upholding their part of the agreement. Tell him no one is interested in punishing him. Everyone wants to help him get along better in school.

Following the individual conferences, all involved parties, including the student, meet to discuss the way the plan will work. The principal directs this conference and may wish to type up planned remarks to read or refer to. For example:

"We've called this meeting because Terry has been having a lot of difficulties in school and it looks as though we just don't know how to help him. We've all agreed that Terry is the only one who can decide to change his behavior. And we realize, Terry, that sometimes you're pretty miserable at school with people trying to tell you what to do.

"So we've all agreed to be friendly towards you and to help you only if you want help. We're not going to bug you about your behavior or your work. You're going to be your own boss. You can do anything you please as long as your behavior doesn't bother anyone or harm others or yourself. If you decide to bother or harm anyone, your teacher will hand you one of these passes. You'll bring it to the office and we'll call your father or mother to come and get you. Do you understand so far? Any questions?" (If Terry refuses to answer any questions, tell him you assume he understands. Then proceed.)

"Terry, here's a list of those things that will let us know you've decided to take some time off from school. Follow along with me as I read it and ask questions if you have any."

(After each point, ask Terry if he understands. At the end, ask him to repeat the kinds of unacceptable behavior you've listed. Again, if he refuses to talk or begins to argue, simply proceed.)

"We'll know you've decided to leave us when you:

1. Interfere in any way with the teacher's job of teaching. You'll be interfering when you talk without permission, make *any* kind of noise, talk back, throw a temper tantrum, call the teacher names, hide, or make messes.
2. Leave your seat without permission, unless you're changing classes at the appropriate time.
3. Start fights.
4. Throw things.
5. Misuse other people's property or school property. You'll be misusing property when you take or destroy anything, jump or climb on chairs, tables, or sinks, tip chairs, or write on furniture or walls.

"In case you're worrying about your parents punishing you when you get home, you can stop worrying because they've agreed not to. Isn't that right, Mr. and Mrs. Bechtle? When you get home you can read, watch TV, or do anything else you'd normally do on a day off from school. Your parents have also agreed not to talk with you about your leaving school unless you bring it up.

"Maybe you're wondering what will happen if you refuse to leave the classroom. You're thinking, 'Other kids fool around. How come I'm the only one who has to leave?' Just remember there's a difference between you and the other students. You are in charge of your own behavior. They are not. You know exactly what will happen when you misbehave. If you must leave the classroom, it's because you've *chosen* to leave.

"We'd like you to leave on your own. If you refuse, your teacher will call me and we'll arrange to carry you out, if necessary. If we have to do that, though, you'll need to go home for three days instead of just one, because you'll be disrupting the classroom and the office. You'll also need to stay home three days if you don't bring us a 'Time Out From School' pass, or if you do anything dangerous or disrupting as you leave the classroom, or if you don't arrive at the office within five minutes of leaving the classroom, because then we'll have to spend time looking for you."

Ask Terry to repeat the behavior that will result in his staying home three days. If he refuses, proceed.

"It's up to you, Terry. If you behave properly you can stay. If you decide not to behave, you will need to leave. Do you have any questions?"

Terry may well tire of this procedure. He'll get no reinforcement for his misbehavior from teachers, administrators, or parents. He'll be removed from his social group at school. He won't be "punished"; he'll simply be excluded from school, a logical consequence of his decision to misbehave.

Guidelines for Removing Students from the Group

At any of the five levels, the following guidelines apply:

1. The student has a *choice* of behaving appropriately or leaving the group.
2. The student is presented the choice verbally only *once*. We can easily get trapped into too much talk. If misbehavior recurs after the student has been removed once, assume the student knows the options and act on that assumption: "I see you've decided to leave the group." With levels 4 and 5, the choice has been set up in advance and no words are needed.
3. Act at the first sign of disturbance. Once you've decided that removal is the only reasonable option (and it should be a last resort), don't allow second chances at the time of removal. Let students take the consequences of their own chosen behavior.
4. Negotiate consequences if you can. Ask, "What do you think would be a fair thing for us to do if you disrupt the class?" If the disturbance is minor (levels 1 and 2), you may not need to negotiate. Level 3 is a good place to talk with students. You may be able to negotiate with certain students at levels 4 and 5.
5. Once the student's behavior shows he or she has chosen to leave, the decision stands. The student then can decide whether to leave willingly or be "escorted." Ask, "Would you like to go on your own or shall I help you?" If the student is too big for you to escort, or if he or she resists, you may need to call on other staff members: "Would you like to go on your own or shall I call Mr. Hernandez to assist you?" In level 5, and sometimes in level 4, plans for an escort are built into the procedure.
6. Most important, remain *friendly* as well as *firm*.

Corrective discipline, then, can be an integral part of a democratic classroom. We can discipline for the purpose of increasing students' self-discipline. By listening sensitively, responding clearly, and offering logical choices, through individual, small-group, and class discussions, we promote personal responsibility.

Typical Misbehavior and Effective Approaches

The following typical situations use the four main approaches and some additional methods. Most of these problems could also be handled through individual and small-group conferences, and in class discussions. The alternatives listed could be suggested by students or teachers.

Problem: Smart talk, insults, swearing, obscene gestures.
Probable goals: Attention, power, revenge.
Problem owner: You and the class.

Some alternatives

If for attention:

1. Ignore. Be unimpressed, as if you didn't hear the comment or see the gesture.
2. Use reflective listening to calm the student down and reach agreement.
3. Give permission. Invite swearing students to tell you privately all the swear words they know. Ask younger students to explain the words they used. (This can be hilarious since their meanings often aren't the right ones!)
4. If the misbehavior continues, hold a conference, giving the student the choice of stopping the misbehavior or leaving the class for a while.

If for power or revenge:

1. Be unimpressed. Walk away or busy yourself with other tasks.
2. Use reflective listening and negotiate.
3. If the misbehavior continues, hold a conference, giving the

choice of stopping the misbehavior or leaving the class for a while.

Problem: Disruptive behavior (shouting out, whispering, throwing things, constantly leaving seat, etc.).
Probable goals: Attention, power, revenge.
Problem owner: You and the class.

Some alternatives

If for attention:

1. Ignore or send an I-message.
2. Give permission for students to bid for attention a limited number of times per day.
3. Create alternatives by noticing when the student is behaving appropriately or by saying, "I will only call on those who raise their hands."
4. If misbehavior continues, remove the student from the group, using the level of removal best suited to the situation.

If for power:

1. Acknowledge the student's power and ask the class to help: "I can't teach. What shall we do?"
2. Create alternatives by putting the student in charge of something.
3. If misbehavior continues, remove the student from the group, using the level of removal best suited to the situation.

If for revenge:

1. Build a trusting relationship by treating the student in a friendly way.
2. Hold a class discussion and enlist the help of the other students.
3. Ask volunteer "buddies" to take turns bringing the student back into the group.
4. If misbehavior continues, remove the student from the group, using the level of removal best suited to the situation.

Problem: Tattling.
Probable goals: Attention directed to teacher. ("See how good I am and how bad she is.") Power directed at teacher. ("I'll make you take care of my problem.") Revenge directed at student tattled on, using teacher as weapon.
Problem owner: Tattling student and student being tattled on.

Some alternatives

All goals:

1. Discuss with the class the difference between tattling and reporting possible danger. Tell them you'll ignore tattling, since the problem is between the students involved.
2. With young students, create alternatives by inviting them to tell good things about one another. When a student reports something good, draw a smiling face and write both students' names under it.

Problem: Cheating.
Probable goals: Attention, power, revenge, display of inadequacy.
Problem owner: Students involved. But you have an obligation to discourage cheating.

Some alternatives

If for attention, power, or revenge:

Give students a choice. Since each did only half the work, they can either take half the grade or do a makeup test or activity during their own time. Each student may choose either alternative.

Note: Even though one student may have done all or most of the work, treat them equally. It takes two to cheat. If one or both of them choose to make up the work, it could be a bit inconvenient for you. But they also will be inconvenienced and will probably stop cheating.

If for display of inadequacy:

The student may be under tremendous pressure. Discuss the problem with the student and possibly the parents. Explore alternatives. Plan success experiences for the student by setting achievable goals.

Problem: Lying.
Probable goals: Attention (to impress you), power or revenge (to evade punishment, to fool you), display of inadequacy (to escape tasks the student feels incapable of doing).
Problem owner: You and the class if the lie is disrupting or interferes with rights. The student if the lie harms no one.

Some alternatives

General procedures for all goals:

1. Don't challenge a lie. The student will rarely confess and may retaliate.
2. Avoid creating conditions that invite lying. ("Did you throw that spitball?")
3. Realize that students may learn lying from adults' "little white lies."

If for attention:

1. Act on the truth, rather than challenging or giving the opportunity to lie. If you see Aaron with paint on his hands, don't ask him if he's spilled the paint. Ask him to clean up.
2. Be unimpressed with exaggeration. Later, discuss with the class why people exaggerate.
3. Create alternatives by giving attention for constructive behavior.

If for power or revenge:

1. Acknowledge the student's power: give an unexpected response by admitting how gullible you can be.
2. Even if you know or suspect strongly that the student has misbehaved, proceed on the available evidence only. If paint is spilled, ask a volunteer to clean up. This gives the misbehaving student no opportunity to lie.

If for display of inadequacy:

Treat as you do cheating. Discuss the problem with the student and possibly the parents. Explore alternatives. Create success experiences.

Problem: Stealing.
Probable goals: Attention, power, revenge.

Note: Young children may steal because they haven't learned the difference between "mine and thine." Impoverished students may steal for survival (at least as they see it). Some may steal for the excitement of it, for the attention of adults and peers, for power, or for revenge. The following considers stealing as related to attention, power, and revenge.

Problem owner: You. Members stolen from.

Some alternatives

If for attention:

1. The student will make sure to be caught. Simply remove the item and return it to the owner without comment.
2. Create alternatives by noticing the student for constructive behavior and by involving the class: "Look at the picture Lance has drawn!"

If for power:

1. If the student wants to be caught to show you he or she can't be stopped, simply return the item to the owner without comment.
2. Create alternatives by finding useful ways for the student to use power. Put the student who steals money in charge of class funds or collecting lunch money. Put the student who steals books in charge of returning books to the library.
3. If the student wants to demonstrate power by being a "mystery thief," acknowledge to the class that the unknown student does have power and has won. Emphasize that you'll not play detective. You're only interested in having the articles returned. Arrange for the mystery thief to return the items anonymously.

If for revenge:

1. If the student wants to be caught and punished so the cycle of revenge can continue, return the object to the owner without comment. Build a trusting relationship, enlist "buddies," get the group's cooperation in helping the student.
2. If the student wants a private revenge, tell the class that the unknown student has the ability to hurt people's feelings and no one can force this student to stop taking things. Treat as a "mystery thief" and arrange for the items to be returned anonymously.

Note: Always discuss with the class how they can protect their belongings.

Problem: Improper conduct on the bus (pushing, fighting, leaving seat, etc.).
Probable goals: Attention, power, revenge.
Problem owner: You if you're expected to remedy the situation and if safety is involved.

Some alternatives

All goals:

Disruptive behavior becomes a safety problem. Ask the bus driver to identify all students involved. Let all share the responsibility to avoid resentment. Deny students the privilege of riding the bus for a few days. Increase the time they can't ride, if necessary.

Problem: Verbal or physical fighting between students.
Probable goals: Attention, power, or revenge directed at teacher. Attention directed at rest of group. Power or revenge directed at antagonist.
Problem owner: Students involved. You if the fight is disruptive or dangerous, although the actual disagreement belongs to students. Avoid reinforcing mistaken goals by taking away students' responsibility for solving their own problems. Whenever possible, let students settle their own disputes.

Some alternatives

If verbal, and for attention, power, or revenge:

Let students who complain about each other settle their own disputes. Tell them to do this only once; ignore future complaints.

If physical, and for attention, power, or revenge:

On the playground, if the fighters aren't attracting a crowd, ignore them and deprive them of an audience. Or establish a "no fighting" rule: students who fight are demonstrating their decision to "sit on the sidelines" until they're ready to stop fighting. They can spend their time discussing how to get along if they choose to.

If students fight in the building, establish a place for them to talk over their conflicts. With young students, designate two chairs the "talk-it-over chairs." Let students work out their problems independently. Stay silent and uninvolved. Your only concern is that they stay away from the group until they're ready to stop fighting.

Accept any solution (except fighting), including complete silence while they're supposedly "talking it over." If they return too soon, say, "I see you've still not decided how to get along. Please leave the group and decide how you'll get along. I'll come over in a few minutes to see if you've solved your problem and are ready to return." Keep returning students to the negotiation area if fighting continues, gradually increasing the time away.

Separate students who are too angry to negotiate. Say, "I can see that you two need to cool off. Christine, you go _____ and Geraldine, you go _____ . I'll check with you in a while to see if you're ready to talk it over or return to the classroom."

Problem: Crying.
Probable goals: Attention, power, revenge, display of inadequacy.

Note: Crying can also reflect an appropriate emotion.

Problem owner: The student. You and the class if the crying is disruptive.

Some alternatives

If for an appropriate emotion:

Use reflective listening and explore alternatives to help the student cope.

If for attention:

1. Reflect feelings or ignore, if frequent.
2. Express faith in student's ability to solve the problem.
3. Create alternatives by involving the student in an activity or project.

If for power or revenge:

1. If you feel you can negotiate, reflect feelings and explore alternatives.
2. Say, "I'll be glad to talk with you when you're ready to discuss it calmly." Then walk away or busy yourself with other tasks.
3. If the crying is disruptive, remove the student from the class or divert the class by arranging an activity for them.

If for display of inadequacy:

Students will not come to you; you'll notice them crying and will need to go to them. Such behavior may be for attention so check your feelings and your experience with the students.

1. Use reflective listening and explore alternatives.
2. Create alternatives by encouraging any sign of progress.

Problem: Disruption and destruction in rest rooms.
Probable goals: Attention, power, revenge.
Problem owner: You. Students also if they complain.

Some alternatives

If making noise, and for attention:

1. Send an I-message about your concern.
2. Remove noisy students from the rest room until others have used the facility. If necessary, have noisy students use the rest room one at a time. If the problem continues, have them use the rest room last for a day or two — longer, if the behavior continues.

If making noise, and for power or revenge:

Escort students or ask other staff members to escort them. Allow students to use the rest room unescorted when they're ready to be orderly.

If leaving rest room messy, and for attention:

Have the students involved clean up. If you don't know who the messy students are, the group shares the responsibility for cleaning up.

If leaving rest room messy, and for power or revenge:

Don't aggravate the conflict by asking students to clean up. Instead, use escorts.

If damaging rest room, any goal:

Have students make restitution.

Note: If this problem remains chronic and nothing seems to work, use staff escorts whenever the group uses the rest room. Establish rotating cleaning committees so students may influence each other to correct the problem.

Works Cited

Dreikurs, Rudolf; Grunwald, Bronia; and Pepper, Floy. *Maintaining Sanity in the Classroom.* NY: Harper & Row, 1971. 2nd ed., 1980.

Keirsey, David W. "Systematic Exclusion: Eliminating Chronic Classroom Disruptions." In *Behavioral Counseling,* edited by John D. Krumboltz and Carl E. Thoresen. NY: Holt, Rinehart and Winston, 1969.

Thompson, Charles, and Poppen, William. *For Those Who Care: Ways of Relating to Youth.* Columbus, OH: Charles E. Merrill, 1972.

Recommended Readings

Carlson, Jon. *The Basics of Discipline.* Coral Springs, FL: CMTI Press, 1978.

Spiel, Oskar. *Discipline Without Punishment.* London: Faber and Faber, 1962.

Thompson, Charles, and Poppen, William. *For Those Who Care: Ways of Relating to Youth.* Columbus, OH: Charles E. Merrill, 1972.

Study Questions

1. How can determining the goal of misbehavior help you choose the most effective approach to discipline? What goal(s) is best handled with reflective listening? I-messages? Natural consequences? Logical consequences?

2. In what way is encouragement the key to any approach? How do we show an encouraging attitude?

3. How can you best approach student-owned problems? Teacher-owned problems? When is reflective listening inappropriate for student-owned problems?

4. What are some things to be aware of when using I-messages? If an I-message doesn't work and you follow with a consequence, what must you keep in mind?

5. Describe a situation calling for a combination of approaches.

6. How do we "give permission to misbehave"? Why is this approach effective in certain situations? Describe a situation from your classroom in which this approach would apply.

7. How can acknowledging the student's power thwart the goals of power and revenge? Describe a situation from your classroom in which this approach would apply.

8. How can we "turn a minus into a plus"? Give some examples of creating positive alternatives for students in your classroom.

9. When is removal from the group necessary? Briefly describe your understanding of each of the five levels of removal.

10. What are the guidelines for removing students from the group?

11. Discuss effective approaches to "smart talk," disruptive behavior, tattling, cheating, lying, stealing, improper conduct on the bus, fighting, crying, disruption and destruction in rest rooms.

Problem Situation

Jeff is a student who operates on his own schedule, regardless of the expectations of authority. The class has had a required project that each student has worked on for a month. You've reminded Jeff several times that he hasn't even begun the assignment. When you call for the projects, Jeff gives you a defiant grin. He has no project.

1. What is the purpose of Jeff's behavior?
2. What may be the source of his discouragement?
3. How would your communication skills be best used with Jeff?
4. What would be a logical consequence for his not having the project finished?

Activity for the Week

Practice selecting appropriate approaches to classroom challenges. Bring examples of the approaches you chose.

Recommended Resource Book Material

Chapters 1-8, stories for group discussion; Chapter 5, "Separate the deed from the doer"; Chapter 12, "Individual student misbehavior"; Chapter 13.

Chart 8

Effective Approaches to Classroom Challenges

Approach	Purpose	Example
Reflective listening.	Communicating understanding of students' feelings about problems they face.	"You feel very sad because your friend says he doesn't like you anymore."
I-message.	Communicating your feelings to students about how their behavior affects you.	(To the class) "When you are not interested in my lesson, I feel very discouraged because I've worked hard to prepare it."
Exploring alternatives.	Helping students decide how to solve a problem they own or negotiating agreements with students for teacher-owned problems.	"What are some ways you could solve your problem?" Or, "How could we settle our disagreement?"
Natural and logical consequences.	Allowing students within limits to decide how they will behave and permitting them to experience the results of their decisions.	Natural: Students who fight may get hurt. Logical: Students who fight go to the talk-it-over area.
Giving permission to misbehave.	Doing the unexpected by permitting misbehavior under certain conditions.	A student who swears is invited to go to a corner of the room to practice swearing.
Acknowledging the student's power.	Admitting defeat or vulnerability in an effort to defuse the student's attempt to overpower, get revenge, or show superiority.	"You've proved your point. I can't force you to work."
Creating alternatives: turning a minus into a plus.	Channeling misbehavior and mistaken goals in constructive directions.	The student who uses humor to disrupt can be put in charge of a comic classroom play.

Recording Worksheet

Selecting the Appropriate Approach

As you listen to each scene, consider the student's goal, the problem ownership, and the appropriate approaches a teacher might use. Be prepared to discuss your responses with the group.

NOTES

Chapter 8

Points to Remember

1. The four main approaches to classroom discipline are reflective listening, I-messages, exploring alternatives, and natural and logical consequences.

2. Encouragement is the key to any method of discipline.

3. To determine the most effective approach to a particular discipline problem:
- Determine the goal of misbehavior.
- Decide who owns the problem.
- Recognize that more than one approach can apply.
- Choose an approach based on your experience with it.

4. Giving permission to misbehave lets humor serve as an unexpected response to misbehavior.

5. Acknowledging the goals of power-seeking or revenge-seeking students thwarts their goals.

6. Creating alternatives by turning a minus into a plus directs negative or destructive behavior into positive, constructive channels.

7. Sometimes we must remove a student from the group, the room, or the building. Removal can be presented as a logical consequence of disruptive misbehavior.

8. Five levels of removal are:
Level 1. The student moves to another part of the room.
Level 2. The student goes to a part of the room where he or she can't see the group.
Level 3. The student goes to a place outside the classroom.
Level 4. The student is systematically removed to a designated "time-out" place in the building every time he or she misbehaves.
Level 5. The student goes home when he or she misbehaves.

9. When removing a student at any of the five levels:
- Offer the student a choice.
- Present the choice verbally only once.
- Act at the first sign of disturbance.
- Negotiate consequences if you can.
- Let the decision stand.
- Remain friendly as well as firm.

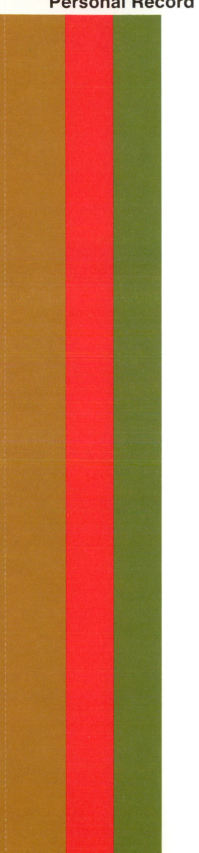

Personal Record Chapter 8

1. My experience with the weekly assignment

2. My reactions to the reading

3. Topics to discuss with the group

4. Skills I intend to improve

5. My beliefs which impede progress

6. My successes in applying program ideas

7. My difficulties in applying program ideas

8. My progress this week: A specific example

9. This week I learned

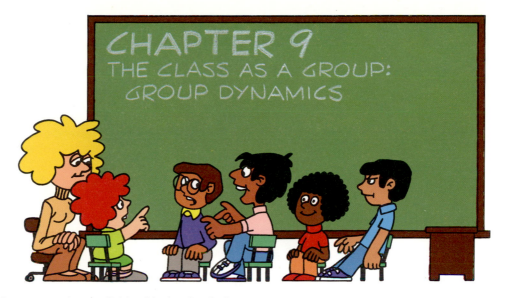

CHAPTER 9
THE CLASS AS A GROUP:
GROUP DYNAMICS

How can the principles governing individual behavior help me
understand the behavior of groups?
How can I build a cohesive group?
How can I direct peer pressures toward the common good?
Which therapeutic group forces can I learn to identify and promote?

Understanding the individual student is important. Yet the goals of our students become clearer when we consider the *social meaning* of behavior. Although most of our teaching experience is with groups, we receive far less training in group leadership than we do in individual instruction. Working *with* the group rather than *against* it can help us influence individuals more easily. Our students are members of a group, they want to feel they belong in that group, and we need to understand how groups work.

Students As Group Members

Some of the principles governing the behavior of individuals help us understand the behavior of individuals in groups:

1. *Students are social beings.* Like people of every age, our students want to belong to a group. The family, the class, the peer group, the team, and the club: Students only feel secure when they're part of or identified with groups.

2. *All behavior has social meaning and purpose.* When Sarah decides, ''I'll only do what I want,'' she establishes her place in the class just as much as Tom does when he decides, ''I'll only do what the teacher wants.'' The behavior and misbehavior we see in our classrooms reflect students' efforts to create a unique identity within the group. The goals they adopt, whether they're aware of them or not, express their beliefs about how they belong to the classroom group.

3. *Behavior reflects lifestyle.* A student's goals express that individual's unique interpretation of where she or he stands in relation to others. Sarah may *say* she wants to cooperate, but her passive resistance to all instructions speaks louder than her words. Students' psychological movement, their goal-directed behavior, and the way they get along with their peers can reveal the purpose of their behavior. We can see what students want and so understand their goals. What people *do* is more significant than what they *say*.

4. Students can learn to feel more accepted by cooperating with others than by fighting with others. The stimulation of our students' *social interest* (Adler, 1938), their willingness to cooperate with others for the common good, is essential to their growth and development. When our students learn to feel accepted by working for the good of the class, they help us create a cohesive classroom atmosphere.

It's easy to see why developing skills for dealing with the class as a group can make us better teachers. We can become the victim of group expectations, pressures, and forces, or we can understand and use group dynamics in a democratic, encouraging way.

Group Dynamics

We need to understand and *use* the group forces in our classroom. Only then will we teach cooperative students who care about each other. Students can be taught that cooperation meets their own goals better than competition. They can come to benefit from peer support and encouragement. They can make choices that benefit themselves *and* the group.

Group dynamics can tell us why students seek attention, power, or revenge, why they display inadequacy. Assuming that all behavior has a social purpose, we can learn to redirect our students' energies toward cooperation and useful behavior. We can then avoid reinforcing their mistaken goals. Much of the time our students misbehave for our "benefit."

Once we gain the respect and cooperation of our class, we can encourage students to help those who misbehave find ways to belong that benefit the whole class. Misbehaving students can learn that they need not be uncooperative to establish their significance.

Building a Cohesive Group

We want a group that cares about its members and works together. Yet because students sometimes have mistaken goals, our classroom can be a place of conflict and excessive competition. The skills explored earlier — reflective listening, I-messages, exploring alternatives, logical consequences — along with the vital process of encouragement, can create the satisfying, constructive atmosphere of a democratic classroom. Students who feel they belong and are accepted work together; they don't need to establish their identities through misbehavior.

A class without social interest is filled with competition, selfishness, a concern for the individual, and "vertical" or superior to inferior relationships among students and between students and teacher. A socially interested class cooperates, encourages each other, works for the good of the group, and maintains the mutual respect needed for "horizontal" or equal relationships.

You can help build a cohesive group.

Peer encouragement. The group can become a force for recognizing and encouraging positive behavior. If Jackie plays the clown, you might ask the class, "Why do you suppose Jackie is doing that?" Their perceptions will probably be accurate: "She wants us to notice her" or "She wants to make us laugh at her." Then you can ask, "How else could Jackie get our attention or get us to laugh without disturbing us?" Jackie can be brought into the discussion as the group helps her channel her energies into constructive behavior.

When we enlist the aid of the group, we recognize the powerful influence of peer approval on students' behavior. In contrast, when we make rules unilaterally, we risk rebellion. In a democratic classroom, students have a voice in all negotiable issues. Common goals can be established through open discussions. Students, with your guidance, can decide to have a free reading period, to use peer tutors, to rotate their seating arrangements, and so forth.

You may decide to form a *steering committee* made up of elected class members. Such a committee meets regularly to discuss their feelings about the way things are going in class and their ideas for change. (You spell out clearly which topics they can and cannot have a voice in.) You meet with them regularly to discuss their plans and concerns. Any proposals they come up with and you approve need to be implemented. Members of the steering committee can have set terms of office, perhaps four weeks, so all students can have a chance to participate. In this way you can encourage individual responsibility and group cohesiveness.

Another way to direct peer pressures toward the common good is to establish a weekly "Encouragement Day." Hold the first one on the topic, "A time when someone encouraged me." Get them started by taking the first turn yourself: "A good friend told me she liked the way I smiled. I really felt good about that! Who else will tell about a time they were encouraged?"

If some people say they feel embarrassed when they're encouraged, discuss why positive comments sometimes embarrass us.

Emphasize that everyone is worthy of encouragement and that we all like to feel good about ourselves.

Next session, discuss "A time when I encouraged someone." Again, focus on what the encouragement was for, who it was given to, and how it felt to give it.

Ask students if they'd like to experiment with a way for all class members, including you, to give and receive encouragement each week. Write everyone's name on a slip of paper and put them all in an "Encouragement Box." On Encouragement Day, everyone, including you, draws a name. Everyone writes on the back of the paper an encouraging sentence about the person named and drops the slip in the box. Since this is like exchanging gifts, you could call each slip an "Encouragement Gift."

Afterwards, distribute everyone's slip of paper. Ask each student to read silently his or her own encouragement. For those who want to talk about what they received, hold brief, small-group discussions; students are usually more comfortable talking in small groups.

How about a "Student of the Week" program? Each week a different name is drawn; that person's picture is placed on the bulletin board, along with a story about his or her interests, talents, and ambitions, written by another chosen student, the "reporter." The student of the week may choose to display any schoolwork, interests, or hobbies; the exhibit stays on the bulletin board all week. Make sure everyone gets a turn to be student of the week.

You'll probably think of other ways to promote cooperation and cohesion among your students. Such programs can improve the classroom atmosphere tremendously.

Therapeutic Forces in the Classroom

Some classrooms are dominated by competition and fear of failure. You can develop a climate for growth by understanding and fostering certain therapeutic, or growth-enhancing, procedures. You needn't be a psychologist to concern yourself with students' feelings, values, and attitudes. Just as a democratic classroom doesn't just happen, so too does group cohesion demand your conscious effort. The time you spend learning to promote students' social and psychological growth can have a dramatic impact on students' willingness and readiness to learn. Students who feel safe and comfortable in their group — your class — aren't likely to misbehave.

Therapeutic forces to promote include:

1. *Acceptance.* You may accept all your students but they may not accept each other. They need to learn how to listen and respond to their peers. Only then can they develop mutual respect and empathy. Students are used to the typical classroom where they're expected to pay attention only to the teacher.

If you think your students are old enough, teach them reflective listening (as discussed in Chapter 4). Then have someone role play an emotion-filled situation, like the death of a pet, and have the others try to guess the feeling and circumstance, phrasing their guesses using the "You feel _____ because _____" format.

Students of any age can become more aware of feelings; listening for others' feelings promotes acceptance. Use the lists in Chapter 4 and add your own words. Introduce one word a week. Ask volunteers to pantomime a feeling and then have students guess the emotion and suggest synonyms. Adding to students' vocabularies of words that name feelings can help them recognize what they and others feel.

As students grow more comfortable about talking of feelings, you'll probably notice a more accepting atmosphere in your classroom. Then you can promote mutual respect by:

a. Having each student pick a classmate to get to know better. The two talk about their interests, ideas, and hobbies; then each person introduces the other to the group.

b. Having discussions where everyone tells the group one personal strength. Then students describe one strength they've noticed in a classmate.

c. Encouraging empathy among students by noticing when they're being responsive to one another — "I can see you're being sensitive to Jerry's feelings, Ron" — and by pointing out common interests and abilities — "Nicole is interested in science experiments just like you are, Brenda."

2. *Ventilation.* In an encouraging classroom, students feel free to express, or ventilate, their feelings, thoughts, and values. Painful emotions may be replaced by excitement, pleasure, and enthusiasm when students know it's safe to say what they feel. Sometimes anger or sadness are reduced when we talk about our feelings with people who care. You can foster ventilation by:

a. Again, helping students expand their vocabularies of words describing feelings.

b. Sharing your own feelings through I-messages and teaching students how to do so. For example: "I feel discouraged when you hold private conversations while I'm trying to teach. I'm afraid we won't finish."

c. Observing unexpressed emotions and commenting on them: "You seem satisfied with that map you drew, Amy."

d. Holding discussions where students express feelings about particular events, such as losing a ball game, seeing someone cut in line, attending a pep assembly, and so forth. Encourage them to think of other situations in which we feel happy, angry, embarrassed, and so on.

3. *Spectator learning.* Students can become more aware of their own troubles and dilemmas by hearing how the group solves similar problems. If Jerry isn't ready to talk about his shyness with the group, he can learn from Gloria, who's had the same feelings and will discuss them. Promote spectator learning by:

a. Sharing some of your own concerns with the class.

b. Making group discussions of students' concerns and feelings a planned part of the day or week, with a specific time.

c. Asking the group, "What did you learn from that?" or "How would you have done that differently?" Discuss with students the advantages of being a spectator.

4. *Feedback.* Sometimes students need to know how they're coming across at a particular moment. When feedback is offered without blame, accusation, or sarcasm, students' self-awareness can be enhanced.

Students who have learned I-messages can use them to offer feedback. "I feel hurt, Chloe, when you tease me about my glasses, because I can't see well without them." "Donald, I really get mad when you're so stubborn." Chloe and Donald may not stop their teasing and arguing, but now they know what others think of their behavior. Remind students to keep anger and blame out of their I-messages. They are to share what they're feeling, not demand change.

Feedback depends on mutual respect, sensitivity, and an encouraging classroom atmosphere: without these, feedback can be ineffective or cruel. Feedback is to replace gossip or tattling; it should never be perceived as an attack. In teaching it, remember to emphasize that we show how much we *care* about another person when we express such feelings. Proper feedback neither labels people nor demands change; it simply expresses how someone feels about someone else's behavior at a particular time.

Because feedback must be offered carefully, you will want to supervise its use. Encourage proper feedback by:

a. Giving feedback (I-messages) to students for both positive and negative behavior.
b. Asking the group at times of conflict, "What are you feeling now?"
c. Explaining that everyone creates different impressions, depending on what we're doing or saying. Someone may feel angry at us at 10:00, and grateful to us at noon.
d. Having each student express a good feeling about someone else. Be prepared to give positive feedback to anyone left out.
e. Asking students to role play a scene and then tell the group what kind of impression they believe they've created. The group discusses whether the student has perceived his or her own behavior accurately or not.

5. *Universalization.* We feel accepted and part of the group when we're aware that others experience what we do. What we have in common binds us together; "you are not alone" sounds good to everyone. Cliff says, "I never have enough time to finish the arithmetic problems." Alison replies, "I never do either." Cliff no longer feels different from the others.

A cohesive group depends upon students realizing that they have a lot in common. You can encourage expression of shared experiences and feelings by:

a. Becoming aware of similarities among students so you can call their attention to feelings, goals, beliefs, and values they have in common. (For example, many may feel nervous about tests, think cheating is wrong, value athletic ability.) Plan to do this daily.
b. Asking, "Has anyone else ever _____?" and "How many of us have experienced this?"
c. Expressing some of your own fears, interests, and experiences, and then asking if others feel the way you do.

184

6. *Reality testing.* When we're experimenting with new ways to respond to people, or when we're attempting to change beliefs and behavior, it helps to try out new behavior in an accepting, non-threatening atmosphere. Reality testing is active problem solving. We don't merely talk; we act out.

For example, Alicia is afraid to read aloud because she fears mispronouncing a word. In a group discussion, she finally reveals her feelings; the class realizes that their giggling when she reads increases her discomfort. Together they agree that when Alicia feels ready, she'll volunteer to read, and the class will help by not giggling.

On Thursday, Alicia reads. She does mispronounce a word, but no one giggles and the teacher simply asks her to continue. Then the class discusses what they liked about her reading, and the teacher points out the courage people need to take chances. All students begin to see the value of an accepting class atmosphere. Alicia will very likely improve her reading with practice.

Suppose you notice Christopher standing on the sidelines during the baseball game at recess, even trying to miss his turn at bat in gym class. You talk with him about practicing with you, other students, or at home. He agrees to practice after school with you and a few friends. A week later, you notice that he's joined the game at recess. He still doesn't play well, but he's developed the courage to take risks.

Introduce reality testing by:

a. Discussing with students specific things about themselves they'd like to improve upon or change. Help all interested students set specific plans of action. Emphasize the importance of everyone's support and acceptance.
b. Reading and discussing stories that show people courageously attempting to improve themselves.
c. Noting and encouraging all efforts of students to work out their problems.

7. *Altruism.* We want to encourage our students to help each other, rather than compete. When Nancy independently decides to help Audrey with her geography, without expecting extra credit or praise, her teacher might say, "I appreciate your helping Audrey. I'll bet you can both learn from each other." If the class points out to Calvin that his quick wit can sometimes hurt other people, his teacher might suggest that he help Kathy inject humor into her pantomime project.

Foster altruism by:

a. Asking students to name or write down things they do well and would be willing to help others with. Ask them also to list things they'd like to learn from others. Then develop a "Talent Index" and match students up.
b. Exploring with students ways they might help other people in school or in the community.
c. Discussing what students enjoy doing for others and how they feel when they do those things.
d. Noting and encouraging all spontaneous altruism; for example, when someone lets another go first in line.

8. Interaction. Some of us may need to reexamine our efforts to create a *silent* classroom. We want our students to interact with each other, to foster their social skills and to help establish a creative, encouraging class atmosphere. If students talk only to us, they're not learning how to function socially outside the classroom.

Encourage positive interaction by:

a. Getting students to talk directly to each other in class discussions. When Sherrie talks to you, even though she's commenting on something Bryan said, tell her, "Sherrie, please talk directly to Bryan."

b. Turning questions addressed to you back to the class, and then having students respond to each other. When Ramon asks why the United States was unprepared for the Japanese attack on Pearl Harbor, say, "That's an interesting question, Ramon. Hilda, can you suggest one reason to Ramon?"

c. Providing opportunities for students to work together without your supervision.

9. Encouragement. Once again, you can best instill hope, stimulate courage, and promote social interest by encouraging. An encouraging atmosphere where students focus on the positive and search for possibilities can be the most therapeutic learning environment of all.

Suppose Glenda has trouble learning her spelling words. You suggest she use the tape recorder to practice, and you help by recording the week's spelling words so Glenda can quiz herself as often as she wants. You arrange for her to have a peer tutor; all your students have been taught to encourage one another, especially when they tutor. Heartened by all the encouragement, Glenda feels eager to improve.

Encourage by:

a. Focusing on strengths and assets.
b. Seeing possibilities for progress in even the most difficult situation.
c. Noting all improvement.

d. Forming positive, realistic expectations.

e. Marking the right answers instead of the wrong ones.

f. Using peer tutors and cooperative learning.

The Cohesive Group in a Democratic Classroom

As you work to build cohesion and promote cooperation among your students, recall these principles of the democratic classroom:

- The group develops its cohesiveness around guidelines offering a wide range of individual freedoms and responsibilities.
- Group members help to set goals, make decisions, and institute changes.
- Wherever possible, students progress at their own levels of interest and readiness. Competition is reduced and success emphasized.
- Discipline is an educational process, rather than a procedure for establishing control. Self-discipline is the goal.
- Students and teacher communicate openly and honestly as equal partners in the learning process.
- Students and teacher work to create an atmosphere of mutual trust and respect.
- Encouragement is the prime motivator.

Works Cited

Adler, Alfred. *Social Interest: A Challenge to Mankind.* London: Faber & Faber, 1938.

Recommended Readings

Dinkmeyer, Don, and Muro, James. *Group Counseling: Theory and Practice.* 2nd ed. Itasca, IL: F. E. Peacock, 1979.

Hawley, Robert. *Value Exploration.* Amherst, MA: Educational Research Associates, 1974.

Schmuck, Richard, and Schmuck, Patricia. *Group Processes in the Classroom.* 2nd ed. Dubuque, IA: Wm. C. Brown, 1971.

Stanford, Gene, and Roark, Albert. *Human Interaction in Education.* Boston: Allyn & Bacon, 1974.

Study Questions

1. Why is it vital for teachers to understand how groups work?

2. Briefly explain how the following principles can help us understand our students' behavior in groups:
   a. Students are social beings.
   b. All behavior has social meaning and purpose.
   c. Behavior reflects lifestyle.

3. What is social interest? How can we foster it in our classrooms?

4. What are the characteristics and techniques which distinguish the democratic classroom from the autocratic and permissive classrooms? What steps can you take to move toward a democratic classroom?

5. How can peer encouragement help build a cohesive group? Discuss the use of steering committees, encouragement days, and student of the week programs as ways to direct peer pressures toward the common good.

6. What are the nine therapeutic forces? How can we promote them in our classroom? Give some specific examples.

Problem Situation

Ms. Jackson is a new teacher in your school. You do some team teaching with her in math and notice a lot of competition in her class. Her students often don't get along with each other. One student, Carmen, is having trouble understanding percentages and asks for help. Another student, Willy, tells her, "You're stupid. You never pay attention and you're too dumb for this work."

1. How might you approach this problem with Ms. Jackson?
2. What are some indications that her class is not democratic?
3. If this were your class, what are some simple things you might do to develop a democratic, less competitive classroom atmosphere?
4. Which therapeutic forces would you use to begin to improve the group atmosphere? How specifically would you use those forces?
5. How would you respond to Willy's remark?

Activity for the Week

Practice using therapeutic forces in your classroom to improve group interaction. Bring examples of how you used specific forces.

Recommended Resource Book Material

Chapter 2, "Belonging"; Chapter 3, "Encouraging ourselves and others," "Encouragement," "Promoting peer encouragement"; Chapter 4, "Building a feeling vocabulary," "Listening for feelings," "A potpourri of exercises"; Chapter 5, "I-messages"; Chapter 8, "Helping," "Social interest," "Friendship," "Developing trust, " "Relating to others"; Chapter 9, "Sociometrics."

Chart 9

Therapeutic Forces

Force	Purpose	Example
Acceptance	To develop mutual respect and empathy among group members.	"I can see you're being sensitive to Joshua's feelings."
Ventilation	To acknowledge and promote the expression of feelings, often by using reflective listening.	"You seem very angry about this idea."
Spectator learning	To help students understand their own concerns as they listen to other group members discuss similar concerns.	"How can you apply our discussion of Jim's problem to your brothers and sisters?"
Feedback	To let students know how others perceive their behavior, often by encouraging the use of I-messages.	"Could you please tell Carlos how you feel when he teases you?"
Universalization	To help students become aware that they are not alone in their concerns, that most students have similar concerns.	"Who else has wondered about that?"
Reality testing	To let students experiment with new behavior.	"Let's role-play this problem and try out new ways of dealing with it."
Altruism	To encourage students to help each other, rather than compete.	"Beth, I really appreciate your helping Ricky with the math problems."
Interaction	To foster students' social skills and help establish an encouraging classroom atmosphere.	"Meg, please share with Joyce how you felt when she said she enjoyed playing with you at recess."
Encouragement	To stimulate students' courage and social interest. To help students become more optimistic about solving problems.	"I think your study habits will help you with your project."

Recording Worksheet

Promoting Therapeutic Forces in the Group

As you listen to the class discussion, consider which therapeutic forces you would promote at various points and how specifically you would promote those forces.

If necessary, refer to Chart 9. Be prepared to discuss your responses with the group.

NOTES

Chapter 9

Points to Remember

1. Our students' goals become clearer when we consider the social meaning of behavior.

2. The following principles can help us understand the class as a group:
- Students are social beings.
- All behavior has social meaning and purpose.
- Behavior reflects lifestyle.
- Students can learn to feel more accepted by cooperating with others than by fighting with others.

3. Social interest is a willingness to cooperate with others for the common good.

4. Group dynamics can help us understand why students seek attention, power, or revenge, and why they display inadequacy.

5. The group can become a force for recognizing and encouraging positive behavior.

6. Ways to direct peer pressures toward the common good include steering committees, encouragement days, student of the week programs.

7. Promote the following therapeutic or growth-enhancing procedures:
- Acceptance.
- Ventilation.
- Spectator learning.
- Feedback.
- Universalization.
- Reality testing.
- Altruism.
- Interaction.
- Encouragement.

Personal Record Chapter 9

1.   My experience with the weekly assignment

2.   My reactions to the reading

3.   Topics to discuss with the group

4.   Skills I intend to improve

5.   My beliefs which impede progress

6.   My successes in applying program ideas

7.   My difficulties in applying program ideas

8.   My progress this week: A specific example

9.   This week I learned

CHAPTER 10
THE CLASS AS A GROUP:
GROUP LEADERSHIP SKILLS

How does the democratic style of group leadership differ from
permissive and autocratic styles?
What leadership skills can help me hold successful discussions?
What is the value of guidance-oriented class discussions?
How can I best organize and use class discussions?

Teachers are always group leaders. It is essential for us to practice specific, effective ways of leading our groups. The democratic classroom promotes active participation by students, but we still guide and direct them. We need to understand group dynamics so we can enhance communication among class members.

Autocratic teachers make all decisions and structure their classrooms so rigidly that they promote either rebellion or dependency among students. Permissive teachers provide little or no structure and few guidelines. Neither style provides the combination of flexibility and guidelines necessary for a productive class.

In the democratic classroom, teacher and students decide on guidelines together. Group members know their rights and responsibilities. The teacher's style of leadership helps students learn to treat people as equals, to be responsible for their own behavior, and to function well in a democratic environment.

The following skills will help you hold successful discussions:

1. *Structuring.* Groups sometimes stray from the subject unless someone keeps them on track. When we structure, we remind our group in various ways of the topic they've temporarily lost sight of. Having set specific guidelines for discussion, we can let students know in what way they've departed from the agreed-upon procedures.

Teach your class to hold orderly, productive discussions by enlisting their help in formulating guidelines. You could adapt the guidelines your STET group uses or devise others such as the following (Dinkmeyer, 1970, 1973):

For younger students

Raise your hand.
Stick to the point.
Don't clam up.
Listen carefully.
Think together.

For older students

Listen for feelings.
Tell how you feel about things.
Don't interrupt.
Be with it.
Talk with each other.
Be positive.

Introduce the guidelines by telling the class that these are some rules others have found helpful. Then ask them to comment on the rules and add to the list if they think something is missing. After you and the students decide what's needed for discussions, write out and post these guidelines. Then, when someone barges into the middle of someone else's sentence, you can ask the group, "What guideline are we forgetting?"

Structuring may be called for when students seem unaware of their own strong feelings. Sometimes the real topic of discussion is replaced by a secondary, usually more emotional one. If the group is deciding how to get ready for dismissal on time, and several students keep blaming each other for keeping the class late, you can say, "Aren't we getting off the topic?" or "What is happening now in our group?" Or you can ask, "Which guideline have we forgotten?"

If the topic is the Constitutional Convention but somehow last night's basketball game keeps coming up, you can ask, "Which guideline are we forgetting?" Someone will point to "Stick to the point."

2. Universalizing. Many of the therapeutic group forces discussed in Chapter 9 are also useful as leadership techniques. Universalizing, for example, promotes careful listening and group cohesion as students learn their concerns are shared. We can ask, "Who else has felt the same way?"

It's especially important to universalize in early meetings so students are encouraged to listen closely to each other. You might ask students to raise their hands when they share a feeling or concern being expressed. Then call on several students to explain their shared concern. Soon the raising of hands will become a show of support for the student who is speaking. You too can participate.

3. Linking. We can facilitate discussions by verbally making connections between different people. Pointing out similarities and differences in opinions, beliefs, and values can help keep discussions moving. Linking also promotes closeness among class members as they realize others share their concerns.

Linking demands that we listen carefully to what students say. We're also sensitive to nonverbal expression. The sad feeling Abby expresses may be reflected in the sad faces of her classmates. You might say, "Abby has said she's feeling sad about her father's leaving home. Leonard and Clare, it looks like you're feeling sad also."

Linking can help get discussions going; it also helps move things along by encouraging careful listening. For example, you say, "Shelley gets very upset and discouraged when she can't do her math assignment. This seems similar to what Jay and Delores feel about their reading."

4. *Redirecting.* Groups are most effective when all members are actively involved. We can promote involvement in discussions by redirecting questions or statements away from us and back to the class: "What do others think about that?"

For example, when Gordon says that farm kids have it a lot harder than city kids, you can ask the group, "What do the rest of you think?" or "How do you feel about what Gordon has said?" Give your own opinion last, and then only if needed. Phrase what you say as an opinion, not a fact: "It seems to me . . . ."

Redirecting can also help when students offer unworkable solutions to problems. Ask, "What might happen if that is done?" Learn to trust your group enough to redirect a negative comment made about you or about a classroom procedure. If Maggie says, "You give us more homework than anyone else and it's all busywork!" you might reflect her angry feelings and then ask, "How do others feel?" You'll be surprised how readily students will be honest and fair if you've established a mutually respectful classroom.

Redirecting, then, serves two purposes: It encourages students to get involved in discussions, and it allows you to step out of the role of authority figure, creating a more democratic environment.

5. *Goal disclosure.* We often use goal disclosure and look for the student's recognition reflex during individual conferences (as explained in Chapter 6). With sensitivity, we can also help students begin to understand behavior by asking the group to guess at someone's goal. If done in a respectful, caring way, open discussion of students' goals can help students decide to change.

Always be tentative and cautious. No one likes to be trapped, lectured to, or embarrassed. Ask Herman if he'd like to find out why he comes in late from recess, if he'd like to discuss the situation with his classmates. If he seems interested, ask the group, "Who has an idea why Herman is usually late from recess?" If anyone ventures a guess, ask, "Does everyone agree? Herman, what do you think about Darla's idea?" If no one has any ideas, offer your own *tentative* interpretation. Begin with, "Herman, could it be . . ." or "Is it possible . . ." or "I have the impression . . . ." Then suggest the goal: ". . . you want us to notice you?"

If you're on the wrong track, you'll get no reaction from the student. But if Herman's recognition reflex suggests you're correct, open the discussion to ways students can be noticed without bothering others. Take the spotlight off Herman, except perhaps to say, "Herman, how do you feel about Ernest's suggestion?" Group consideration of individual misbehavior, if handled carefully, can be a valuable force for group cohesion.

6. *Brainstorming.* Learn to lead brainstorming sessions, inviting students to share *any* ideas they have about issues, questions, or problems. Emphasize that there will be no right or wrong answers and no evaluation until all suggestions are given. Brainstorming encourages students to participate unhesitatingly in discussions.

For example, ask students what to do about rest room vandalism. Write down all suggestions: post guards; take the doors off; suspend anyone caught; have an all-school assembly; take a school vote on what to do; appoint a student committee. Then discuss.

Or brainstorm about academic subjects. Ask, "What value is poetry to us?" Students may suggest: it's worthless; it says a lot in a few words; it helps us see things in new ways; it gives English teachers something to do; it teaches us to rhyme. You can direct an interesting discussion based on these responses. Just remember not to evaluate or judge any suggestion. Encourage creative thinking.

Brainstorming can also be useful when the group is helping a student solve a problem. "Lester, would you like some suggestions from the group? Let's brainstorm."

7. *Blocking.* Sometimes the group's discussion may degenerate into attacks or destructive behavior. You'll then want to intervene. If students have been taught to use I-messages, you can recommend they state their feelings in that form. Or simply block the remarks by letting students know the group won't accept such comments.

For example, Fran keeps asking, "Why do we have to do that?" Try to get her to express her feelings more clearly. Say, "You seem annoyed, Fran. Will you explain your feelings?" Suggest that she use an I-message. Or open up the discussion to the class: "What is another way Fran could express her anger?"

Ed tells Rita, "You're always ruining our games at recess. I wish you'd never come to this school!" You block by encouraging Ed to use an I-message and to be *specific* about what bothers him. You refocus Ed's feelings away from the negative and toward the constructive.

Suppose Krista shouts at Stanley, "Why did you say that, you dummy?" You step in and remind Krista kindly but firmly that personal attacks have no place in the classroom. You show her a respectful way to differ with people, saying , "I wonder how Stanley felt when you said that?"

TO SUM UP...

8. *Summarizing.* It's very helpful to summarize a discussion at various points. Give your summary from the students' perspective: "So far we've learned that conservation programs only work when they have wide public support." It's even more valuable to teach students to summarize. Summarizing helps them clarify the discussion and lets you know what they're learning. Students' summaries can begin with "I learned," and focus on content, feelings, beliefs, or attitudes.

9. *Task setting and obtaining commitments.* Our students often enjoy talking but are unwilling to commit themselves to a specific plan of action. As group leader, you can focus students' attention on what needs doing. For example, after Dennis and the class discuss his

tardiness, he decides to leave home so he will arrive five minutes before school starts. He agrees to begin the plan Monday and stick to it for a week. You suggest that he report his progress to the group at the next discussion. You can also help the class as a whole set definite goals, devising a strategy for the United Way campaign, perhaps, or scheduling the rehearsals for the class play. Mutually deciding on specific tasks can help align the goals of students and teachers. This alignment is crucial so students and teachers can work together toward goals they share.

10. *Promoting feedback.* Students explore how they are perceived and how they perceive others when they learn to give and receive feedback. They begin to focus on behavior, not on personalities. We can promote feedback ourselves during class discussions or extracurricular activities. For example, say, "I feel discouraged when we take so long to get to work because our school newspaper has to be out by Friday. How do the rest of you feel?"

11. *Promoting direct interaction.* Get students to speak directly to each other so you won't feel like a "translator" relaying messages from student to student. When Elizabeth makes a suggestion to Patsy through you, ask, "Would you please tell Patsy directly?" Include instructions for students to speak to each other when you promote feedback: "How do you think Larry is feeling right now? Speak directly to him." Continue these requests until students begin addressing each other without prompting.

12. *Promoting encouragement.* We can encourage and teach students to encourage each other. Ask them, "What do you like about . . . ?" "What do you enjoy about . . . ?" "Who has noticed Jonathan's improvement in . . . ?" We can institute Encouragement Days and Student of the Week campaigns.

Show students how to encourage by noticing their improvements: "I liked the way you people settled that argument." "I'm glad to see you're able to stay with us all period." "Cassandra, we all appreciate your efforts to be on time." Encouragement is contagious!

Using Group Leadership Skills

Now you want to put the techniques of group leadership into action. Consider the following class discussion about pets:

You're talking about taking care of pets. Alexandra says, "I have a dog but I hate to walk it." You *universalize* by asking, "Who else has felt pets are a lot of work?" After several other students agree that pets are hard work, Madeleine remarks, "I saw a zebra at the zoo." Now you'll need to *structure:* "I believe we were talking about animals we have as pets."

As the discussion proceeds, listen for opportunities to request feedback. Ralph and Sean have been vehement in their defense of animals' right to live without being "put to sleep." You *redirect* and *request feedback* by asking, "How do you feel about what Ralph and Sean have said?" You *promote direct interaction* by saying, "Speak directly to them about your feelings."

At this point, Pearl says to Ralph and Sean, "You guys must be crazy. If they didn't kill animals, dogs and cats would be all over the place.'' Now you *block* by reminding Pearl to stick to the issue and avoid attacking people: ''Pearl, I get concerned when we call each other names because people's feelings could be hurt.''

To forestall a class argument about whether it's better to be ''unrealistic'' or ''cruel,'' you decide to hold a *brainstorming* session. What are the alternatives to the present system of handling stray animals? You record the results of the brainstorming: Don't allow the humane society to kill animals; put all strays up for adoption indefinitely; put all strays up for adoption for two weeks only; require that all pets be neutered.

During the discussion that follows, Ralph asks you what you'd do if your cat had a litter. You *redirect* the question to the class. Esther says she would give the kittens to friends. You *link* her comment with several other similar remarks.

For a while, Eddy keeps interrupting by saying, ''They should kill all cats.'' He laughs and looks at the class everytime he says this. The class has been taught about goals, and Eddy agrees to discuss his motivation for interrupting. You promote *goal disclosure* by asking, ''Who has an idea why Eddy keeps interrupting?'' After Eddy's goal is disclosed, you ask, ''What are some useful ways we can get the group's attention?''

Finally, the group decides to visit the Humane Society as part of their study of the problem of excess pets: they make that decision because you encouraged *task setting and obtaining commitments.* The class divides into committees that will report on different aspects of the subject within three weeks.

As the discussion ends, you ask several students to clarify what the group has said. You help them *summarize* the discussion, including the commitments made: ''Who can sum up what we've decided? What suggestions did we make about the problem of stray animals?''

Throughout the discussion, you *encouraged:* ''Thank you for sharing that idea, Diane.'' ''I can see you're all really thinking about this problem.''

BLOCKING   GOAL DISCLOSURE
BRAINSTORMING
UNIVERSALIZING   STRUCTURING
TASK SETTING   FEEDBACK
LINKING
REDIRECTING   ENCOURAGE
SUMMARIZING

Becoming a Successful Group Leader

Memorizing group leadership skills will not guarantee you successful discussions. You need to feel comfortable leading discussions democratically, rather than autocratically. Effective group leadership also takes practice. You may want to list on a card those skills you consider most important for you or those you tend to forget. You can glance at the card as a reminder during discussions.

You may find it helpful to have another teacher observe your group and then tell you how the discussion seemed to go. You might also observe other classrooms for comparison.

Many of the topics covered in previous chapters will be helpful as you work to improve your leadership skills. Deepening your understanding of behavior and your recognition of the goals of misbehavior will help you react appropriately to students. Recognizing the purpose of emotions in the group setting allows you to guide and redirect students. You'll begin to predict conflicts and be able to block them. You'll see when your own feelings or beliefs are interfering with the group's activities.

Remember that you're not totally responsible for the success or failure of a discussion. But you can encourage all students, notice all improvements. In this way, you clarify what you expect and help students feel valued.

The communication skills of reflective listening, I-messages, and exploring alternatives are basic to successful group work. Promoting responsible behavior through natural and logical consequences that students helped decide will let the class know what you and their peers expect. Peer approval and disapproval can also help set limits.

Why Are Class Discussions Valuable?

Discussions with your whole group can be extremely worthwhile. Such discussions may:

- Help students develop better relationships with each other.
- Teach students to solve problems together.
- Allow students to share feelings, intentions, and beliefs, as well as ideas.
- Help students establish guidelines for classroom behavior.
- Increase group cohesion and individual feelings of belonging and acceptance.

When we are skillful group leaders, we can avoid two common pitfalls: dominating discussions with our own ideas and opinions; allowing discussions to become free-for-alls without structure or purpose.

Uses and Organization of Class Discussions

Topics particularly suited to class discussion include:

a. Academic issues and questions: causes of the French Revolution; ways to use arithmetic in everyday life; ways we can use what grows in the ocean for food.

b. Particular behavior: students' progress in keeping classroom supplies orderly; someone's increasing ability to finish assignments on time; problems in working together.
   c. Stories, poems, plays, and essays that deepen students' knowledge of human behavior.
   d. School and classroom issues: how students can encourage each other; how the school can combat littering.

You'll want to set aside times for discussion, perhaps 10-10:30 every Monday, or fourth period every Wednesday and Friday. You and the class may decide to use every other meeting of the Class Council for discussions of classroom policies.

It's best to start regular class discussions early in the year, even during the first week. Whenever you start, you might tell students that you need their help in deciding certain classroom issues or exploring various topics. List the issues and topics you'd like to talk over, and ask the group if they're willing to discuss these things. If they're interested, ask them to add to the list of possible topics. Write down and display all suggestions. As a group, decide where to begin.

Remember that students will learn only gradually how to hold successful discussions. Take time to teach them how to participate. Offer them a good model by using the skills of group leadership yourself.

Prepare students for effective group participation by encouraging them to express clearly their own and others' feelings. Point out similarities in feelings. Ask students to notice and comment upon their classmates' strengths and improvements. Help them explore their own feelings and values.

If you decide to teach students some of the group skills you've learned, help them practice by:

   a. Demonstrating or giving an example of how the technique works.
   b. Having two students demonstrate the technique. For example, ask Phil to express his anger about the project he's working on. Ask Ruth to give Phil feedback or reflective listening on his comment.
   c. Supervising a larger group, perhaps four students, as they practice a technique. Have them reverse roles after a while.
   d. Asking students who have caught on quickly or who already know the technique to help others practice.

Learning to be successful group leaders and teaching our students how to participate in discussions ought to be vital parts of any curriculum. Such training can greatly enhance the value of group guidance activities and classroom meetings, subjects of the next two chapters.

Works Cited

Dinkmeyer, Don. *Developing Understanding of Self and Others. D-1, D-2.* Circle Pines, MN: American Guidance Service, 1970, 1973.

Recommended Readings

Dinkmeyer, Don, and Muro, James. *Group Counseling: Theory and Practice.* 2nd ed. Itasca, IL: F. E. Peacock, 1979.

Gazda, George, et al. *Human Relations Development.* 2nd ed. Boston: Allyn & Bacon, 1977.

Gorman, Alfred. *The Interactive Process of Education.* 2nd ed. Boston: Allyn & Bacon, 1974.

Study Questions

1. What is *structuring* and when is it needed? How can we involve students in formulating discussion guidelines?

2. How can *universalizing* be a useful leadership technique?

3. What is the value of *linking*?

4. When, how, and why do we *redirect*?

5. How can *goal disclosure* bring the class closer together?

6. What is the value of *brainstorming*? Name some topics or situations suitable for brainstorming.

7. When is it necessary to *block*? How can we block and still maintain mutual respect?

8. How can *task setting* and *obtaining commitments* help align the goals of teachers and students?

9. How can we *promote feedback* during class discussions?

10. How can we teach students to *encourage* each other?

11. How can we *promote direct interaction* during class discussions?

12. Why is *summarizing* useful for teachers and students?

13. How can teachers become successful group leaders?

14. Why are class discussions valuable? Describe their uses and organization.

Problem Situation

Mr. Sanders has taught for a number of years. Lately he's been having a lot of trouble getting his class to cooperate with him. He has always established classroom rules and lesson plans; when students did not cooperate, he sent them to the principal, called their parents, or found some way to punish them. But he sees that these methods don't change the students' attitudes. When he asks the group why they won't cooperate, some students say nothing. Others begin talking all at once, complaining about each other and him. Mr. Sanders comes to discuss the situation with you.

1. What do you think is the basic problem?
2. What are the first corrective steps Mr. Sanders might take?

3. What are the specific skills Mr. Sanders needs? How can he acquire these skills?
4. What are the skills his students need? How might they be acquired?

Activity for the Week

Practice using group leadership skills in class discussions. Bring examples of how you used specific skills.

Recommended Resource Book Material

Chapter 3, ''Encouraging ourselves and others,'' ''Encouragement,'' ''Promoting peer encouragement''; Chapter 9, ''Sociometrics''; Chapter 10, ''Linking,'' ''Learning to link,'' ''Summarizing''; Chapter 12, ''Individual student misbehavior.''

Chart 10A

Styles of Leadership and Classroom Atmosphere

Democratic	Autocratic	Permissive
Mutual trust. Mutual respect.	Control through reward and punishment. Attempt to demand respect.	Students may do what they want without concern for others.
Choices offered wherever feasible.	Demands. Dominates.	Anarchy.
Motivation through encouragement. Identification of the positive.	Focus on weaknesses and mistakes.	All behavior tolerated.
Freedom within limits. Balance between freedom to work and responsibility to work.	Limits without freedom. Promotion of dependency and/or rebellion.	Freedom without limits. Confusion.
Intrinsic motivation. Teachers and students set goals together.	Extrinsic motives and punishment.	Motivation erratic, unpredictable.
Success-oriented activities designed to build self-confidence.	Activities focus primarily on producing superior products.	Some activities help students make progress and others do not.
Cooperation, shared responsibility.	Competition.	Individual rights without regard for rights of others.
Discipline as educational process. Self-discipline encouraged.	Discipline is to establish external control.	No discipline is expected.
Goals are aligned.	Goals are set by teacher.	No positive goals.
Ask for ideas, contributions.	Teacher decides all issues.	No formal decisions reached.

Chart 10B

Group Leadership Skills

Skill	Purpose	Example
Structuring.	To establish purpose and limits for discussion.	"What's happening in the group now?" "How is this helping us reach our goal?"
Universalizing.	To help students realize that their concerns are shared.	"Who else has felt that way?"
Linking.	To make verbal connections between what specific students say and feel.	"Bill is very angry when his brother is late. This seems similar to what Joan and Sam feel about their sisters."
Redirecting.	To promote involvement of all students in the discussion and to allow teachers to step out of the role of authority figure.	"What do others think about that?" "What do you think about Pete's idea?"
Goal disclosure.	To help students become more aware of the purposes of their misbehavior.	"Is it possible you want us to notice you?" "Could it be you want to show us we can't make you?"
Brainstorming.	To encourage students to participate unhesitatingly in generating ideas.	"Let's share all our ideas about this problem. We won't react to any suggestion until we've listed them all."
Blocking.	To intervene in destructive communication.	"Will you explain your feelings?" "I wonder how Stanley felt when you said that."
Summarizing.	To clarify what has been said and to determine what students have learned.	"What did you learn from this discussion?" "What have we decided to do about this situation?"
Task setting and obtaining commitments.	To develop a specific commitment for action from students.	"What will you do about this problem?" "What will you do this week?"
Promoting feedback.	To help students understand how others perceive them.	"I get angry when you talk so long that the rest of us don't get a turn. What do others think?" "I really like the way you help us get our game started."
Promoting direct interaction.	To get students to speak directly to each other when appropriate.	"Would you tell Joan how you feel about what she said?"
Promoting encouragement.	To invite students directly and by example to increase each other's self-esteem and self-confidence.	"Thank you for helping us out." "What does Carol do that you like?" "Who has noticed Jamie's improvement?"

Recording Worksheet

Group Leadership Skills

As you listen to the class discussions, consider which group leadership skills are needed at various points and how specifically you would use those skills.

If necessary, refer to Chart 10B. Be prepared to discuss your responses with the group.

NOTES

Chapter 10

Points to Remember

1. In a democratic classroom, the teacher's style of leadership helps students learn to:
- Treat people as equals.
- Be responsible for their own behavior.
- Function well in a democratic environment.

2. The following skills will help you hold successful discussions:
- Structuring.
- Universalizing.
- Linking.
- Redirecting.
- Goal disclosure.
- Brainstorming.
- Blocking.
- Summarizing.
- Task setting and obtaining commitments.
- Promoting feedback.
- Promoting direct interaction.
- Promoting encouragement.

3. Effective group leadership takes practice.

4. Class discussions may:
- Help students get along better.
- Teach cooperative problem solving.
- Promote the sharing of feelings, beliefs, and ideas.
- Help students establish classroom guidelines.
- Increase group cohesion.
- Encourage feelings of belonging and acceptance.

5. Use class meetings to discuss:
- Academic issues and questions.
- Behavior problems.
- School and classroom issues.

6. Prepare students for effective group participation by encouraging them to express their feelings clearly.

7. Consider teaching your students some of the group skills you've learned.

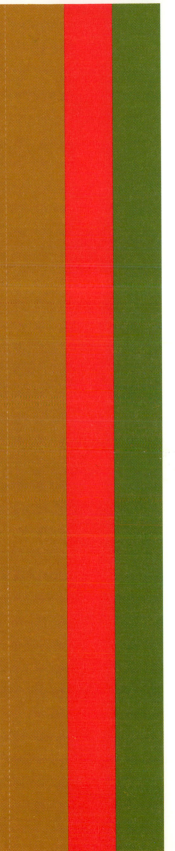

Personal Record Chapter 10

1. My experience with the weekly assignment

2. My reactions to the reading

3. Topics to discuss with the group

4. Skills I intend to improve

5. My beliefs which impede progress

6. My successes in applying program ideas

7. My difficulties in applying program ideas

8. My progress this week: A specific example

9. This week I learned

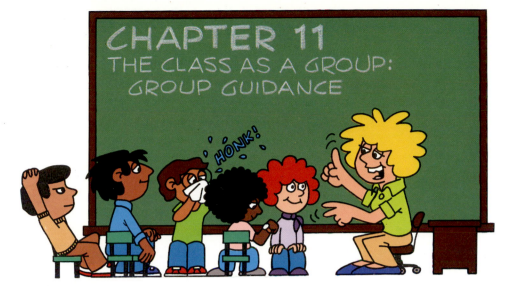

What are some of the principles of group guidance?
What is the teacher's role in guidance?
How can I offer my students career guidance?
How can I make connections between school and the world outside?
What are some specific ways to conduct group guidance activities?
In what sense is group guidance a form of experiential learning?

We can't realistically say, "I'm a teacher, not a counselor. I'll leave the 'guidance' to professionals." While counselors, psychologists, and social workers provide essential services for our students, we teachers have the most direct and sustained contact with the individuals and group members who make up our classes. One of our most important responsibilities is the creation of an encouraging classroom climate. Students are more likely to learn in a place where they feel accepted and successful. Using some *group guidance* techniques can help us create such a place.

Group guidance activities involve the whole class. They focus on attitudes, feelings, beliefs, and goals, on self-image and human relationships. They can be discussions, role-playing exercises, art, music, and writing activities, and field trips. These activities aren't usually part of the core curriculum of school, although the regular curriculum can easily accommodate group guidance. No matter where these activities "fit," they should never be secondary or auxiliary. If we agree that emotions and goals are as important to education as mathematics and language arts, then group guidance activities become an integral part of the curriculum.

Principles of Group Guidance

Teachers tend to think that the student who meets regularly with a guidance counselor or psychologist must have some special problem. He or she may not appear to fit in with other students, behaviorally or intellectually. But guidance in the classroom is *for all students.*

Group guidance is as well-organized as other parts of the curriculum. It is a continuous program.

Although teachers organize and structure group guidance activities, we do so in partnership with students. Students participate by suggesting discussion topics and by working with the teacher to formulate individual and group goals that can be addressed in group guidance sessions.

Whether activities deal with personal, social, educational, or career concerns, group guidance focuses on identifying individual strengths, setting goals, aligning the goals of students and teacher, building self-confidence, and nurturing social interest and cooperation.

Finally, group guidance is both preventive and developmental. We discuss situations and issues before they become problems, and problems before they become unmanageable. Our discussions begin where students are, addressing topics that concern or interest them now.

In essence, group guidance treats education as more than the accumulation of information. The *context* of learning influences students' academic success. If Marty learned arithmetic in a mistake-centered classroom where he often failed, he very likely hates arithmetic. Had he learned in an atmosphere of success and encouragement, his feelings would probably be different. It may be easier for him to ''relearn'' arithmetic than to learn to feel more confident about arithmetic. Our feelings about what we learn can determine how much and how fast we learn.

Teachers' role in guidance includes:

a. Working to align students' goals with our own, accomplished by identifying those goals and then working toward greater cooperation, perhaps by developing individual and group contracts.
b. Identifying and meeting students' individual needs, accomplished through conferences and personalized assignments.
c. Working with counselors to promote successful guidance programs.
d. Conducting group guidance activities and discussions.

This chapter will explore two of the three main kinds of group guidance activities: sessions devoted to specific topics about self-understanding, getting along with others, and adapting to the world of work; and sessions devoted to particular subjects and to the relevancy of school. The third kind of activity, the classroom meeting, is the subject of Chapter 12.

Human Relationships and Career Education

In partnership with the family, teachers hope to prepare students for responsible, responsive, and productive lives. We can do that most successfully by combining academic instruction with attention to basic human relations. Students who aren't happy with themselves and who can't get along with others often are unsuccessful learners. They may grow up to be dissatisfied adults.

We can help students learn to make good decisions about themselves and their future lives by offering them ''career guidance'' throughout their time in school. Career guidance is more than simply

information about specific jobs. In fact, in elementary and junior high school, career education means helping students develop a realistic self-image, an ability to make responsible decisions, the capacity for successful human relationships, and an awareness of the world of work. In junior high, students begin exploring many careers through work experience which earns academic credit. Students' eventual career choice has a lot to do with their feelings about themselves and others and their attitudes toward work.

Remember: *Any activity that addresses self-concept, human relationships, responsibility for one's own actions, and self-motivation contributes to career awareness.*

Some discussion topics about human relationships include:

Why do we behave as we do?
How can we get along better with our families? brothers and sisters? friends? teachers?
How can we encourage each other?
How can we say what we mean without discouraging others?
How do we make friends?
What can we do if our friends try to pressure us into doing something we don't want to do?
Who has a better deal — boys or girls?
How can we avoid power struggles with our parents, our friends, our teachers?
How can we get along with our boss and our fellow employees?

Students can also discuss the meaning of the family constellation, the purpose of emotions, the principles of democracy and social interest, how to deal with feelings of inferiority, with divorce, with death, and so on.

You'll probably think of other topics suitable for your students. As students become experienced in these kinds of discussions, they can choose their own topics. Older students may begin to lead discussions; with younger students, you'll probably want to take a more active role.

We can aid our students in career development by helping them to:

• Discover and use their strengths.
• Understand how their abilities and interests point to possible careers.
• Express their feelings and be sensitive to others' feelings, an ability that is essential to relationships with employers and employees.
• Become independent, resourceful, and flexible so they can adapt to career changes.
• Understand the connections between school and career.
• Cope with stress and change.
• Develop their own value system, make choices, and accept the consequences of their decisions.

Career opportunities are best met by people skilled in human relationships, people who see themselves as contributing members of society.

Particular Subjects and the Relevancy of School

These group guidance discussions focus on specific academic topics, terms, or concepts, and how these connect with students' present interests and concerns. For example, students can learn what democracy is by discussing, "What does democracy mean to you?" You can follow this by having them suggest ways of making their classroom more democratic. They can understand the Constitution by discussing questions like, "What does the Constitution have to say about education? What does it say about families? about religion? about newspapers?" Mathematics can take on new meaning through discussions and projects about the use of numbers in post offices, supermarkets, gas stations, television studios, hospitals, and so forth. Students can operate a classroom store or build something that calls for exact measurements.

These kinds of group guidance activities help broaden the curriculum by making close connections between school and the world outside.

Specific Group Guidance Activities

Here are some specific ways to conduct group guidance activities.

Discussions. Arrange students in a circle and encourage them to talk to each other as well as to you. Resolve, as the leader of most discussions, to respect all answers and ideas.

Do not dominate discussions. Instead, use your group leadership skills to stimulate and guide. Ask thought-provoking, open questions. Encourage students to evaluate their own feelings, values, and beliefs as they share their thoughts with classmates.

Suppose you're discussing name-calling. You might stimulate discussion by asking:

How do you feel when someone calls you a name?
What do you usually do when someone calls you a name?
What happens when you do that?
Since you say that getting angry when people call you names doesn't help, what do you think would work better?

216

Class discussions can be lively and informative ways of getting students to consider human behavior.

Stories and problem situations. Stories are good ways to get students of all ages to consider feelings, attitudes, and beliefs. You can also use stories to illustrate the four goals of misbehavior and ways students can recognize and redirect such goals (as in the resource book, Chapters 1-8).

Similarly, 'problem situations,' sharply focused vignettes dealing with a single issue, can stimulate discussion of students' typical concerns. Each chapter of this handbook is followed by a problem situation and each chapter of the resource book includes five others. You might adapt these to the interests of your students or else make up new ones.

For example: The class admired Jerry's social studies project and the teacher encouraged his ideas. But one student, Bob, remarked, "That's not so great. In my class last year, we did lots of projects better than that."

After reading this vignette to your students, ask them, "What do you think about what Bob said? Why do you suppose he said that? How would you feel if you were Jerry?"

ELEMENTARY, MY DEAR WATSON!

Role playing. Children at play often pretend to be someone else — astronauts, professional athletes, disc jockeys, or comic book characters. We all play roles, no matter what our age. In role playing, we have students act out specific scenes so they can feel what it's like to be someone else. They can act out their own ideas and feelings and then discuss them. They can consider alternatives. As members of an audience, they can learn through observation and empathy.

We set the scene, direct the "production," and guide the discussion that follows. Students volunteer to participate and may help determine the "script," the direction the scene will take.

The steps in role-playing include:

1. Decide on a particular problem or issue, a specific situation to enact. For example, present two students showing off during Parents' Night.
2. Ask for volunteers to play specific parts: students, teachers, parents, principal.
3. Discuss each part and plan each person's role in the scene. There is no written script. Actors are to behave as they believe their characters would. If you want, use simple props like hats or tools. For example, have the person playing the teacher carry a notebook and pencil.
4. Discuss with the class the scene about to be acted out. Help them understand what to look for. Ask them to notice showing off behavior: loud talking, running back and forth, interrupting.
5. Have the participants act out the scene. Give guidance, if necessary, but encourage spontaneity. Accept the inevitable nervous silliness; for example, when the student playing the father giggles everytime someone calls him "Mr. Wolfe."
6. After the performance, discuss each character's feelings and motivations. Compare the audience's perception of a

character with what the actor hoped to convey. Ask an observer how it felt to watch people showing off; ask an actor how it felt to show off. Discuss why people show off. Explore ways for the two show-offs to get attention in positive ways; act out those alternatives.

Discussion pictures. Interesting pictures often stimulate lively discussions. Collect pictures from books and magazines that point to feelings, attitudes, values, motivations. Ask questions like the following:

What's happening in this picture?
Why are these people doing what they're doing?
How do you think this person feels? Why do you think so?
What might happen next?
How would you feel if you were this person?
What would you do if you were in this situation?
Who will tell us about a similar experience they've had?
What did you learn from our discussion of this picture?

Remember that students' perceptions — not what the picture "really" shows — are what count.

Films and filmstrips. Check your library for lists of appropriate films and filmstrips. Use audiovisual materials to promote discussion and role play.

Exercises and games. Collect and use activities that deal with emotions, communication, motivation, and so forth. (Many examples can be found in the resource book.)

Art, music, and writing. Have students draw pictures to illustrate emotions. Ask them to write paragraphs on topics such as, "I feel lonely when _____" and "I feel angry when _____." Discuss, asking, "What can you do if you're lonely? if you're angry?" Invite them to illustrate and express emotions through music or dance. Then discuss the creative expressions.

Guest speakers. Career education becomes more real when you bring in people who actually hold certain jobs. Combat sex role stereotyping by inviting people who hold non-traditional jobs, like male nurses or female electricians.

Field trips. Take students to see various businesses and agencies. Visit a school for the severely handicapped, a day-care center, a factory, a farm. Let students try "shadowing," following individual workers on the job. Involve parents and other relatives in this activity. Spread such trips out over several weeks and have students discuss their experiences with the class.

Guidance units. Plan a series of activities around a specific topic, like making friends. You might start out with a film or story, followed by a discussion of the characters' actions, feelings, and motivations. This might lead to an open discussion about what it means to be a friend. Then have students role play various scenes, or use puppets to illustrate how to make and keep friends. Create art, music, or writing projects about friendship.

Evaluate such a guidance unit by having students write essays about "My Best Friend" or "Why I Think I'm a Good Friend." Ask them to read and discuss a story about friendship. Have them write and produce a skit. Invite them to list five characteristics of a good friend, with a specific example of each.

Group Guidance as Experiential Learning

Because group guidance activities address students' feelings, motivations, goals, and beliefs, students' response to the activities becomes the content of the lesson. For example, if students respond with anger to a film about drug abuse, that experience of anger *is* the lesson — not drug abuse but students' anger about drug abuse. We respond to our students' anger and encourage them to see how their beliefs, goals, and values led to that anger. Students learn not only about drug abuse but about how drug abuse can provoke angry feelings. We encourage them to focus on how information — in this case, about drug abuse — affects people's minds and emotions.

Group guidance activities train students to express and examine their feelings; as they do, we teachers keep in touch with the emotions that so strongly influence learning. Because there are no right and wrong answers in such experiential learning, students are encouraged to be spontaneous and creative. They listen to each other, not merely for the content of what is said but for the emotions expressed. Gradually, the interest, involvement, support, and acceptance of the group, rather than of the teacher, become most important. Learning then depends less on the approval of the teacher, more on the student's personal desire to be a valuable member of the group. Motivation becomes less extrinsic, more intrinsic.

Group guidance, as experiential learning, tends to be valued and retained. By making guidance part of our curriculum, we teachers can involve our students in highly motivating experiences.

Recommended Readings

Canfield, Jack, and Wells, Harold. *100 Ways to Enhance Self-Concept in the Classroom.* Englewood Cliffs, NJ: Prentice-Hall, 1976.

Dinkmeyer, Don, and Caldwell, Edson. *Developmental Counseling and Guidance: A Comprehensive School Approach.* NY: McGraw-Hill, 1970.

Dreikurs, Rudolf; Grunwald, Bronia; and Pepper, Floy. *Maintaining Sanity in the Classroom.* 2nd ed. NY: Harper & Row, 1980.

Hillman, Bill W. *Teaching with Confidence: Getting Off the Classroom Wall.* Springfield, IL: Charles E. Thomas, 1980.

Muro, James, and Dinkmeyer, Don. *Counseling in the Elementary and Middle Schools: A Pragmatic Approach.* Dubuque, IA: Wm. C. Brown, 1977.

Raths, Louis; Harmin, Merrill; and Simon, Sidney. *Values and Teaching.* Columbus, OH: Charles E. Merrill, 1966.

Shaftel, Fannie, and Shaftel, George. *Role Playing for Social Values.* Englewood Cliffs, NJ: Prentice-Hall, 1967.

Study Questions

1. What is the teacher's role in guidance?

2. What is involved in career education for students in elementary and junior high school?

3. What are some possible discussion topics about human relationships?

4. "Any activity that addresses self-concept, human relationships, responsibility for one's own actions, and self-motivation contributes to career awareness." Explain.

5. What is the value of group guidance discussions focusing on specific academic topics, terms, or concepts?

6. What are some specific ways to conduct group guidance activities?

7. "Group guidance, as experiential learning, tends to be valued and retained." Explain.

Problem Situation

You are initiating group guidance by having the students learn to express their emotions and listen for each other's feelings. After a brief demonstration, you have the class pick partners for a discussion of topics they feel strongly about. You note that several pairs are having problems expressing and listening for feelings. Some students seem embarrassed and unwilling to join in.

1. What would you do?
2. What is a way to reduce the possibility of this happening?

Activity for the Week

Use at least one of the specific group guidance activities discussed in this chapter (for example, stories, discussion pictures, films). Bring questions and comments about group guidance activities and techniques appropriate for your students.

Recommended Resource Book Material

Chapter 2, "Understanding the family constellation," "How people create their own emotions"; Chapter 7, "Peer pressure and responsible choices"; Chapter 8, "Friendship"; Chapter 11, "Career education"; Chapter 12, "Operating democratically in the classroom."

Chart 11

Group Guidance Procedures in the Classroom

Activity	Purpose	Example
Discussion of human relationships.	To increase students' self-understanding and improve their social skills.	How can we get along better with our friends?
Career education.	To help students discover their resources and become aware of the world of work.	Personal exploration of the relationship between student's interests and the world of work.
Discussion of particular subjects and the relevancy of school.	To make connections between school and the world outside.	How do we use numbers when we go shopping?
Stories and problem situations.	To consider feelings, attitudes, and beliefs.	Discuss a problem situation showing typical misbehavior.
Role-playing.	To experience the feelings and goals of other people and to consider alternate ways to behave.	Role-play ways of handling teasing and ridicule.
Discussion pictures.	To learn to recognize feelings, attitudes, values, motivations.	How do you think this person feels? How would you feel if you were in this situation?
Films, filmstrips.	To develop empathy and to consider alternatives. To explore the world of work.	A film about conflict between siblings.
Exercises and games.	To provide experiential ways of learning about emotions, communication, motivation.	"I appreciate": Students, in turn, tell something they appreciate about the person on their right. The teacher also participates. Follow up discussion: "How does it feel to be appreciated?"
Art, music, and writing.	To illustrate and express emotions, behavior, and relationships.	Draw a picture illustrating an emotion.
Guest speakers.	To introduce students to people who hold certain jobs.	Invite a male nurse and a female firefighter.
Field trips.	To give first-hand experience with various jobs and human relationships.	Visit a day-care center.
Guidance units.	To take part in several activities around a central theme in order to reinforce the theme.	Unit on cooperation with several activities requiring cooperation. Discussion of what cooperation is.

Recording Worksheet

Role-Playing

As you listen to the role-playing activity, note how the teacher proceeds through the steps listed below. Be prepared to discuss each step with the group.

Steps in Role-Playing

1. Decide on a particular problem or issue, a specific situation to enact.
2. Ask for volunteers to play specific parts.
3. Discuss each part and plan each person's role in the scene.
4. Discuss with the class the scene about to be acted out. Help them understand what to look for.
5. Have the participants act out the scene.
6. After the performance, discuss each character's feelings and motivations. Consider and act out possible alternatives.

NOTES

Chapter 11

Points to Remember

1. Group guidance activities involve the whole class. They focus on:
- Attitudes.
- Feelings.
- Beliefs.
- Goals.
- Self-image.
- Human relationships.

2. Group guidance is both preventive and developmental.

3. Teachers' role in guidance includes:
- Working to align students' goals with our own.
- Identifying and meeting students' individual needs.
- Working with counselors to promote successful guidance programs.
- Conducting group guidance activities and discussions.

4. Any activity that addresses self-concept, human relationships, responsibility for one's own actions, and self-motivation contributes to career awareness.

5. Group guidance activities focusing on specific academic topics help broaden the curriculum by making close connections between school and the world outside.

6. Specific ways to conduct group guidance activities include:
- Discussions.
- Stories and problem situations.
- Role-playing.
- Discussion pictures.
- Films and filmstrips.
- Exercises and games.
- Art, music, and writing.
- Guest speakers.
- Field trips.
- Guidance units.

7. Because group guidance activities address students' feelings, motivations, goals, and beliefs, students' response to the activities becomes the content of the lesson. As experiential learning, group guidance tends to be valued and retained.

Personal Record Chapter 11

1.   My experience with the weekly assignment

2.   My reactions to the reading

3.   Topics to discuss with the group

4.   Skills I intend to improve

5.   My beliefs which impede progress

6.   My successes in applying program ideas

7.   My difficulties in applying program ideas

8.   My progress this week: A specific example

9.   This week I learned

CHAPTER 12
THE CLASS AS A GROUP: CLASSROOM MEETINGS

What are the basic functions of class meetings?
How can I involve students in planning?
How can I introduce students to problem solving?
How can I get students to encourage each other?
What are some guidelines for class meetings?
How can I start class meetings?

One of the most worthwhile group activities is the class meeting, a structured get-together of all students at a specific time each week. Like group guidance activities dealing with human relationships and with particular subjects, class meetings are concerned with helping students understand behavior and group dynamics. Since misbehaving students are discouraged and feel they don't belong, class meetings can give such students the peer encouragement they need. Students who give such encouragement learn empathy and social maturity. Class meetings can also enhance the communication of teachers and students.

Class meetings are democratic forums where we and our students share ideas, feelings, opinions, and plans. The group becomes an agent for forming values, developing cooperation, and instilling trust and empathy among class members. Everyone functions as an equal at such meetings. Participants encourage and help each other.

The three basic functions of a class meeting are planning, problem solving, and encouragement.

Planning. Class meetings are opportunities to involve students in deciding policies and setting guidelines. Tell them which matters they and perhaps you cannot decide: school hours, curriculum, school board policies. (However, if students have strong opinions on these subjects, we can encourage them to contact the appropriate person or committee.) Certain areas that traditionally have been the teacher's responsibility can be shared by the students in a democratic classroom: ways to study certain subjects, alternative ways to evaluate learning, classroom duties and jobs.

Consider all students as resources during your planning sessions. Norma may have slides and souvenirs from her trip to Mexico.

Russ' uncle is a carpenter; other students also have parents and relatives who might be willing to visit the class and discuss their jobs. Such guest speakers can be scheduled into the regular curriculum during planning sessions.

Allow students to participate actively in their own evaluation. Ask them to submit test questions. Give tests to small groups; plan the format with students. Solicit students' ideas about panel discussions and projects.

When we involve students in planning their own learning, we help them take responsibility for their own learning. They become our partners. They needn't have to guess at what we want them to learn; they needn't be surprised by test questions or grades.

Discuss the type and distribution of classroom jobs during planning sessions. Let students use their creativity to devise an equitable system for helping out.

Problem solving. Enlisting the help of the class in solving misbehavior problems can be more effective than imposing a solution yourself. Students who misbehave become aware that the class has certain expectations and that their behavior isn't acceptable to the group. The class encourages those who misbehave to seek acceptance in more constructive ways.

In order to solve problems of misbehavior, we must first discover the student's goal. As in other forums for goal disclosure, we first ask the student involved if he or she agrees to discuss the situation with the group. If not, the student may choose either to stop misbehaving or to have the class help decide how to deal with the misbehavior. If the student agrees, we solicit from the class their tentative hypothesis or guess: "Why do you think Jorge keeps throwing the softball over the fence?" Members of the class offer: "He knows we'll have to go get it." "He doesn't like to play softball and wants to make sure no one else plays." "He's just a brat." "He only wants to play soccer."

You block name-calling ("I feel concerned when we call each other names because name-calling doesn't solve any problems.") and help the class explore the purpose of behavior: "Let's discuss the reasons Jorge behaves as he does." Then you or a student puts together the group's conclusion: "Jorge, could it be that you throw the softball over the fence because you're getting even with us for not letting you play soccer?"

Jorge's recognition reflex tells you the guess is correct. You then ask all students, including Jorge, to suggest a solution to the problem. The class brainstorms, during the course of which everyone notices that other students share Jorge's desire to play soccer. The class decides to play soccer on Wednesdays, softball on the other days. They will continue this schedule until the next class meeting, when the plan will be evaluated. Jorge agrees not to throw the ball over the fence on "softball days."

Such problem-solving ventures often reveal that misbehaving students aren't alone in their feelings. They realize the group disapproves only of their response to those feelings, their behavior — not them as people. The class learns to accommodate varied opinions and emotions within the group. You keep in touch with your students' thoughts, opinions, feelings, and motivations.

At problem-solving class meetings, students can also discuss troublesome relationships with parents, siblings, teachers, or friends. The group provides encouragement and suggestions. Students can also discuss problems involving the whole group: not returning materials to their proper place, for example.

Encouragement. This function of class meetings can't really be separated from planning and problem-solving. No matter what the focus, emphasize the positive: "How can we solve this problem together?" Guide students toward the positive, educational side of experiences. Help them see each other's strengths: "Who noticed how Edward's been improving in his spelling?" Notice and comment on contributions: "I really appreciated your help today."

We can help students develop confidence by getting them to express faith in one another: "How many think Naomi can solve this problem? Let's see a show of hands." In an encouraging, respectful classroom, such a display of support can be heartening.

In addition to giving spontaneous encouragement, consider beginning each class meeting with "good news time." Say, "Before we decide on a field trip, I have some good news. Anessa has improved in her handwriting, particularly in her a's and e's." You'll soon be able to begin meetings by asking students if they have any good news. Ask them to mention what is positive and new in their lives. Plan to make each student the subject for good news at least once.

Guidelines for Class Meetings

Successful class meetings require our commitment and patience. We'll probably not have instant success. Students may test our sincerity, especially about involving them in decision making. They may start lengthy discussions on matters they can have no voice in. If they do, ask in a friendly, tentative way, "Could it be that when you talk so long about the length of the schoolday, you're trying to take up part of our geography period?"

Let students see your interest and involvement by paying close attention to what everyone says and by taking a seat within the circle. You will probably play a larger role in early meetings than you will after students learn how to participate and discuss. But no matter what your role, be an interested group member.

Let students know that class meetings aren't to be "gripe sessions," that they have a positive purpose. Emphasize that the meetings are to bring about change, not merely to review complaints. Keep the focus positive by blocking all personal attacks. Focus students' attention on helping, on making everyone feel accepted. For example, tell complaining students, "I appreciate the topics you've brought up. Who can suggest ways we could solve this problem?"

Help students uncover the real issues behind what people say and do: use class meetings to discuss the goals of misbehavior. If students are arguing about who should do a particular classroom job next, and you notice that power and defeating other students are the real purposes of the discussion, alert students. Lead them into a discussion of how people use the goal of power.

Redirect discussions when they keep coming back to certain people's problems and gripes. Say, "We seem to be having trouble today staying on the topic. Why do you suppose that's happening?" Especially in early meetings, you'll want to refer often to the discussion guidelines the class has set up. Everyone needs to practice clear speaking and careful listening: they can do so at class meetings.

Strive for consensus, delaying decisions until all students agree. If necessary, take a vote and let the majority rule (but be aware that the minority may be uncooperative). Make the decision yourself when the problem demands immediate action and students don't seem near a decision. Those who disagree with the results can offer new ideas at the next meeting. Place any unfinished business on the agenda for the next meeting. Encourage students to add to the agenda during the week. Set up an "Agenda Box" for written suggestions.

Review for yourself the techniques of group leadership and the ways you can use therapeutic forces in your classroom. Show students by example how to participate and how to discuss.

A Sample, Problem-Solving Class Meeting

Mrs. Chapman's class is discussing the behavior of two boys, Max and Anthony, who disrupt recess by chasing each other around and running through ongoing games.

Mrs. Chapman: Does anyone have an idea about why these boys are doing this?

Student 1: They're just trying to show off!

Mrs. Chapman: Any other ideas? (Redirecting)

Student 2: They think they're real smart!

Mrs. Chapman: I'm getting concerned that we might not solve this problem if we keep calling Max and Anthony names. They may want to get even with us. (Blocking with an I-message) Could these boys be trying to show us something? (Redirecting, leading to goal disclosure)

Student 3: Maybe they're trying to make us mad.

Mrs. Chapman: How many of you feel angry when they run through your games? (Several students raise hands.) What do some of you do when you get angry at Max and Anthony? (Several students report that they call them names and chase them.) What happens when you do this? (Several admit it doesn't help.) Is it possible that Anthony and Max want you to get angry and chase them? (Several nod.) Why would they want to do that? (Redirecting, leading to goal disclosure)

Student 4: Maybe they want to show us they can do what they want and we can't stop them?

Mrs. Chapman: Boys, what do you think about that? (Max and Anthony grin.) Seems like we've figured it out. You've said that trying to make Max and Anthony stop doesn't work. So what can we do? Who has a suggestion?

Student 5: We could ask them nicely not to do it.

Student 2: Aw, that won't work!

Mrs. Chapman: Wait a minute; let's brainstorm. I'll write down everything we think of. We won't say anything about any idea until we're finished. "Ask them nicely not to do it" is one suggestion. Who has another? (Blocking and brainstorming)

Student 1: Make them stay in from recess!

Mrs. Chapman: Okay. Other ideas? (Pause.) Joyce, we haven't heard from you. What do you think? (Redirecting to silent members)

Joyce: We could ask them to join our games.

Mrs. Chapman: Any other ideas? (No one has anything else to add.) All right, our ideas are: Ask them nicely not to run through the games; make them stay in from recess if they do it; ask them to join the games. Since the decision we make involves you, Max and Anthony, do either of you have anything to say? (Redirecting) (Silence.)

Well, if you're not willing to talk about it, we'll have to decide ourselves. Which plan do we want? (Most students want them to stay in from recess. A few say they'd like the boys to join their games.)

I have an idea too and I'd like to know what you think. I think if you invited Anthony and Max to join your games and they did, the problem would be solved. If they didn't join the games and kept disturbing you, then they'd have to come in for the rest of recess. What do you think? (Most indicate agreement.)

How many are willing to go along with this combination plan until our next meeting? (Task setting and obtaining commitments) (Most raise their hands.) All right, Anthony and Max, do you want to comment? (Silence.)

Let's review our plan. We decided to invite these boys to join the games. If they keep up the disturbance, they'll have to come in. Is that right? (Summarizing)

Student 2: What if they don't join the games when we ask them to?

Mrs. Chapman: Well, what about that? (Redirecting)

Student 5: They don't have to join the games. Just as long as they don't bug us.

Mrs. Chapman: Is that all right? (Students agree) I'm glad we've got a plan. Let's see how it goes and talk about it at our next meeting. Now, I think we need to show Max and Anthony that we're not angry at them all the time. What are some things they do that we like? Please speak to Max or Anthony. Say, "I like it when you _____ ." (Encouragement and promoting direct interaction) Who will begin?

Student 3: I like it when Max tells jokes.

Mrs. Chapman: Excuse me. Please speak to Max. (Promoting direct interaction)

Student 3: Okay, Max, I like it when you tell jokes because they're funny.

Mrs. Chapman: Thank you. What about Anthony?

Student 6: Anthony, I like it when you help me with my math. (The teacher continues to promote encouraging comments.)

Notice how a skillful leader and a responsive class can solve problems together. Mrs. Chapman decided not to promote direct interaction at first; the boys may have felt attacked. Instead, she decided to have the first comments directed at her. The ideas of what to do came from the students. Mrs. Chapman then helped them implement their ideas. She did make a suggestion; she convinced the students to ask the two boys to join their games. She took this opportunity to pull Max and Anthony back into the group.

Had the group disagreed with their teacher's idea and made unproductive suggestions, wanting to punish the offenders, Mrs. Chapman might have expressed her own feelings in an I-message: "When you want to punish others, I feel sad because we want everyone in our class to be treated fairly." She might then ask students if they'd want the proposed punishment themselves, if the punishment will help the situation. In the example, the suggestion to send the boys in from recess was a logical consequence.

Mrs. Chapman finished the session by inviting everyone to encourage Max and Anthony. Showing students how to separate the deed from the doer and helping misbehaving students feel liked is *extremely* important. We must be prepared to encourage if the group doesn't. We can remind the class of positive things the misbehaving students have done.

Starting Class Meetings in Your Classroom

Introduce your students to class meetings gradually, holding informal meetings now and then. Don't expect them to know how to solve problems immediately. Instead, use this "three-phase" approach:

Phase 1. Before each meeting, arrange your chairs or desks in a circle so students can see and talk to one another. Begin the meeting by informally letting the class decide how to handle routine tasks. Discuss low-key issues such as room arrangement, bulletin board committees, classroom jobs, planning field trips and parties, and so forth.

Introduce students to decision making by letting them decide how certain chores will be done. Say, "I've been making most of the decisions about what happens in our classroom. Now I'd like you to help me. Let's talk about what jobs need to be done in our room and how we can divide them up fairly. Shall we make a list? What jobs need to be done?"

If no one responds, be more specific. "I'm talking about jobs like erasing the chalkboard and passing out papers. Besides those two jobs, what are some others that have to be done?" If students overlook some jobs, add them yourself.

After the class gets more accustomed to planning, move on to more complicated issues like the order of study, different ways of covering certain subjects, various ways to evaluate learning. With very young students, you might start by giving them two choices: "Would you like your snack before or after storytime?" Gradually increase the number of alternatives to three or four. Eventually, students will be ready to propose their own.

Phase 2. Introduce problem solving when you feel the group is ready. Describe a problem and appeal to the class for help. For example: "Class, we have a problem and I need your help in deciding what to do. It seems some students are forgetting to return the playground equipment to the box. Mr. Morstad's class has had to use some of their recess time finding the equipment. I'm not interested in knowing who's not returning the equipment or in punishing anyone. I only want to solve the problem. Who has an idea about what we could do?"

As the group learns to solve such problems, you can begin to discuss how the class can help misbehaving students feel accepted by behaving constructively. Never allow students to punish each other. Instead, let them see the logic of the logical consequences you propose. Gradually, involve them in formulating consequences.

The group has been learning cohesion through group guidance activities, discussions of human relationships and of specific academic subjects. Continue to encourage cooperation and closeness as students learn to plan and to solve problems.

Phase 3. After the class has successfully worked through some problems, it's time to set up regular, formal class meetings. You might say, "For quite a while we've been discussing our problems and making certain decisions about what goes on in our classroom. Now I'm wondering how you'd feel about making our class meetings a regular part of each week. What do you think?"

Most students will like the idea. Then suggest some guidelines: "I've learned about other class meetings and certain groups found it helpful to meet every Monday morning. What do you think?" Offer ideas about having an agenda, formulating guidelines for discussion, planning the frequency and length of meetings, and so on. Stress that students will now share the task of suggesting topics.

Hold the first official class meeting soon after the planning session, preferably the next day. You be the chairperson for the first few meetings. Sit in a different place in the circle each meeting to emphasize the equality of all participants. (The leader needn't sit at the "head.")

Set up an outline for the meetings if you feel more comfortable doing so. Here's one suggestion (Dreikurs and Cassel, *Discipline Without Tears,* 1972, page 80):

1. Good news of the past week.
2. Ways in which we can improve next week.
3. Personal problems.
4. Responsibilities.
5. Future plans.

As points are raised, record them under the appropriate heading. You might limit the discussion of each area — to six minutes, perhaps, or 10 minutes, depending on your students' maturity.

At first, ask students to raise their hands. Invite silent members to comment. As students get used to the format, rotate the responsibility for leading the meetings. Suggest co-chairpersons so everyone will have a chance to share the leadership.

Let the class decide how chairpersons will be selected and how long each pair will serve. Stress that everyone will have a chance to lead. Before each meeting, consider holding a brief session with the new chairpersons in which you explain their responsibilities. You might want to train four students at a time, perhaps while the class is working on a different project.

Explain briefly and simply some of the leadership skills discussed in Chapter 10. Review the discussion guidelines; go over reflective listening and I-messages too if students are familiar with them.

The point is not to make students well-trained group leaders. But some training in leadership will benefit your class meetings. Further, you'll be teaching students some valuable ways to participate in a group. And you'll be reviewing leadership techniques for yourself.

At the first meetings with student chairpersons, you might sit near the leaders and give assistance as needed. Act as a consultant only (Dreikurs, Grunwald, Pepper, 1971). Whisper suggestions occasionally: "Ask Erica what she thinks." But let the students address the group. Gradually, sit away from the leaders and let them take full charge.

You can also introduce the job of recorder, so you'll have a written record of each meeting. You can be the recorder the first few times, writing notes on the board. Then select, or have the class select, student recorders. You might also tape-record the meetings or help young student recorders tape-record their own summaries.

It may take some classes only a few weeks to reach "Phase 3." It may take others a semester. Set an appropriate pace for your students.

Some Dos and Don'ts of Class Meetings

1. *Do adhere to time limits.* Begin and end meetings at the agreed-upon time. Meetings with primary students may only last 10-15 minutes. Older students may discuss for 30-50 minutes. If everyone

knows the limits, members will be less inclined to waste time. Do allow a few minutes at the end for a summary.

2. *Don't skip meetings.* Cancelling meetings affects cohesiveness and group morale. Students must know you consider the meetings important. Whether or not to hold meetings during short weeks can be up to you and the class to decide.

3. *Do block personal attacks.* Even when promoting feedback, make sure students understand that they're not to be critical, fault-finding, or rude. Emphasize the positive purpose of the meetings.

4. *Don't permit meetings to become gripe sessions.* Explain the difference between complaining (which is easy but not productive) and proposing changes (a more difficult but more beneficial procedure). If students gripe, say, ''Do you want to change this? What are some things we can do?'' If you see that they only want to complain, say, ''It seems to me you really don't want to change things. The discussion is going nowhere. I understand you feel angry about this, but let's move on to more productive topics. What's next on our agenda?''

5. *Do become an equal group member.* Resist the temptation to bring up your own issues at every meeting. Let students know these are class meetings, not teacher-dominated discussions. Refrain from lecturing and making rules. Listen to what your students are saying and feeling.

6. *Don't allow anyone to monopolize the meeting.* Some people insist on being the center of attention. If Louise talks on and on about her troubles with the gym teacher, you'll want to intervene. Suggest that time is going and the group needs to discuss other topics. Review your discussion guidelines. If Louise doesn't get the message, and there isn't time to explain, meet with her privately. Suggest more constructive ways for her to behave. If her behavior during meetings doesn't change, the logical consequence would be to exclude her until she's ready to follow the group's guidelines.

7. *Do put agreements into action.* When the class has decided something appropriate for them to decide, be sure to follow

through as soon as possible. Students will then see that their decision-making power is real. As long as you have carefully defined what students may decide, you should have no difficulty implementing their decisions. You have the opportunity at all meetings to voice your own concerns or questions.

8. *Do evaluate meetings.* Class meetings need to be evaluated like any other part of students' education. Consider holding a regular evaluation after every third meeting. Have students help you put together an evaluation form to fill out or simply discuss. For example:

> What have we done especially well during our last three meetings?
> What have we not done especially well during our last three meetings?
> Has everyone participated? Do people seem interested? How can you tell?
> Are we following our discussion guidelines?
> Are there any guidelines we don't always follow? Which ones?
> Are we following through on our agreements?
> What improvements can we make in our next meetings?

When we make a firm commitment to regular classroom meetings, we put our desire for an encouraging, democratic classroom into action.

Works Cited

Dreikurs, Rudolf, and Cassel, Pearl. *Discipline Without Tears.* Rev. ed. NY: Hawthorn Books, 1972.

Dreikurs, Rudolf; Grunwald, Bronia; and Pepper, Floy. *Maintaining Sanity in the Classroom.* NY: Harper & Row, 1971.

Recommended Readings

Dreikurs, Rudolf. *Psychology in the Classroom.* NY: Harper & Row, 1968.

Dreikurs, Rudolf, and Cassel, Pearl. *Discipline Without Tears.* 2nd ed. NY: Hawthorn Books, 1972.

Dreikurs, Rudolf; Grunwald, Bronia; and Pepper, Floy. *Maintaining Sanity in the Classroom.* 2nd ed. NY: Harper & Row, 1980.

Glasser, William. *Schools Without Failure.* NY: Harper & Row, 1969.

Stanford, Gene. *Developing Effective Classroom Groups.* NY: Hart, 1977.

Study Questions

1. What are the three basic functions of class meetings?

2. How can students take part in the planning function?

3. Why is it useful to involve the class in solving misbehavior problems? What are some other functions of problem-solving class meetings?

4. How can we promote encouragement during class meetings?

5. What do we do if:
   a. Students start lengthy discussions on matters they can have no voice in?
   b. Meetings become gripe sessions?
   c. The real issues behind what people say and do during meetings remain hidden?
   d. Certain students monopolize meetings?
   e. Consensus isn't forthcoming and a decision must be reached?

6. What is the "three-phase approach" to starting class meetings? How can you begin to introduce problem solving?

7. Why is it important to adhere to time limits? Hold meetings when scheduled? Block personal attacks? Become an equal group member with students? Put agreements into action? Evaluate meetings?

Problem Situation

You have started class meetings after studying therapeutic group forces and learning group leadership skills. In the second meeting, students discuss how teachers' helpers are selected. Many complain that these helpers are only teachers' pets. You notice the students are not listening or responding to each other. Some hold private conversations; others look bored.

   1. What might be the reason for this type of interaction?
   2. What would you do to change it?
   3. What do you believe is the most systematic and effective way for you to introduce class meetings?

Activity for the Week

Conduct a class meeting. Bring notes or a tape recording of the meeting.

Recommended Resource Book Material

Chapter 1, "Cooperation and responsibility," "Classroom jobs"; Chapter 3, "Encouraging ourselves and others," "Encouragement," "Promoting peer encouragement"; Chapter 6, "Exploring alternatives"; Chapter 12, "Individual student misbehavior."

Chart 12

Phases in Establishing Class Meetings

Phase	Purpose	Procedures
1. Informal planning discussions.	To provide initial training in making cooperative decisions.	Discuss low-key issues: room arrangement, bulletin board committees, sharing classroom jobs, planning field trips and parties, deciding on the order of studying subjects. Then move to more complicated issues: units of study, learning activities, methods of evaluation.
2. Introduction of problem solving.	To give students practice in solving group-owned problems.	Begin with general problems by appealing for students' help: "We have a problem about cleaning up after art." ("I have a problem and I need your help.") When the group is ready, discuss the misbehavior of individual students.
3. Setting up regular class meetings.	To get students involved in classroom management and planning, and to provide a safe environment to discuss personal concerns.	Discuss how to set up the meetings: rules and procedures. Stress that students, not just you, will have the opportunity to bring up topics. Hold the first class meeting soon after the planning meeting. Train students in leadership so they can take charge of meetings.

Recording Worksheet

Class Meetings

This recording presents a teacher's attempts to win her students' cooperation for studying a grammar unit. Consider what you would say or do at various points to motivate and encourage the students. Be prepared to discuss your responses with the group.

NOTES

Chapter 12

Points to Remember

1. The three basic functions of a class meeting are planning, problem solving, and encouragement.

2. Planning sessions are opportunities to involve students in deciding policies and setting guidelines.

3. Enlisting the help of the class in solving misbehavior problems can be more effective than imposing your own solution.

4. The encouragement function of class meetings can't really be separated from planning and problem solving. No matter what the focus, emphasize the positive.

5. Guidelines for class meetings include:
- Adhere to time limits and don't skip meetings.
- Become an equal group member with students.
- Strive for consensus. Put agreements into action.
- Don't allow anyone to monopolize meetings.
- Don't permit meetings to become gripe sessions.
- Block personal attacks.
- Evaluate meetings periodically.

6. Start class meetings using a three-phase approach:
Phase 1. Begin with low-key planning sessions.
Phase 2. Introduce problem solving when you feel the group is ready.
Phase 3. Set up regular, formal class meetings.

Personal Record Chapter 12

1. My experience with the weekly assignment

2. My reactions to the reading

3. Topics to discuss with the group

4. Skills I intend to improve

5. My beliefs which impede progress

6. My successes in applying program ideas

7. My difficulties in applying program ideas

8. My progress this week: A specific example

9. This week I learned

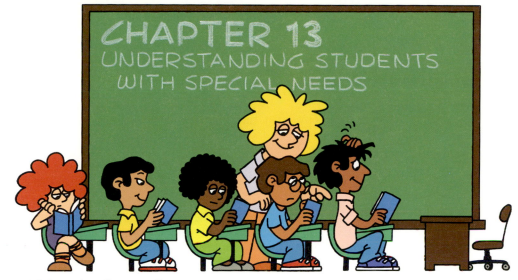

What is an Individualized Education Program?
How do I work with the special education teacher and consultant?
What do I need to know about teaching "special" students in my mainstreamed classroom?
How do I handle the special behavior problems presented by handicapped students?

Floy Childers Pepper
Coordinator, Program for the Emotionally Handicapped
Multnomah County Education Service District
Portland, Oregon

Teachers face a variety of special students in today's mainstreamed classrooms. Some have involuntary learning problems, and some can learn but don't. Often the two conditions occur together.

Often these students have developed a mistaken idea of how they can become recognized members of their classrooms. They think in terms of status and achievement, comparing their performance to that of others. They do not realize that when they measure their contributions by the achievements of others, they progressively undermine their ability to value their own contributions and themselves. The more students strive to gain status and recognition, the more deeply discouraged they become if they fail to achieve these goals.

Students with special needs who feel their self-worth depends on achieving some kind of superiority over others may misbehave. They may argue, blame or accuse others, become defensive, or fight. They experience a constant threat of failure and defeat and may strive to control every situation.

This chapter will attempt to illustrate how these desires for power and superiority are transferred to behavior in the classroom, to give suggestions about how to work with this behavior, and to discuss other "special" students and problems.

Please note: In order to identify clearly various differences among students, descriptive labels (slow learner, underachiever, pseudo-retarded) will be used. *This in no way implies that students should themselves be labeled. Labeling students sets them apart as "different" and damages their self-esteem.*

Special Education

Teaching handicapped students requires special training. The term 'handicapped' refers to the full range of physical, mental, and emotional conditions that interfere with the student's learning and require special education. The provision for special education is based on the unique needs of individual students, rather than on the handicapping condition itself.

Special education is now interpreted to mean the individualized education program (IEP). It employs a variety of techniques, procedures, instructional materials, and equipment to advance the student's rate of cognitive, affective, and motor development. Special education recognizes that all handicapped students have a wide range of educational needs, varying greatly in intensity and duration.

Special educators, psychologists, counselors, social workers, and other specialized staff are taking on new consultative roles, emphasizing the training of regular educators to work competently with handicapped students. This new consultative function is one of the main duties of the specialized staff. "Consulting," then, is a relationship undertaken to help improve the instruction of one or more students.

The special education teacher and consultant provide additional instructional material for use by the regular teacher. They work as partners with the regular teacher and schedule time to be in the classroom. They are available for consultation, planning, providing additional curriculum, and giving general support to the regular classroom teacher, including prescriptive teaching methods and materials.

Regular classroom teachers must understand the characteristics and needs of their "special" students. Some students in the regular classroom could be considered handicapped, but they have not been previously identified as such. Others may have been placed in the regular classroom as the most appropriate setting for their particular need.

The type and degree of handicap will vary with each student. Reynolds and Birch (1977) provide these distinctions:

Impairment is the physical defect itself, the actual condition of the tissue, such as the absence of fingers, a severed nerve, diabetes, a heart condition.

Disability is a matter of function, a lack of some ability. It is a limitation of the behavior directly dependent upon the impairment.

Handicap is the extent to which an impairment, a disability, or both get in the way of normal living, including getting an education. 'Handicap' is highly personal; it describes an individual's own reactions to the presence of an impairment or disability.

246

What Training Will Regular Classroom Teachers Need?

Regular classroom teachers need to know:

1. An overview of Public Law 94-142 (PL94-142).
2. The various categories of handicaps, such as emotionally disturbed, hearing impaired, physically impaired, learning disabled, and so on.
3. The flow chart for referrals from their own district.
4. How to write an IEP according to their district guidelines.
5. Where to find curriculum materials to meet the handicapped student's needs.
6. How to handle severe behavior problems.

Each district, county, and state will have its own policies and procedures concerning the first five above. The techniques of handling behavior problems also vary greatly.

Retardation

All retarded people have the capacity to learn, some more quickly than others. The "educable" mentally retarded (EMR) student has an assessed IQ of 50-70 and is usually capable of learning academic skills between the third- and sixth-grade levels. These students can achieve vocational, personal, and marital independence.

The appropriate, least restrictive environment for an educable retarded student is the regular classroom. Most of the student's education can be conducted in this setting, with specialized instruction coming from speech therapists, physical and occupational therapists, counselors, and so on. These specialists may need to train the regular classroom teacher to carry out the student's instructional program.

Because educable retarded students learn slowly, many teachers and parents treat them as if they were totally incompetent and incapable. Because they are deferentially or specially treated by significant adults, these students may despair or become extremely discouraged. They may begin to believe they are stupid and inadequate. They may become more and more dependent, give up all hope of succeeding, and may choose to display inadequacy in school.

Richard was this kind of student. He had been properly placed in a regular classroom. However, his teachers felt sorry for him because he was slow and they equated slowness with stupidity. They did everything for Richard until he became convinced he couldn't do anything. So he gave up. Instead of achieving and becoming a happy, well-adjusted student, Richard regressed even to the point of soiling. When one teacher finally figured out what had happened, she began a program of encouragement. Soon Richard's self-esteem started to increase.

Encouragement is a continuous process aimed at giving the student a sense of self-respect and accomplishment. The teacher encouraged Richard to develop self-confidence and to recognize his own abilities. She gave him verbal recognition for doing the things he was supposed to do: "Richard, you followed instructions on your language assignment." "It's nice to see you enjoying your math." "You were settled and ready for reading within one minute." "You really worked hard!" Richard learned that he was recognized and valued as a person, regardless of his most recent behavior or his previous failure. His teacher realized that she needed to do more than teach Richard skills. She had to reach Richard and help him find his place in the group.

By participating in class discussions, Richard began to realize that some of his behavior was unacceptable to his classmates and that he needed to change. The group asked themselves, "What can we do to help Richard so he doesn't have to act as if he can't do things?" They suggested that Richard tutor another student in something he knew well. The youngsters also let Richard know they noticed his improvement in personal hygiene and his attempts to accept responsibility for his behavior. Richard was able to, find his place in the group and become a more responsible person.

Teachers must be aware that students like Richard can easily become discouraged and give up. It's best to keep their interest high by having them work at specific activities for brief periods of time. Like all students, EMR students need to be treated with mutual respect and equality to help bolster their self-esteem. The expectations of the teacher are crucial. Through encouragement and class discussions, these students can adjust to school and eventually become self-supporting citizens. Their academic program needs to build on strengths and minimize limitations.

The curriculum for the educable retarded student does not differ greatly from that of the regular student. It is directly related to the school's published curriculum and accommodates the learning characteristics of the individual student. These students do a better job when learning *concrete* rather than abstract material. They need to be asked to learn and retain material in very small units or sequences. They have difficulty when the learning materials are reversed or the order is changed. Reducing distractions, drawing attention to the task, and encouraging frequently will help them learn. Programming them on their own success level, sequencing the learning tasks, and breaking some tasks into smaller steps can be effective teaching methods. Specific task analysis and specific behavioral objectives need to be emphasized in order to teach these students to carry out instructional sequences.

The objective for educable retarded students is to increase their functioning and to overcome the educational lags that led to the initial assessment. The hope is that these students will be able to continue through school with little or no special help. More and more educable retarded young people are being merged into the mainstream of instruction while still receiving high-quality special education.

The ability to attain functional literacy is the main difference between educable mentally retarded (EMR) students and trainable mentally retarded (TMR) students. By adulthood, the trainable retarded student's intellectual ability is between that of a five- and a nine-year-old, with an assessed IQ of 49 or below. These young people will probably not be truly mainstreamed. However, they do need a continuum of services so they can go to school in a setting where their needs are served and their restrictions minimized.

Their training emphasizes oral communication and attaining the social graces. These students very often have social and/or physical characteristics that set them apart from others. For example, they may chew on their shirt sleeves, shuffle when walking, talk right into your face, and interact inappropriately. They need intensive social training to minimize their differences so that they will be accepted by the non-handicapped.

The Slow Learner

Another group of students have IQs between the upper edge of the mentally retarded range and the lower edge of the range for so-called normals (normal IQ assessed at 71-109). Realizing that an IQ score is not necessarily a true measure of a child's potential, we may come to a different conclusion about these students' abilities if we tailor the curriculum to their individual needs. Test scores are influenced by how students feel about themselves, what their goals are, how they feel about the tester, and what information they decide to give on any particular day.

This group of "no-man's land" youngsters form approximately 15% of the school population. They usually can't or don't keep up and are probably doing the poorest work in the average classroom. It is generally in the intellectual arena, in the highly complex mental operations or reasoning processes, where the slow learner finds difficulty.

These students are sometimes termed "leaky buckets": the teacher pours facts in, but the student never seems to retain anything. Nonetheless, they are essentially normal in their motor, physical, social, and emotional development.

The slow learner is educated in the regular classroom and is usually not identified as needing special education. However, many could profit from changes in curriculum. The content can be the same, but the materials must be presented in simple sentences and directions need to be clear and brief. Slow learners need encouragement to change their behavior; they may constantly lose their pencils, misplace their papers, and in general be disorganized.

Sonia was such a student. She would finish about three-fourths of her reader by the end of the first year, return in the fall, and need to start all over again. Given a math assignment or concept, she would learn it, be able to do her work correctly, and two days later would approach the same task as if she had never seen it before. She could never find anything and was always disorganized. But her teacher noticed that Sonia would hold up a piece of paper and ask, "What do you want me to cut out?" No matter what anyone suggested, a car or a wagon or whatever, Sonia would take the scissors, and cut, and snip, and cut. She would then assemble the pieces and they would all fit together properly.

Through training and class discussions, Sonia's teacher was able to help her become responsible for her own belongings. Discussion, the democratic interchange of ideas, is one of the most effective means of eliciting behavioral change. Since all behavior has social meaning and is strongly influenced by the reactions of others, the group provides an excellent setting for bringing about change.

Sonia's class discussed her ability to cut out shapes and put them together. Since she was so good at that, they wondered why she was constantly losing her pencil, eraser, hat, jacket, and so on. Someone asked, "Why is Sonia always losing things?" Another student said, "I don't know, but it's a great way to keep everybody busy with her. You know, we're always looking around for her lost things." The group decided to help Sonia be responsible. They helped her organize her desk and label a place for each item she kept there. They encouraged Sonia by commenting on how straight her desk was, how well she was remembering to put everything back where it belonged. They decided not to comment on or look for things Sonia lost. Heartened by the group's interest and concern, Sonia's self-esteem rose and she became more organized.

Slow learners have difficulty in reasoning and in complex mental operations. Assigning these students a peer tutor can be helpful. They also need to learn organizational skills. The teacher can help by breaking all tasks down into their component parts and having the student check them off when they're done. It is a good practice to post the list of tasks either on the student's desk or on a bulletin board.

Pseudo-Retardation

It is important not to confuse the slow learner with the pseudo-retarded student. Slow learners have genuine reasoning difficulties. Their deficiencies are usually not excuses for non-performance.

Pseudo-retarded students may have any IQ score but act as if they cannot learn. They often get special service, special attention, exemption from things they don't want to do. They can dominate the family and the classroom, using their "deficiency" for personal benefit. We must remember, however, that they are seldom aware of their psychological goal.

If one accurately observes these youngsters, one can see how cleverly they manipulate adults and how systematically they use every situation for their own benefit. They demand repeated explanations, constant help and reminders. Directly or indirectly, they tell us, "It's time to come and scold me"; "It's time to help me"; "I'm too little"; "It's time to take care of me again." They feel no need to give up their way of living and acting because they get attention without having to do what others do. They get special treatment and have tremendous power to defeat any pressure from adults. They can be told what to do each day, but they won't listen. They don't learn what is required of them, but they make their teacher do what they want.

Leon, for example, never seemed to get directions straight. The other students would start working. He would sit, look at his book or paper, and then raise his hand for help. The teacher would go over the task again with him. Leon would begin work and then ask for additional assistance or want to have his work checked to see if it was right. This same scenario was played and replayed many times a day. One day the teacher decided to tell Leon that she was going to explain the assignment one time and one time only.

A few days later, Leon and his mother came in for a conference. The mother said Leon had told her that his teacher wouldn't help him anymore and he couldn't do his work. His mother said it was the teacher's job to teach, she paid her taxes, etc., etc.

The teacher asked Leon if he remembered their talk about his really not listening when she gave instructions. He slowly nodded. The teacher asked the mother if Leon ever wanted her to repeat things. The mother said, "Yes! As a matter of fact, I seem to have to repeat a lot of things for Leon." The teacher said, "I think Leon is a bright boy and can understand things the first time. What do you think about that, Leon?" Leon said, "Sure, I can — oh, I mean, no . . . I need you to help me." His mother understood. The teacher said, "Could it be, Leon, that you want to keep your mother and me busy with you?" Leon grinned but shook his head. His mother said, "This is certainly an eye-opener for me. I see I need to make a few changes in what I'm doing."

As teachers, we need to be able to recognize the specific goals of these students. Usually the student who is using pseudo-retardation has adopted the passive-destructive goal of attention (service) or is displaying inadequacy. When Leon said, "I can't do it. Help me," his teacher felt annoyed. She usually helped Leon, even though he was clearly capable of helping himself. A better response to his goal of attention would be to ignore the behavior, walk away, and become busy elsewhere, remembering to notice Leon's positive behavior. Had Leon not asked for help, but rather sat quietly, only talking when his teacher asked a direct question, had the teacher felt despair, the student may have been displaying inadequacy. In that case the teacher could refuse to give up on Leon, encouraging any positive effort.

Rex was 12 years old and large for his age. He moved slowly and looked awkward when he walked or ran. Sometimes adults and peers said hurtful things to him: "You big lummox!" "Can't you move faster than that?" "You're just plain stupid and dumb." "Dummy!" In class, whenever the teacher attempted to help Rex, he would say, "I can't do it. I'm too dumb."

Rex was convinced that he was stupid and couldn't learn. He had given up. His teacher discussed the problem with his parents and they all agreed to say encouraging things to Rex to help him feel better about himself. They also asked the physical education teacher to help Rex attain more skill in body movement and control.

In the classroom during discussion, the teacher brought up the general topic of name calling and how people often feel when someone calls them names. Then she asked if there was anyone in the class who called people names or who were called names. After some discussion, one of the students said people did that to Rex. The class began to suggest ways they could help Rex. Then they discussed what Rex could do himself: he could hold his head up so he could see where he was going, wear his belt tighter so his jeans wouldn't droop, and act a little more lively.

A few weeks later, the group noted how Rex had improved and made another suggestion: they would teach him to dance. They had noticed he was having a tough time dancing in gym class because other students teased him. Throughout the year the class continued to encourage Rex. Gradually Rex began to feel better about himself. He even began to learn at a faster rate.

"Pseudo-retarded" students who display inadequacy need to be encouraged to do *something,* academic or not. Regular encouragement of any positive movement stimulates their courage.

Underachievers

Underachievers quite often test in the top third of their class but are unsuccessful in school and usually make poor grades. Surveys show that approximately 40% of all students are underachievers, performing below their abilities. Although these students are not identified as needing special education, they may be a problem for the regular teacher. Underachievers are quite often impulsive, want instant gratification, may have poor interpersonal relationships. They usually have high social aspirations, but quite often have low self-esteem.

Francis X. Walton (1978) stated: "Students usually agree that apathetic behavior is a passive and subtle use of power and that the private logic of the apathetic student is substantially as follows: "You (Mr. and Ms. Teacher/Administrator) are going to tell us what to do, when to do it, and how to do it. It's clear that we can't change anything. We can't fight city hall, so I'll tell you what you can do, Mr./Ms. Teacher. You can have it! It's your classroom. It's your school. On the other hand, I want to get out of this place some day, so I'll do enough academic work to get by (that's for me). You can bet I won't do any more than enough to get by (that's for you)."

Underachievers may fall into four basic categories: the dependence seeker, the independence seeker, the approval seeker, and the security seeker (Pecaut, 1973). However, they all have something in common. They are shifting the responsibility for themselves and their actions onto some other person, usually an adult.

Students who seek dependence spend their time attempting to convince others that they can't control what is happening in their lives. They see themselves as victims of circumstance and strive to gain attention by keeping adults busy with them. In contrast, students who seek independence are usually in a power conflict. They are determined not to do what adults want — a kind of reverse dependence. The approval-seekers want approval from significant adults in their lives. They always attempt to please so others will like them. They run into trouble when they believe they must please two or more authority figures with different demands. The security-seekers, feeling lost, unloved, and alone, may try to get even with others as they fight their way through life hunting for an adult they can trust and who will trust them.

Underachievers may seek attention, power, or revenge, but they all have underlying feelings of inadequacy. Maureen, for example, disagreed with the social studies curriculum. Regardless of the assignment, she complained, refused to do the work, argued, and harassed the teacher. At mid-term a new teacher took over the social studies class. For a two-month project, Mr. P. asked the students to select an issue that was of national interest, but also one that they were really interested in and would enjoy. Their task was to examine all sides of the issue and to present their findings.

Maureen could not believe her ears! She immediately said she wanted to work on marijuana. Mr. P. said, ''That's fine. All I ask is that you present all sides of the issue.'' Maureen replied, ''Aw, I was only kidding.''

A few days later, Maureen said she wanted to make a study of the problems of senior citizens, specifically dealing with the southeast area of town where she lived. She planned to compare her findings with the national average. A few other students had been unable to decide on a problem and said they wished they had thought of senior citizens. Mr. P. said, ''Maureen, you really have an interesting idea. If you would like to enlarge your project, perhaps you could get a committee together. You could be the chairperson. If you'd rather work alone, that's fine — it *is* your idea.'' Maureen said, ''That's okay, I'd like to work with a committee.'' Had Mr. P. picked up on and moralized about Maureen's first choice, marijuana, he would not have won Maureen. Instead, Mr. P. gave Maureen space to breathe, to think, to come to her own decision, and to decide to cooperate.

The underachiever may wear many hats and behave in many different ways. It is up to us, their teachers, to recognize the symptoms and to understand the dynamics behind the underachiever.

Classroom Strategies for Hard to Reach Youngsters

Students who are in some way emotionally disturbed or learning disabled often use psychological mechanisms to avoid confronting and solving their problems. We as teachers must understand the psychological dynamics of these students. We need to see that they are striving to find their places on the useless side of life using a ''psychology of deficiency.'' We must also remember that in using their ''deficiency'' for their personal benefit, they are unaware of their goals. We can help them understand their goals and change their behavior.

We are too much affected by names others use to describe students: aggressive, slow, trouble-maker. All are labels which affect youngsters more than most adults realize. A slow learner, an underachiever, or an emotionally disturbed student often gets undue service, even though such attention isn't helpful. It takes a great deal of courage, perseverance, and confidence not to be sold on what some students have to sell — namely, their deficiency.

Emotionally Disturbed

The terms 'emotionally disturbed' and 'learning disabled' have been the subjects of controversy for several years. To add to the dilemma we also have labels such as hyperactive, brain injured, minimal brain dysfunction, autistic, aphasic, dyslexic, aggressive, disruptive, neurologically impaired, socially maladjusted, perceptual problems, delinquent, educationally disabled, emotionally disabled, emotionally and/or educationally handicapped, incorrigible, and hyperkinetic. Regardless of what these students are called, experience has shown that two educational problems are prevalent:

1. They seem to have a slow rate of learning and are behind their peers academically two years or more.
2. Their behavior interferes with productive learning. They seem to be lacking in personal and social relationship skills and quite often have disturbed family relationships.

In an attempt to distinguish among all the labels, let us consider the legal differences. Those young people who have committed crimes are usually termed 'socially maladjusted,' 'delinquent,' or 'incorrigible.' They are frequently confined by law in reform schools or other detention facilities. Some may need special education; many others need solid, high-quality regular education.

Youngsters who become status offenders (those who run away, who are promiscuous, and who create behavior problems) may also be termed 'mentally retarded,' 'mentally ill,' 'emotionally disturbed,' and 'behaviorally disordered.' They may or may not be institutionalized, depending upon the degree of their deviant behavior. If they are institutionalized, they are usually sent to some form of mental health-managed, residential facility. The present trend is to maintain the status offenders in the mainstream of school and society.

Emotionally handicapped youngsters usually have family problems. Students with ''problem parents'' seem to be unable or unwilling to function adequately in the home, school, or community.

254

The young people termed 'emotionally disturbed' are misnamed. It is not their emotions that are disturbed, but their *use* of their emotions. These students can use their emotions to get what they want. They quite frequently vacillate from one goal to another: from attention to power, back to attention and into revenge or to a display of inadequacy. They can be extremely good manipulators and are often so clever and bright that teachers must really be on their toes to stay out of their traps!

Experience has shown that learning problems usually precede behavior problems. The most prevalent reason for learning problems (besides the student's mistaken self-evaluation) is the lack of appropriate individualized instruction.

Regular classroom teachers may have two or three students who need special education and are termed 'emotionally disturbed.' There may also be another student or two with similar problems who have not been labeled as such, but who still need special instruction. A special education teacher can assist the classroom teacher in developing an IEP and/or in preparing curriculum materials for these students commensurate with their academic level.

It has been found that emotional tensions, aggressiveness, anxious behavior, and other disturbing symptoms seem to disappear when encouraging remedial techniques are used and the student begins to achieve in school. When we relieve students of the pressure to excel, they can concentrate on learning. Many students are so angry with their parents, other adults, and society that they use insults and refuse to learn as a way to demonstrate their power and defeat others.

Mel was this kind of angry student. One afternoon, the teacher's aide was escorting four students to the bus when one of the boys accidentally stepped on Mel's heel. Mel whirled around and hit the boy behind him. When Mel got to the bus, the aide asked him to stand aside while others got on. He turned on her and let fly with a string of obscenities. The aide ignored this barrage and helped get all the students seated on the bus, including Mel. When the aide came back into the building, several teachers reproached her because she had done nothing in response to Mel's hitting and swearing.

Within a few days, the entire school was buzzing about how nothing is ever done to ''those emotionally handicapped kids.'' But the principal knew that Mel's parents and teachers were working together to help Mel.

As the teacher's aide realized, Mel's behavior was intended to shock his adult audience. He is quite angry with home, school, community, and society at large, and wants revenge. The aide decided to ignore Mel's revengeful behavior and concentrate on her job: getting all the students on the bus.

The teacher or teacher's aide who has students with difficult problems has to do a good public relations job with the principal and the staff. Everyone must realize that these students receive special education because they have special needs, that it takes time to fulfill those needs, and that methods of discipline used with some students may not be appropriate for all.

Disturbed students in any classroom need special understanding. They will complain, blame others, make excuses, display inadequacy, and use many more techniques to get out of doing what they have been asked to do or to have their own way. Teachers need to be unimpressed by the anger, the tears, the blaming, and the complaining. These are the emotions used by students to manipulate. But teachers do need to recognize the deep discouragement felt by these students. It's important to remain firm, calm, and kind, and not to become emotionally involved.

Consider Jessie, who returned to the special classroom from a mainstreamed math class, obviously upset. She came in the classroom, slammed the door, stomped over to her desk, jerked it around, and sat down. She took her pencil, broke it into pieces, and threw the pieces at the wall. She took her books and papers out of the desk and scattered them on the floor. During all this, the teacher and the aide kept the rest of the class working. Eventually Jessie cooled down, picked up her mess, and raised her hand. The teacher went over to Jessie and they quietly discussed what had happened in the math class. Neither of them mentioned Jessie's behavior when she entered the classroom.

In order to effect change in students, teachers must change their own behavior and expectations first. Teachers cannot control students' behavior or make students do anything. Rather, teachers can assist students in learning self-discipline and cooperation.

Hyperactivity

A hyperactive person is usually overactive, distractible, impulsive, and excitable, and has been that way since birth or early life. The hyperactive student is unpredictable and is caught in a downward spiral of defeat and low self-esteem.

At the present time there seems to be no single, precise, identifiable cause of hyperactivity. Most theories mention abnormalities of the brain such as minimal brain damage, biochemical effects, epilepsy, or brain tumor. Hyperactivity has a marked preponderance among boys, for unknown reasons. Since people tend to react negatively to hyperactive behavior, the condition may lead to emotional disturbances.

It is most helpful for teachers to assume that hyperactive behavior has a purpose and can be changed. The student with a short attention span has chosen to be easily distracted; she or he may maintain long periods of concentration if the task is interesting.

For example, Brian, according to the psychologist, was supposed to have an attention span of 30 seconds. By proper academic programming, by setting the tasks at Brian's success level, his teacher got Brian to work steadily for two and a half hours. First he was given an assignment he liked, followed by a short difficult one, followed by a long neutral one, followed by an easy one, followed by a long one he liked, and so on. All assignments lasted from two minutes to eight minutes each and were immediately checked. Brian was given encouragement and recognition all along the way.

Teachers can structure the material, program the student's assignments, and schedule the day so that a longer attention span is encouraged and the student can successfully finish the tasks. If looked at in this way, hyperactivity becomes a behavioral and instructional problem to be solved.

Learning Disabilities

Much has been written about the learning disabled youngster and there is some confusion surrounding the condition. One of the reasons for the confusion is that professionals from many disciplines have been associated with this handicap and they usually do not agree on the etiology, diagnosis, or treatment. The medical profession has added labels such as dyslexia, minimal brain damage, perceptual handicaps, and developmental aphasia.

The term 'learning disabilities' describes many different kinds of behavior. Learning disabled students may have average or above-average intelligence, but something prevents them from learning and the disability is not the result of other handicapping conditions. Students with learning problems are usually the ones behind in almost every subject. They often have difficulty with reading and math skills and frequently take the attitude, "I can't learn, so why should I try?"

Research suggests that most learning problems are due to ineffective teaching, lack of individualized instruction, students' faulty notions about themselves, and their low self-esteem. Although it can be difficult to individualize instruction in large classes, careful planning can overcome some of the deficiencies in the students' educational foundation. Many learning disabled students can be successful in school.

The learning environment needs to be structured so that these students will work at the top of their capacity. For the teacher, this means giving clear, concise directions, providing a variety of curriculum materials, establishing classroom guidelines and limits with the students, and arranging the room to increase social interchange and peer tutoring. Alternate ways to achieve objectives need to be considered. For example, to aid socialization, the students' desks should be clustered in groups of twos and threes. Most troubled youngsters have social problems and we are doing them a disservice if we do not provide them with the necessary skills to alter their behavior. It is important to view students in their social setting and to look at their behavior in terms of its social context. Class discussions can also help students solve interpersonal relationship problems.

Many of the behavior problems of learning disabled students are psychological rather than organic. These students may behave in negative and self-defeating ways. They may show anger, hostility, anxiety, fear, jealousy, antagonism — all kinds of behavior designed to put distance between themselves and other people.

Teachers need not take these outbursts personally. Students may be expressing their feelings of unfairness, their inability to live up to their own and others' expectations, or general discontent with society and the world. Learning disabled students usually have low self-esteem and see themselves as inferior. Viewed from a psychological point of view, these students may be operating from any of the four goals. Once the goals are disclosed, teachers can use remedial methods and techniques to program the student's learning experiences for success.

Reading Difficulties

Reading ability is the basis for any academic progress. Most reading and learning problems are due to a lack of fundamental skills, a refusal to accept responsibility, dependency on others, feelings of inadequacy resulting in low self-esteem and poor self-concept, failure in school, distorted ambition based on competition, and mistaken goals.

Reading difficulties can be seen as one facet of disturbed interpersonal relationships. Lack of cooperation, unwillingness to follow directions, feeling sorry for oneself, poor attitude toward learning, and defiance of order and organization are all problems common to the reluctant reader.

The manner in which teachers work with learning disabled students and students with reading difficulties is the same. The classroom atmosphere needs to be encouraging. The teacher needs to understand the psychological dynamics of the student in order to stimulate a change in motivation. Students with reading and learning problems often feel inadequate, demand special attention, defy the demands of adults; their fears and frustrations are all part of the psychological dynamics their teachers must understand.

The foundation for effective education is an effective interpersonal relationship. The teacher needs to give encouragement, to accept students as they are, to treat students with mutual respect and equality, to use discussions as a means of encouragement, and to help students increase their self-esteem and belief in themselves. At the same time, the teacher needs to find the deficits in the student's learning and provide remedial instruction in those areas.

Conclusions

Obviously we cannot discuss all the "special" youngsters, nor can we discuss all the special problems a teacher may find in a classroom. We have attempted to give a bird's-eye view of dealing with some special problems. Changes need to be made in teachers' behavior but that alone is not enough. The most highly motivated teacher must have carefully planned administrative support, and the cooperation and shared responsibility of all educators concerned.

The following points must be emphasized: First of all, while certain students are termed handicapped or special, we must not lose sight of the fact that these students, like all students, are *whole* persons. They function according to beliefs (private logic) and purposes (goals), as do all human beings. Those who attempt to explain special students' behavior with special theories which do not apply to the so-called "normal" population do these students a disservice. A handicapped student is provided choices of adaptation. One can decide to succumb to the handicap, to overcome it, or to compensate for it by becoming proficient in another area. View your handicapped students as you would other students. Consider their view of themselves and the goals they pursue.

Many of us have grown up isolated from people with handicaps. When we first come in contact with a student having special problems, we often have some very difficult feelings: feelings of insecurity about being able to help the youngster; feelings of resentment about having to make special efforts to help one student when there are "so many other things to do"; feelings of rejection toward a student who acts or looks different from the others in the class; and guilt feelings about having so many negative thoughts (Mayer 1974).

We must remember that our attitudes about a handicapped student will rub off on others. If we baby or avoid a special student, so will the other students. If we are warm, positive, and encouraging — if we can see the student as an individual, not as a special problem — the other students will follow our lead.

To help handicapped students, again like all students, we must focus on their strengths. Most people, when asked to describe a particular handicap, will offer a list of liabilities instead of assets. We all have liabilities; we don't need to have them emphasized. But we can benefit when others emphasize our strengths.

Works Cited

Mayer, Colleen. ERIC Newsletter. Fall, 1974.

Pecaut, Linnus. "Underachievement Personalities." In "Underachievers — The Children Who Don't Do as Well as They Can" by Carol Costello. *Woman's Day,* October 1973.

Reynolds, Maynard, and Birch, Jack W. *Teaching the Exceptional Child in All American Schools.* Reston, VA: CEC Publishers, 1977.

Walton, Francis X. North American Society of Adlerian Psychology Newsletter, March 1978.

Recommended Readings

"Counseling Handicapped Persons and Their Families." Special issue of *Personnel and Guidance Journal* 58 (December, 1979).

Gearheart, Bill, and Weishahn, Mel. *The Handicapped Child in the Regular Classroom.* St. Louis: C. V. Mosby Co., 1976.

President's Committee on Employment of the Handicapped. *People . . . Just Like You: About Handicaps and Handicapped People.* Washington, DC, 1979.

Yura, M. *Raising an Exceptional Child.* NY: Elsevier-Dutton, 1979.

Study Questions

1. What is the difference between impairment, disability, and handicap?

2. What is harmful about labeling students as "slow learners" or "underachievers"? What can such labels do to students' self-esteem?

3. "The provision for special education is based on the unique needs of individual students, rather than on the handicapping condition itself." What is your understanding of this statement?

4. Discuss ways of encouraging handicapped students in mainstreamed classrooms. How can we devise a suitable curriculum for these students?

5. How can the class help encourage and change the behavior of students with special needs?

6. What is "pseudo-retardation"? How can we help these students without reinforcing mistaken goals?

7. What are the four basic categories of underachieving students? What do they all have in common?

8. How can emotionally disturbed and learning disabled students use the goals of misbehavior to avoid confronting their problems?

9. How can we structure the learning environment so learning disabled students will work at the top of their capacity?

10. Why are teachers' attitudes toward students with special needs so important to these students' success in school?

11. What similarities do you see in the approaches to all "special" students? How are students with special needs the same as all other students?

Problem Situation

You have a new student who has been mainstreamed into your class. Scott has been diagnosed as educably retarded. During social studies period, your students are working in small groups. You ask Scott what project he would like to work on. He decides to work with the map-making group. You take him to the group and one of the boys shouts, "I'm not working with a retard!"

    1. How would you feel?
    2. What might be the purpose of the name-calling?
    3. What would you do?

Activity for the Week

Identify a student who has special needs or presents exceptional problems. Use some of this chapter's suggestions for working with the student and bring a record of your progress. Note the student's behavior and purpose, your response, and the student's reaction.

Recommended Resource Book Material

Chapter 3, "Encouraging ourselves and others," "Encouragement," "Promoting peer encouragement"; Chapter 8, "Focusing on positive qualities," "Friendship," "Developing trust," "Relating to others"; Chapter 9, "Sociometrics"; Chapter 12, "Individual student misbehavior"; Chapter 13.

Chart 13

Encouraging the Student with Special Needs

NOTE: The ''labels'' or categories are for teachers' convenience. Remember that each student
is a whole person with beliefs and purposes to consider.

Exceptionality	Ineffective Procedures	Effective Procedures
Educable retarded	Assuming students to be less capable than they really are. Treating students as if they were totally incapable. Doing things for students they can do for themselves.	Verbal encouragement of effort and improvement, no matter how small: ''You've improved in spelling. Last week you got five correct, this week you got seven correct!'' Focus and build on student's strengths. Have student teach a skill to another student who needs help. Group discussions to build confidence and acceptance: ''We all learn at our own rate.'' Tailor curriculum by focusing on concrete rather than abstract material. Divide lessons into small units. Don't reverse sequence. Expect student to learn.
Pseudo-retarded	Falling for students' ''ineptness.'' Expecting too little. Giving undue service.	Recognize goal — usually passive attention and service or display of inadequacy. If purpose is attention, ignore; walk away when student bids for service. Refocus attention on positive behavior. If purpose is to display inadequacy, accept *any* effort and focus on assets. Develop plan of regular encouragement.
Emotionally disturbed	Allowing self to be manipulated. Attempting to control disturbing behavior. Relying on reward and punishment.	Understand student's purposes — may vacillate from one goal to another. Use group discussions and natural and logical consequences to deal with disturbing behavior. Keep assignments short, varied, and geared to interests. Encourage frequently. Remove pressure to learn. Be unimpressed by anger, blaming, and complaining. Expect cooperation.
Learning disabled	Viewing students as disabled rather than focusing on goals and instructional approaches. Overemphasizing disability.	Develop specific teaching strategies. Give clear, concise directions, provide a variety of curriculum materials, arrange room for increased social interaction. Use group discussion, role-playing, and natural and logical consequences. Insure success experiences. Give immediate feedback. Focus on what student can do, rather than on what student can't do.

Recording Worksheet

Working with Students with Special Needs

As you listen to each scene, consider the student's goal, the problem ownership, the appropriate approach, and the positive aspects of the student's behavior. Be prepared to discuss your responses with the group.

NOTES

Chapter 13

Points to Remember

1. Labeling students sets them apart as "different" and may damage their self-esteem.

2. The provision for special education is based on the unique needs of individual students, rather than on the handicapping condition itself.

3. Regular classroom teachers need to know:
- An overview of Public Law 94-142.
- The various categories of handicaps.
- The flow chart for referrals.
- How to help write an IEP.
- Where to find curriculum materials for handicapped students.
- How to handle severe behavior problems.

4. The appropriate, least restrictive environment for educable retarded students is the regular classroom. Their academic program needs to build on strengths and minimize limitations.

5. Slow learners can profit from changes in curriculum. Information needs to be presented simply, clearly, and briefly.

6. Pseudo-retarded students may have any IQ score but act as if they cannot learn. They often adopt the passive goals of attention or display of inadequacy.

7. Underachievers shift the responsibility for themselves and their actions onto some other person, usually an adult. Regardless of their goal, they all have underlying feelings of inadequacy.

8. Emotionally disturbed students usually have two main educational problems:
- They seem to have a slow rate of learning and are behind their peers academically two years or more.
- Their behavior interferes with productive learning.

9. Emotional tensions, aggressiveness, anxious behavior, and other disturbing symptoms seem to disappear when encouraging remedial techniques are used and the student begins to succeed in school.

10. It is most helpful to assume that hyperactive behavior has a purpose and can be changed.

11. In order to help learning disabled students work up to their capacity, teachers need to:
- Give clear, concise directions.
- Provide a variety of curriculum materials.

- Establish classroom guidelines and limits with the students.
- Arrange the room to increase social interchange and peer tutoring.

12. Students with special needs, like all students, function according to beliefs and purposes.

13. Remain calm, kind, firm, and consistent with "special" students. Treat them with mutual respect and equality.

14. Use group discussions as the forum for understanding and influencing behavior.

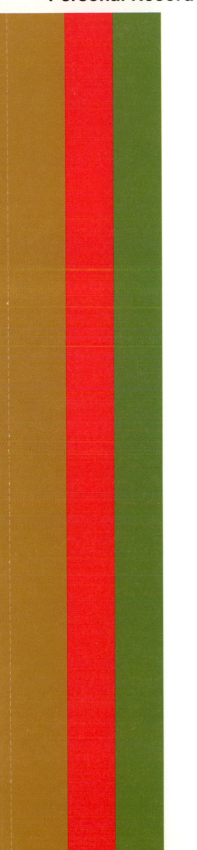

Personal Record Chapter 13

1. My experience with the weekly assignment

2. My reactions to the reading

3. Topics to discuss with the group

4. Skills I intend to improve

5. My beliefs which impede progress

6. My successes in applying program ideas

7. My difficulties in applying program ideas

8. My progress this week: A specific example

9. This week I learned

CHAPTER 14
WORKING WITH PARENTS

How can I improve and strengthen my relationships with my students'
parents?
How can I involve parents actively and constructively in the education
of their children?
How can I hold successful conferences with parents?
What can be my role in study groups for parents?

Parents have a most significant influence on a child's attitudes. Students make their own choices, but no one can doubt the importance of their parents' behavior and attitudes. Teachers can benefit greatly from the interest of their students' parents.

Parents' involvement has become a priority in many school systems, yet exactly how to involve parents remains unclear. Too often, teachers use parents as enforcers of school discipline — although such efforts often invite power struggles, revenge, or dependence — and parents use teachers as targets for their anger and frustration.

How can we improve and strengthen our relationships with parents? How can we involve parents actively and constructively in the education of their children?

Who Are These Parents? What Kind of Involvement?

When we speak of our students' parents, we must include more than biological mothers and fathers. All the adults who care for children, who provide "parenting functions," can be thought of — for simplicity's sake — as "parents."

Grandparents, older siblings, other relatives, and anyone else with whom students have frequent contact can act as parents. Other adults who provide direct role models for children can become involved in school: neighbors, people from the community, clergy. Older students can also serve as role models. We can reach out to all adults having the potential for influence with our students.

There are two general categories of parental involvement: Parents and other interested adults provide services to the school; the school provides services to parents and other interested adults. We can offer specific, useful programs for both.

Parents As Classroom Resources

Running a school is an enormous task. For many years, parents have helped by serving as guest speakers, room parents, field trip escorts, library, office, and cafeteria helpers, and providers of refreshments. These important jobs can be expanded and new ones added: parents visiting classrooms, teaching mini-courses, sharing hobbies and interests, providing on-the-job visits, directing school carnivals, becoming class photographers. One of the best ways to coordinate all these activities is by forming an advisory council.

Advisory councils, composed of parents and school personnel, advise the school about building and curricular matters. For example, such a group would recommend how some of the district's money could be spent, which curricular innovations should be adopted, which school procedures need reviewing or replacing.

Although council members may volunteer or be appointed, it's often best to elect them. Students' parents elect their own representatives; school staffs elect theirs. The principal can be a permanent member of the council.

Councils can be established both for buildings and for districts. The district council is made up of the superintendent and an elected representative from each building council. Beginning at the junior high level, *students* need to be included on building and district councils. Students' opinions and suggestions can be extremely valuable.

You can even establish an advisory council of parents for your own classroom. Or, if you prefer to be more informal, hold periodic group meetings with parents to discuss programs and procedures. The method isn't important; what counts is getting parents involved. A major side benefit may be the positive feelings you create when parents realize how committed you are to their participation.

Parents as school and classroom aides. When we recruit parents to help in the library, the first-aid center, the office, the playground, the cafeteria, we free ourselves to concentrate on teaching. Parents can be effective "safety patrol" members, especially in neighborhoods with high incidences of vandalism and other crimes. Parents can also be valuable classroom aides. They can listen to students read, tutor, work with small groups, arrange field trips, keep records, grade papers, and locate materials. The contributions of aides can be enormous.

Your "Resource File." You'll want first to determine the kind of resource people you have available. Consider setting up a "parent resource file" (as developed by the Pima County Developmental Career Guidance Project, Tucson, AZ). Send home a letter and one or more parent involvement cards (see the following examples) with each student. For schoolwide programs, the letter can come from the principal. From the information you collect, make (or have parents who checked "clerical help" make for you) a set of Occupation Cards and Interest Cards. (See the following examples.) Each parent will have one card giving his or her occupation and different cards for each area of interest checked. If parents indicated they would allow students to visit them at work, or would come to school and talk about their work, list that information on their Occupation Card.

Letter to Parents

Dear Parents,

We need you! You are the primary influence in your child's life and we need you as a partner in the education of your child.

So we have set up a parent involvement program here at Edison. We need parents to come and tell us about their occupations, to host groups of students at "on the job" visits, to help in the library, nurse's office, cafeteria, playground, and buses, to help with field trips, to share hobbies and special interests, to serve as teacher's aides, and much, much more!

Enclosed you will find a Parent Involvement Card which lists ways you can help and has places to check what you want to do. There is also space for you to give us additional ideas on how you can get involved.

Will you come and help the school and your child? Even an hour of your time will be greatly appreciated. If you have any questions, please call. Thanks so much.

Sincerely,

Alva Thomas

Alva Thomas, Principal
888-2020

Parent Involvement Card
(Front of card)

NAME_____ RELATIONSHIP TO STUDENT_____

ADDRESS_____ PHONE_____

CHILDREN IN SCHOOL
             _____ _____   _____ _____
             STUDENT   TEACHER   STUDENT   TEACHER

             _____ _____   _____ _____
             STUDENT   TEACHER   STUDENT   TEACHER

PLACE OF EMPLOYMENT_____PHONE_____

OCCUPATION_____

I would like to have students visit me at work. _____

I would like to come to school and talk about my job. _____

I would like to show pictures (slides) of my job. _____

(Back of card)

I would enjoy helping students and the school in the following ways:

1. Field trip escort _____
2. Work on school carnival _____
3. Be a class photographer _____
4. Telephoning _____
5. Provide refreshments _____
6. Clerical work _____
7. Arts and crafts _____
8. Help with music _____
     Instrument I play _____
     Vocal _____
9. Help with plays _____
10. Cooking _____
11. Sewing _____
12. Nurse's aide _____
13. Library aide _____
14. Playground supervisor _____
15. Cafeteria helper _____
16. Bus supervisor _____

17. Teacher's aide _____
      Grade papers _____
      Listen to students read _____
      Keep records _____
      Locate materials and arrange field
        trips _____
      Tutor _____ Subject(s) _____
      _____
      Work with small groups _____ Subject(s)
      _____
      Teach a special skill _____ What skill?
      _____

18. I have slides of interesting areas of the
      United States or other countries to
      share. _____ Place(s) _____
      _____

19. Special interests and hobbies I would
      be willing to share. _____

Other suggestions and ideas _____

For example, if Mr. Jacobs is a carpenter and Mrs. Jacobs is a real estate salesperson, each would have an Occupation Card with their jobs listed. If Mrs. Jacobs indicated she would like to be a teacher's aide and also checked "sewing," she would have one Interest Card filed under "Teacher's Aide" and one under "Sewing."

Occupation Cards

CARPENTER

Sol Jacobs
444 Any Street
777-1313
Employer: Two By Four Builders (222-1000)

He would have students visit him at work.

He would come to school to talk about his job.

REAL ESTATE SALESPERSON
(Part-time)

Carla Jacobs
444 Any Street
777-1313
Employer: Forsale Realty (999-1000)

She would come to school to talk about her job.

Interest Cards

TEACHER'S AIDE

Carla Jacobs
444 Any Street
777-1313

She would assist by working with small groups
in reading and math.

SEWING

Carla Jacobs
444 Any Street
777-1313

Since new students enter throughout the year, the Parent Involvement Card and its accompanying letter can be made part of the registration material each student receives. At the end of the year, remove the cards of parents whose children will not return next year, or move them to an inactive file. You might want to ask the parents of graduating students if they would continue to help at school. You can also keep the file current by removing the cards of families who leave the school at various times during the school year.

Back of file organized alphabetically by areas of interest.

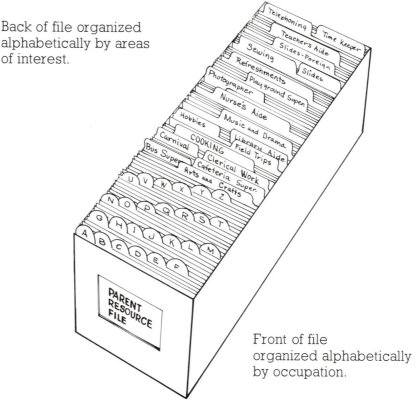

Front of file organized alphabetically by occupation.

As you use the file, record on the backs of cards when the parent was called. This will prevent overusing some parents and neglecting others. Put your name after the date when other teachers use the file; this allows them to ask you about the effectiveness of the volunteer. Include in your resource file all adults involved in students' lives. Reach out also to people in the community who don't have children in school; they may be eager to help. Ask your students, other teachers, and parent volunteers to recommend people in the community.

It's best to have a building-wide parent involvement program so you can have a wider selection. Keep the file in a central place, accessible to all teachers.

Selecting aides. Once you have the resource file, interview volunteers to determine their suitability and level of experience. Find out a little about their views of education and their beliefs about children: since some aides will have considerable contact with you and your students, you'll want to choose with care. You may want to select one classroom aide to help you for a period of time and then change aides. Or you may prefer having several aides performing different tasks.

Sometimes you'll find it advisable to avoid using your own students' parents as aides, depending upon the job you need done and the relationship between parent and child. You are the best judge of the suitability of aides.

It's convenient to draw from the whole school for all services, not just for aides. Suppose your class is studying electricity. You want an electrician to come speak to your students. None of their parents is an electrician but the parent of a student in another class is. With a building-wide program, you can locate that parent.

Your classroom aides may need training. You might invite them to observe your class for a few days to get acquainted with you, your students, and your teaching methods. You might also give them some reading from this handbook, or talk with them about effective ways to get along with students. Discuss the reading with your "aides-in-training."

As aides become more experienced, you'll be able to involve them in planning and problem solving. Making them part of a team effort will benefit all. You retain the final responsibility, but their suggestions and advice can be very useful.

Setting up a parent resource file and then selecting and training aides takes time. But consider the time-saving benefits once your program is set up!

Strategies for Getting Parents Involved

Many parents believe the school only wants them involved when their children get in trouble. Aside from attending PTA meetings, conferences, and other school programs, some parents may be leery of coming anywhere near school. You'll need to motivate them! You might:

- Announce your needs and intentions at Open House.
- Telephone parents yourself or have your room parents telephone others.
- Send home attractive, stimulating flyers. Be sure to mention specific ways parents can help.
- Discuss parent involvement with your students and enlist their help. Do some role playing on how to motivate the busy or reluctant parent. Teach them "positive persistence": "Gee, Dad, I'd be so proud if you'd come over during your lunch hour and tell us how you do your job."

Schools As Parents' Resources

Parent-teacher conferences and parent study groups are two ways to provide services to parents and other interested adults. Both help establish positive relationships between parents and school officials. Both enlist parents' cooperation in working with their children and teenagers. Both provide parents with information on ways to improve their relationships with their children.

Parent-Teacher Conferences

Conferences usually go smoothly with the parents of your "good" students. But meetings with the parents of "problems" are usually dreaded by both parties. These are the parents we most need to talk with, but they may be the most difficult to reach. No parents look forward to bad news, especially if they've heard it year after year. They may already feel like failures. Perhaps they're embarrassed about their "problem child."

Encourage these parents — and all parents — by making conferences a positive part of a positive parent-involvement program. Combat the "bad news syndrome" by sending home regular "Happy-Grams," reports on students' progress and cooperation. (See the example below.) Parents will begin to trust you; they will appreciate your interest and attitude. Even if some parents remain suspicious, you're still a significant person in the lives of their children and your influence will be respected.

Happy-Gram

February 2, 1981

Dear Mr. and Mrs. Charles,

Just a note to tell you that Billy was so cooperative today. He completed all his work and stayed in his seat. I really appreciated his positive behavior.

Sincerely,

Maria Torres

Maria Torres, Teacher

Teacher-initiated conferences. Be prepared. Have a plan. Beyond winning parents' cooperation, what specific points do you want to make? For example, if you want to persuade Lee's parents to ease their pressure on him and let you handle his reading difficulties, know what you're going to say and how you'll say it.

Prepare a written progress report to give parents when they arrive. This can be a one-page evaluation including:

1. A summary of the student's progress.
2. Areas of concern.
3. Areas of strength.

Be sure the report follows this order so parents will read last about their child's strengths. It always helps to leave them thinking about the positive and encouraging things.

Be sure to allow enough time for conferences, especially with parents of students having difficulties. Depending on your district's policies, you might telephone certain parents, mention the student's strengths, and tell them that since things are going well, you see no need for a conference. If your district requires scheduled conferences with every parent, you might shorten some conferences to allow more time for others. With the parents of students you're concerned about, don't wait until the regularly scheduled conference to meet.

It's important for *both* parents of students having difficulties, or all adults acting as parents, to attend conferences. Hold such conferences in the evenings, if that's most convenient. If parents are divorced and the student is in frequent contact with both, invite both to the conference, provided they're willing to meet together and you feel the joint conference will be productive.

Decide whether or not to include the student in the conference. If you decide not to, be sure to meet with the student in advance. Explain the purpose of the conference and what you plan to discuss. Let the student express any negative feelings or reactions. Many students feel threatened by parent-teacher conferences. Explain that conferences are designed to help them at school and at home. Students still may not like the idea, but at least they'll know you respect them enough to brief them in advance.

The Conference

WANT TO TALK ABOUT THOSE PROGRESS REPORTS?

After the introductions, ask the parents to read your progress report. Get their reactions: "Is there anything in my comments you'd like to discuss?" If they seem upset, use reflective listening. Explain anything they don't understand. If the parents don't comment or react, take the initiative yourself: "I'd like to discuss some of the problems I'm having with Sharon and how we can encourage her."

Discuss how you see the student's performance. If the student misbehaves, offer your view of the goals of the misbehavior and what you're doing to redirect those goals. Emphasize your attempts to capitalize on the student's strengths.

For example, "I think Sharon wants to show me by her behavior that she can do as she pleases. She seems very interested in power and often tries to show me who's boss. I used to fight with her but now I'm letting her take responsibility for the consequences of her behavior. For instance, if she decides to disturb the class, I ask her to leave the group for a while until she gets control of herself. I'm also capitalizing on Sharon's real strengths — leadership and reading — by having her tutor other students in reading. Both these procedures seem to be working."

If Sharon's parents seem enthusiastic about your strategies with her, you might see if they're interested in getting along better with her themselves. Most students who misbehave at school also misbehave at home. You could refer them to a school or private counselor and offer to sit in if they want you to. Or, if you've established good rapport with the parents and feel comfortable giving guidance, you might help them explore alternatives during the conference.

Remember that involving yourself as a counselor means a commitment of time. Be prepared for follow-up conferences and phone calls. If you do decide to help the parents, use the following format to discuss specific problems. Ask them to:

1. Describe specifically what the student does.
2. Describe how they feel when the student behaves this way.
3. Describe what they do about the misbehavior and how the student responds.

If one parent is absent, ask how that parent reacts to the misbehavior and how the student responds. Also ask what the other children in the family do when the misbehavior occurs. This will give you information about the goals of misbehavior, the family constellation, sibling rivalry, and competition.

Look for the pattern that points to the student's goal. Then explain that goal and how the parents may be unintentionally reinforcing the behavior. Linking your experiences with theirs will help you illustrate that adults can make mistakes. This also helps universalize the problem and avoids focusing only on the parents' mistakes. For example, ''From what you've told me and from my own experiences, it seems Sharon believes she has to prove that no one can tell her what to do, that she's in charge. She's a very powerful girl. I know she's trapped me into fighting with her at times. You've said she's also provoked you into trying to force her, even though forcing her often doesn't work. Does what I'm saying make sense to you?''

Sometimes, after the student's goal is explained, the parents want instant answers: ''Yes, that makes sense. What do I do about it?'' But refrain from discussing solutions until you have more information. You could structure the interview by saying, ''I know you want answers. But first I need more information so I can understand Sharon's situation.''

Next, ask for more information about the family constellation: ''Since brothers and sisters have such great influence on each other, I need to know about your other children.'' Listen carefully as the parents describe each of their children from the oldest to the youngest, including your student. Ask, ''What kind of person is _____?'' ''What words would you pick to describe _____?''

Suppose Sharon, aged 10, has an older sister, Elena, aged 13. Their contrasting qualities may be listed:

Elena	Sharon
good student	poor student (except in reading)
helps at home	has to be prodded to do chores
neat	sloppy
friendly	friendly
artistic	artistic
quiet	noisy, acts babyish
gets along well with adults	gets along with adults until they tire of her babyish behavior
many friends	few friends

After you consider this information, suggest what you see happening in the family: "It seems to me that Elena plays the 'good' girl in the family and Sharon plays the 'bad' girl. I've learned that most children in a family compete for a place. If one is successful at something, the other may decide to be good at something else.

"Sharon is friendly, a good reader, and artistic, but she's discouraged. We can tell she is because she's learned to be recognized for her misbehavior. While we don't want her to be sloppy and irresponsible, she finds that those characteristics give her a place in the family and the classroom. We know Sharon is around! It also seems like the more Elena succeeds or is recognized for her success, the more discouraged Sharon gets. And, as you said earlier, Elena often tattles on Sharon, which makes her look good and Sharon look bad. Is this an accurate way to describe the relationship?"

If the parents agree with your analysis, help them explore the student's assets. Say, "You mentioned that Sharon is friendly, artistic, and a good reader. What other strengths do you see?" Some parents are so discouraged they won't come up with any strengths. Encourage Sharon's parents by saying, "Both your children are friendly and artistic. That may mean you two have those qualities also." Help them by discussing the strengths you've noticed and encouraged in the classroom.

Next, begin to explore alternatives by seeing how strongly the parents want to make changes. Say, "From our discussion, have you discovered anything you'd like to change?" If they reply, "Everything!" suggest they work on one or two things at a time.

A first step might be to ask the parents to let school problems be between you and the student. Suggest that giving students two or more adults to rebel against or be dependent on doesn't make sense. Encourage them to concentrate on improving the situation at home.

You'll be removing a tremendous burden from them when you ask them to focus only on behavior at home. Review the situation: "Remember, we discovered that Sharon is trying to show how powerful she is when she throws a temper tantrum. You said you often get angry and either spank her, yell at her, or give in. What do you think she's learning if you fight or give in? What else could you do to show her that power plays won't work?" Ask them to brainstorm some ideas.

Refine the parents' ideas if necessary. For example, "How will you ignore Sharon's tantrums?" If they can't think of specific ways, make a suggestion. "What do you think will happen if you leave her alone in her room for awhile? I've found it helpful to leave her alone until she calms down."

Stress the student's assets. Ask, "How could you show Sharon how to use her strengths to help the family?" Encourage them to let Sharon feel accepted as a person. "What can you do to help Sharon feel more worthwhile?" You might suggest the "I appreciate" game. Everyone in the family fills in the blank, "I appreciate it when you _____," about everyone else. You could ask the parents to say at least one positive thing to Sharon each day. Take some time to explain the differences between encouragement and praise.

Next, get a firm commitment and plan a time for evaluation. Remember to watch for the "I'll try" hedge. Ask the parents to experiment: "Are you willing to leave the room and let Sharon be by herself each time she throws a tantrum until we talk about it again in two weeks? At that time, I'll give you a progress report on how things are going at school." Schedule another conference or simply a phone call. At that time, if things are going well, suggest they work on another area of their relationship with Sharon. Check with them again by phone or in person, and so on.

Since your time is limited, ask parents to do some reading or suggest a parent study group. Finally, summarize the conference by spelling out how you're going to treat the student in school and what they're to do at home. Go over when and how you'll evaluate the effectiveness of your plans.

Parent-Initiated Conferences

During conferences that parents have called, you'll want to follow their leads and discuss the issues that concern them. Use reflective listening, especially if they're angry. Then summarize and state your position in an I-message.

For example: "Let me see if I understand what you're saying. You're angry because I allow students to discuss their relationships with their parents and siblings during class meetings. You think such topics are too personal and don't belong in the classroom, that they have nothing to do with education. Is that how you feel? I'd like to explain my feelings about this issue and see if we can come to an understanding. I believe personal growth is part of education. We know students learn more if they feel good about themselves and others. I can appreciate your concern about students bringing up family matters, but the things discussed are *very* typical, such as fighting between brothers and sisters. I don't permit things to be discussed which may be embarrassing to a family. What do you think about my reasoning on this?"

If the parents agree with you, turn to other issues. If they don't agree, negotiate: "It seems we need to find another solution that will suit both of us. Are you willing to see if we can reach an agreement on this? All right, you don't want Brian to have this experience and I think students benefit from it. So what do we do?"

Brainstorm. Give your own suggestions. Then evaluate. Perhaps you'll decide that Brian will visit another classroom during these discussions, if the parents are strongly opposed to his taking part. If you can't reach an agreement, you may want to schedule another conference, to be attended by the counselor and principal.

Including the Student in the Conference

Whether or not to include the student in the conference depends on several factors. First, consider what will be gained if the student attends. How will the parents react? Second, is the student willing to meet with you? If not, benefits may be few and disruption very possible. You might tell students why you want them at conferences, assuring them you'll do your best to prevent their being attacked or embarrassed. Ask them if they're *willing* to come. Finally, decide how comfortable you'll feel conducting a conference with the student present.

Having decided to include the student, begin the conference by distributing your written evaluation of the student's progress. (Read it to the student if necessary.) Then get reactions, bringing up anything of concern to you that's not mentioned.

If the student has been misbehaving, describe *for the parents* what you think the goal is. Talking directly to the student may bring on defensiveness. For example, say, "It seems to me Kurt believes he has to have special attention before he'll go to work. He wants me to remind and coax him."

Observe Kurt's recognition reflex. Then continue, "So I've decided that Kurt is capable of working without my reminding him. I now give the assignment and let Kurt decide whether or not to get busy. He has a choice. He can do the assignment either during the period or at recess. If he doesn't finish during the period I assume he's decided to do it at recess. In the last couple of weeks, Kurt has decided to do his work during the period most of the time. I've also been inviting Kurt to use his building abilities. Did he tell you about the model factory he's building in social studies?"

Get reactions from both Kurt and his parents. Next, if you decide to offer help about their family relationships, ask about any problems they have getting along at home. If the parents respond, ask Kurt occasionally to comment. If he disagrees with his parents, you could say, "It seems you and your parents have different opinions."

Don't ask directly for comparisons between family members since these may embarrass the student. Instead, find out about brothers and sisters by responding to comments about your student. If Kurt's father says, "Kurt was never a good student," ask, "What kind of person is Joanne? Ralph?"

Encourage the parents to point out Kurt's assets. "What does Kurt do that you enjoy?" Add to their list. Then explore alternatives by seeing how willing both Kurt and his parents are to change. Brainstorm, making sure you include Kurt. "Have you got any ideas on how we can settle this, Kurt?" You may need to help them negotiate an agreement.

Get a commitment and plan a time for evaluation. Be sure to ask Kurt how he feels about the plan. Finally, ask the parents or Kurt to summarize the conference. Add your comments if necessary.

Above all, don't permit parents to attack the student. Confront them with the probable consequences of their remarks. "I wonder how Kurt feels when you call him lazy." Then, check with Kurt: "How do you feel when Mom calls you lazy? What do you feel like doing?" You might also ask the parent, "What would it be like for you to be in Kurt's place and be called lazy?"

I-messages can often block attacks. "When you call Kurt lazy, I get uncomfortable because I've found that children often live up to our expectations of them. I wonder if we could look at some ways to help Kurt become more responsible."

If the attacks persist, state your limits. "I feel accusing and labeling Kurt won't help him. I'm afraid we're not making any progress. I'm willing to continue only if you agree to stop making these comments. Otherwise, I want to excuse Kurt so you can speak the way you want to and he doesn't have to hear. What do you want to do?"

Stick to your limits. You have an obligation to protect students from further discouragement.

Dealing with resistance. Sometimes you and parents will have conflicting objectives. For example, you may want them to withdraw from a power contest. They want to force the student to obey. In this case, your long-range objective may be the same: getting the student to cooperate. But your short-range goals are different. You want them to let the student learn from experience and they want instant obedience.

With other parents, your long-range objectives may also be in conflict. The parents of a dependent student may resist your suggestion that their daughter be more independent, because they fear losing their significance in her life.

Your task is to align your objectives with the parents' objectives. You aren't a psychotherapist so you don't deal with their lifestyles. But you can attempt to win their cooperation.

If parents resent your methods and your assessment of their child's behavior, use your listening skills. ''That explanation doesn't make sense to you, does it? You seem really uncomfortable with that procedure.'' Ask for their ideas. After all, they do know their children. If you disagree with a proposal, send an I-message. ''I'm concerned about that plan because _____.'' Ask them for other suggestions. Make one yourself or return to your original idea and explain it again.

If parents continue to resist, or if you expect a particularly difficult conference, call in the counselor or principal. They may be able to suggest ways of overcoming the communication difficulties.

Suppose the parents are cooperative but when you ask if there are any problems with Gabrielle at home, they say no. You think they're too permissive. It may be that your expectations for Gabrielle differ from theirs. You might ask a few questions about her typical day. ''How well does Gabrielle get up, get dressed, have her breakfast, and leave for school? What happens when she comes home from school? At the supper table? Does she eat what's put before her without coaxing? What happens with homework? Bedtime?''

As you go through the routine, listen for areas of conflict. ''How many times do you have to call Gabrielle before she gets up? How do you feel and what do you do when you have to call four or five times?'' Then explain how you see the situation. ''The prodding you give Gabrielle every morning seems very similar to what I do in language arts. It looks to me as if she's got us all trapped in a power struggle.''

If the parents resist making changes, ask them to evaluate their present method. ''Are you satisfied with your present relationship with Gabrielle? Is what you're doing working?'' Some parents will say yes, that their methods do work. Ask, ''When you punish Gabrielle, are you saying she *never* needs coaxing again?'' Follow this by asking, ''Would you like her to be more cooperative? Will you experiment with another procedure for a couple of weeks just to see what happens?''

Sometimes you may have to ask them to do some reading and then discuss the ideas with you. (See this chapter's recommended readings.) A book can make suggestions easier to take. The printed page is more impersonal.

If parents fight with each other during the conference, let them know you understand both their positions. But suggest the disadvantages to the student of the parents' fighting. Be firm. Think of the student. "You're both angry and don't agree on what to do with Gabrielle. Each of you must decide how best to communicate with her. But I wonder if you're aware how your anger toward each other may be affecting her. Gabrielle may be misbehaving because she's confused and discouraged. It's also quite possible that she's learned to play each of you against the other. I'd like to get back to what each of you is willing to do to help Gabrielle."

If they continue to fight, adjourn the conference and reschedule separate appointments. If they seem to have serious marital problems and you feel they'll accept a suggestion from you, recommend that they seek counseling.

Conferences with single parents. Single-parent families are as varied as conventional families. Some single parents enjoy and cope well with their responsibilities; others feel overburdened. Some divorced people feel bitter toward their former spouses; some have cordial, cooperative relationships. Avoid forming any conclusions about a family until you meet and talk with them.

Similarly, never assume that the children of divorced parents are troubled. Children respond to every situation according to their own perceptions. Pity from well-meaning adults is rarely appropriate. If parents and teachers believe in children's ability to handle life's difficulties, then the breaking up of a family — for whatever reason — needn't bring long-term troubles.

You will sometimes need to show special acceptance and understanding to divorced parents. Despite the prevalence of divorce, many people believe they've done their children a disservice, been failures as parents. Your empathy can help both parent and student.

In summary, the parent-teacher or parent-teacher-student conference, called to discuss the student's misbehavior, involves:

1. Presenting your evaluation of the student's progress.
2. Stating your perception of the student's goal of misbehavior.
3. Informing the parents of your response to the misbehavior and your attempts to focus on the student's strengths.

Then, if you decide to help them explore alternatives:

4. Finding out about the student's relationship with parents.
5. Finding out about the family constellation.
6. Exploring alternatives for helping the student get along better at home.
7. Getting a commitment and planning a time for evaluation.

Study Groups for Parents

Few parents were trained for that important job. Being an effective parent was assumed to come naturally. Now we know that parents can benefit greatly from joining study groups to discuss child-rearing. As trained teachers, we can lead or initiate these valuable programs for our students' parents.

Many structured programs and books are available for parent study groups. *Systematic Training for Effective Parenting* (STEP), for example, is a multimedia program applying to parent-child relationships many of the ideas about human behavior found in STET. The program emphasizes discussion, experience, and practice.

Parent study groups can be led by teachers, counselors, psychologists, physicians, social workers, clergy, and informed lay persons. We teachers are in a particularly good position for leading such groups. Improving our relationships with parents can only strengthen our relationships with students. There are few better ways of demonstrating our commitment to strong parent involvement. The time we give each week to parent study groups can be extremely valuable to all concerned.

The leader of such a group helps participants understand and discuss alternative ways of dealing with their children. Groups should be small: no more than ten to twelve participants (Dinkmeyer, McKay, and Dinkmeyer, 1978).

You may want to co-lead such a group with the school counselor or other guidance professional in your school. But do get involved yourself, as leader, co-leader, or participant.

All parents can profit from study groups, not just the parents of "difficult" students. Get everyone interested with announcements, flyers, posters, and phone calls. When your group is formed, use the same leadership and communication skills you use in the classroom. Maintain an informal, relaxed atmosphere. Use first names. Admit you don't know all the answers!

You'll probably discover that several parents are especially quick to grasp ideas or seem particularly good at discussing. These people can be valuable resources for you. They may also become leaders of their own study groups.

Parent involvement is crucial to our success as teachers. Cooperative, supportive parents working with teachers committed to encouraging, democratic classrooms can move us a long way toward those ideals we formed in college. We can then offer our students an education fit for the times.

Works Cited

Dinkmeyer, Don; McKay, Gary D.; and Dinkmeyer, Don, Jr. *CMTI Parent Education Resource Manual.* Coral Springs, FL: CMTI Press, 1978.

Recommended Readings

Dinkmeyer, Don. *The Basics of Adult-Teen Relationships.* Coral Springs, FL: CMTI Press, 1976.

Dinkmeyer, Don, Jr., and Dinkmeyer, Jim. *The Basic Introduction to Parenting Skills.* Coral Springs, FL.: CMTI Press, 1980.

Dinkmeyer, Don, and McKay, Gary. *Raising a Responsible Child.* NY: Simon & Schuster, 1973.

Dinkmeyer, Don, and McKay, Gary. *Systematic Training for Effective Parenting (STEP).* Circle Pines, MN: American Guidance Service, 1976.

Dreikurs, Rudolf, and Grey, Loren. *A Parent's Guide to Child Discipline.* NY: Hawthorn Books, 1970.

Dreikurs, Rudolf, and Soltz, Vicki. *Children: The Challenge.* NY: Duell, Sloan and Pearce, 1964.

Gould, Shirley. *Teenagers: The Continuing Challenge.* NY: Hawthorn Books, 1977.

Walton, Francis X., and Powers, B.D. *Winning Children Over.* Chicago: Practical Psychology Associates, 1974.

Wood, Pat, and Wood, Murray. *Living with Teens and Surviving.* Toronto: Alfred Adler Institute of Ontario, 1979.

Study Questions

1. Why is parents' involvement in school so important?

2. What is an "adult role model"? Why is it advisable to include other adult role models besides parents in students' education?

3. What is the value of an advisory council?

4. How can you develop a "parent resource file"?

5. What can parents do as classroom aides? How do we select aides?

6. Describe some strategies for involving parents and other adult role models in your classroom.

7. How can we motivate reluctant parents to come to conferences?

8. How can a written progress report help begin conferences? What other methods have you found helpful?

9. Why do we meet with students before parent-teacher conferences? Under what conditions might we ask students to attend conferences?

10. If you decide to involve yourself as a counselor, what specific questions would you ask parents about their child's behavior at home?

11. What are some ways to deal with resistant or hostile parents?

12. What do you do if parents verbally attack their child while the student is present? What if parents fight with each other during the conference?

13. What is the value of study groups for parents? Why should teachers participate in such groups?

Problem Situation

You have been having problems with David; he fools around and seldom finishes his assignments. Joan is also a problem for you; she is very bright and finishes all her work early, but then gets in trouble talking with other students. You will soon be scheduling conferences with the parents of all your students.

1. How will the conferences with David's and Joan's parents be similar? How will they be different?
2. What do you hope to accomplish in each conference?

Chart 14

Ten Dos and Don'ts for Effective Conferences with Parents

Do

1. Make "happy-calls" or send "happy-grams" to parents of difficult students.

2. Prepare a report summarizing student's progress, areas of concern, and strengths. Emphasize strengths.

3. Explain and seek agreement for your plan of action.

4. Request that parents let student's school behavior be between you and student.

5. Request presence of counselor and/or principal if you anticipate a difficult conference.

6. Meet with student before parent-teacher conference or parent-teacher-student conference.

7. Use reflective listening skills when parents are upset.

8. Consult parents as resources.

9. In parent-teacher-student conferences, protect student's self-esteem.

10. Understand the unique concerns of single parents.

Don't

1. Dwell on student's mistakes in reporting to parents.

2. Allow parents to focus on student's mistakes.

3. Argue with parents.

4. Ask parents to monitor school behavior or work.

5. Think you have to handle every situation by yourself.

6. Keep student "in the dark," promoting suspicion and disrespect.

7. Rush toward solutions.

8. Overlook parents' areas of strength.

9. Permit parents to attack student.

10. Make assumptions about single parents' situations before getting to know them.

Recording Worksheet

Parent-Student-Teacher Conference

As you listen to the conference, consider what you would say at various points and why. Be prepared to discuss your responses with the group.

The recording begins with the teacher asking for comments about the progress report he's given the parents and their son to read. That report says:

Summary of Student's Progress

Ed is having some difficulty meeting the requirements for science class. He is a very capable boy who lacks motivation.

Areas of Concern

Ed is frequently late to class and doesn't turn in assignments.

Areas of Strength

Ed has a talent for leadership. He enjoys caring for our laboratory animals.

NOTES

Chapter 14

Points to Remember

1. All adults who provide direct role models for students can become involved in school.

2. One of the best ways to get parents involved is to form an advisory council composed of parents and school personnel.

3. Setting up a "parent resource file" can help you determine the kind of resource people you have available.

4. Motivate parents to get involved by:
- Announcing your needs at Open House.
- Telephoning.
- Sending home attractive, stimulating flyers.
- Discussing parent involvement with students and enlisting their help.

5. Make conferences a positive part of a positive parent-involvement program.

6. Send home regular "Happy-Grams," reports on students' progress and cooperation.

7. Prepare a written progress report to give parents when they arrive. Include, in the following order:
- A summary of the student's progress.
- Areas of concern.
- Areas of strength.

8. Always meet with students before meeting with their parents.

9. Include students in conferences if you feel their presence will be helpful, if students want to come, and if you feel comfortable conducting conferences with students.

10. Don't permit parents to verbally attack their children during conferences.

11. Attempt to win the cooperation of resistant parents by using your listening and responding skills. If you expect a particularly difficult conference, ask the counselor or principal to attend.

12. Conferences called to discuss a student's misbehavior involve:
- Presenting your evaluation of the student's progress.
- Stating your perception of the student's goal of misbehavior.
- Informing parents of your response to the misbehavior and your attempts to focus on the student's strengths.

Then, if you decide to help them explore alternatives for changing relationships at home:

- Finding out about the student's relationship with parents.
- Finding out about the family constellation.
- Exploring alternatives.
- Getting a commitment and planning a time for evaluation.

13. Teachers are in a particularly good position for leading parent study groups. Getting involved in such groups can strengthen our relationships with parents and students and can demonstrate our commitment to strong parent involvement.

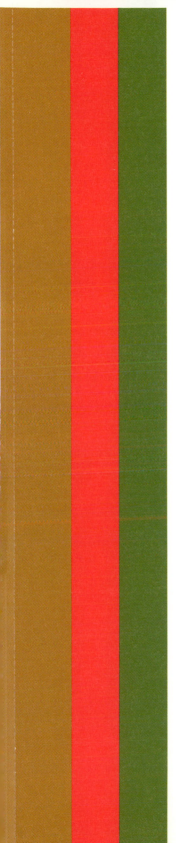

Personal Record Chapter 14

1.   My experience with the weekly assignment

2.   My reactions to the reading

3.   Topics to discuss with the group

4.   Skills I intend to improve

5.   My beliefs which impede progress

6.   My successes in applying program ideas

7.   My difficulties in applying program ideas

8.   My progress this week: A specific example

9.   This week I learned

How Effective Was STET for You?

Date _____

The purpose of this survey is to determine the effectiveness of the STET program, *not* to evaluate teachers. Please give your opinion of the following skills as you attempted to apply them with your students during the time you were in your STET group. Circle the most accurate response (or check the "not attempted" box).

Note: When rating each item, please consider your experience with *all* your students, not just the basically cooperative ones or those with special needs or problems. **Notice that numbers are occasionally reversed.** Refer to the categories listed.

Skill	How Effective?							

Using the four goals of misbehavior as a model for understanding students' misbehavior.

always	very often	often	sometimes	seldom	very seldom	never	not attempted
7	6	5	4	3	2	1	☐

Using the family constellation as a model for understanding students' behavioral characteristics.

always	very often	often	sometimes	seldom	very seldom	never	not attempted
7	6	5	4	3	2	1	☐

Applying encouragement procedures.

never	very seldom	seldom	sometimes	often	very often	always	not attempted
1	2	3	4	5	6	7	☐

Using reflective listening.

always	very often	often	sometimes	seldom	very seldom	never	not attempted
7	6	5	4	3	2	1	☐

Sending I-messages.

never	very seldom	seldom	sometimes	often	very often	always	not attempted
1	2	3	4	5	6	7	☐

Using problem ownership to determine responsibility for problems.

never	very seldom	seldom	sometimes	often	very often	never	not attempted
1	2	3	4	5	6	7	☐

Exploring alternatives for student-owned problems.

always	very often	often	sometimes	seldom	very seldom	never	not attempted
7	6	5	4	3	2	1	☐

Exploring alternatives for teacher-owned problems.

never	very seldom	seldom	sometimes	often	very often	always	not attempted
1	2	3	4	5	6	7	☐

Applying natural and logical consequences.

always	very often	often	sometimes	seldom	very seldom	never	not attempted
7	6	5	4	3	2	1	☐

Promoting therapeutic forces in the classroom (acceptance, ventilation, spectator learning, feedback, universalization, reality testing, altruism, interaction, encouragement).

never	very seldom	seldom	sometimes	often	very often	always	not attempted
1	2	3	4	5	6	7	☐

Using group leadership skills (structuring, universalizing, linking, redirecting, goal disclosure, brainstorming, blocking, summarizing, task setting and obtaining commitments, promoting feedback, promoting direct interaction, promoting encouragement).

always	very often	often	sometimes	seldom	very seldom	never	not attempted
7	6	5	4	3	2	1	☐

Conducting group guidance activities and exercises.

never	very seldom	seldom	sometimes	often	very often	always	not attempted
1	2	3	4	5	6	7	☐

Holding class meetings.

never	very seldom	seldom	sometimes	often	very often	always	not attempted
1	2	3	4	5	6	7	☐